THE BLIND MINDMAKER

EXPLAINING CONSCIOUSNESS WITHOUT MAGIC OR MISREPRESENTATION

C. S. Morrison

QUALIAFISH

ISBN: 978-1-9993393-1-9

"The point which as evolutionists we are bound to hold fast to is that all the new forms of being that make their appearance are really nothing more than results of the redistribution of the original and unchanging materials. The self-same atoms which, chaotically dispersed, made the nebula, now, jammed and temporarily caught in peculiar positions, form our brains; and the 'evolution' of the brains, if understood, would be simply the account of how the atoms came to be so caught and jammed. In this story no new *natures*, no factors not present at the beginning, are introduced at any later stage.

But with the dawn of consciousness an entirely new nature seems to slip in, something whereof the potency was *not* given in the mere outward atoms of the original chaos....

The demand for continuity has, over large tracts of science, proved itself to possess true prophetic power. We ought therefore ourselves sincerely to try every possible mode of conceiving the dawn of consciousness so that it may *not* appear equivalent to the irruption into the universe of a new nature, non-existent until then... *If evolution is to work smoothly, consciousness in some shape must have been present at the very origin of things.*"

William James (The Principles of Psychology, 1890)

"The universe is of the nature of a thought or sensation in a universal Mind... To put the conclusion crudely — the stuff of the world is mind-stuff. As is often the way with crude statements, I shall have to explain that by "mind" I do not exactly mean mind and by "stuff" I do not at all mean stuff. Still that is about as near as we can get to the idea in a simple phrase. The mind-stuff of the world is something more general than our individual conscious minds; but we may think of its nature as not altogether foreign to feelings in our consciousness... Having granted this, the mental activity of the part of the world constituting ourselves occasions no great surprise; it is known to us by direct self-knowledge, and we do not explain it away as something other than we know it to be — or rather, it knows itself to be."

Sir Arthur Eddington (The Nature of the Physical World, 1928)

ABOUT THE AUTHOR

Colin S. Morrison is a science graduate, writer and freelance philosopher who is an expert in consciousness studies. He gained his honours degree in theoretical physics at the University of St Andrews in the 1990s, and currently lives in the UK, where he teaches mathematics. He has studied the mind and the difficulties of explaining subjective experience for twenty years, presented at high-profile international conferences, and discussed his ideas with the world's leading philosophers. He is now confident he has found the only scientifically defensible solution to the mind-body problem.

Unlike all previous theories of consciousness, his proposal – *Position Selecting Interactionism* – explains the image-forming capability of our experiences purely as a product of natural selection acting upon ordinary matter. It invokes no substances, forces or principles that are not implied by successful scientific theories. And most interestingly, it requires none of the strange functionalism to which other theories attribute the astonishing appropriateness in the way particular types of experience represent particular types of data (pain for damage, unpleasant emotions for detrimental circumstances, pleasant feelings for beneficial circumstances, and so on). But what really makes his theory stand out from all the rest is that it provides a full explanation of what experiences are. He never brushes them aside as 'illusions' or 'an issue that will disappear when we have fully understood how the brain works'. His theory explains exactly what they are and what they have evolved to do. It tells us precisely what role they play in the workings of the human brain. And it shows us how and why they acquired that role.

He has previously published parts of this theory in abbreviated form in the *Toward a Science of Consciousness* program book for the years 2010, 2011, 2012 and 2014, and in *The Science of Consciousness* 2016 program book, all published by the University of Arizona Centre for Consciousness Studies. However, the present work is ground-breaking as it is the first full-length account of this theory. It is the first publication that brings all the arguments that support it together in one place, and shows why this author believes it to be far superior to all the many other theories of consciousness that have to date been advocated in the philosophical literature.

To Ruth and Jim

Raindrops reflect the sun's light –
Each wavelength on one line of sight.
But it sends to my brain
Signals similar to pain;
So what the bleep are red, green and white?

C. S. Morrison (Painbow)

CONTENTS

PREFACE

In 1994 the famous biologist Francis Crick, co-discoverer of DNA's molecular structure, published a book entitled *The Astonishing Hypothesis*. In that book he argued that all our experiences – colours, sounds, tastes, smells, feelings of hardness, softness, pain, pleasure, warmth, coldness, emotions, thoughts, dreams, memories, etcetera – are nothing but the firing of neurons in our brain (where neurons are the cells that generate electrical signals). This is what Crick called the 'Astonishing Hypothesis', and it is indeed astonishing. It is astonishing that someone of Crick's calibre could make such a claim when there is so little evidence in its favour. Nothing that science has shown us about the firing of neurons gives us any reason to think they should ever generate any of these experiences. In fact, science strongly suggests they shouldn't *and don't* generate experiences at all. It tells us that they are really all just complex switches triggered by particular patterns of input signals. And it reveals that the information being processed by the vast majority of the neurons in our brain never features in our conscious experience. But even if the firing of neurons did generate experiences, nothing we know about the evolution of the brain suggests that those experiences would be organised to form images and patterns rather similar to the patterns of stimuli impinging upon our sense organs (the light rays hitting our retinas, the acoustic waves vibrating our eardrums, the surfaces pressing against our skin, or the varieties of molecule interacting with the sensors in our nose and taste buds).

If Crick really meant exactly what this hypothesis suggests – that the firing of neurons in the visual cortex is what gives rise to colours, and those in the auditory cortex to sounds, and so on (no matter where in the brain consciousness lies) – he would have to be considered a functionalist, and functionalism, as you will discover later in this book, is a position on consciousness that receives absolutely no support from our current scientific understanding of other things. In no system that science has explained does the performance of distinct functions give rise to distinct properties that are not fully caused by the physical properties of the particles and forces involved, and those of their environment. And nowhere do we find complex forms perfectly designed for a particular function that are not the result of a physical process (such as natural selection or the creative thinking at work within a brain).

I suspect that Crick did not really mean that the types of experience themselves are caused by the firing of neurons. Like most neuroscientists, he probably only meant that the *variations* in our experiences of colour, sound, touch, taste, smell, emotion, thought, etcetera, were caused by that firing. He may merely have been hypothesising that the firing of neurons was entirely responsible for the ways in which our colours, sounds, feelings, and such like, *change with time* and *combine with each other*. Since that is what encodes the information in our experience, those variations and combinations are indeed bound to be the result of that information-processing activity. There is nothing, as far as I can see, that's particularly astonishing about that.

Being familiar with the complexities of neuroscience, Crick is of course perfectly entitled to be astonished by the claim that the firing of neurons could be entirely responsible for that accurate internal representation of so many distinct sources of information. Indeed, the fact that the changes that this firing brings about take place within *experiences* – a medium not yet described by physics – is somewhat unexpected to say the least! However, when your hypothesis is only about how these patterns of colour, sound, pain, and so on *change*, it is quite misleading to suggest that it explains the experiences themselves. After all, you are not proposing any explanation for the fact that there *is* an experience that changes. Nor are you suggesting a reason for why the thing that changes in response to those neural firings is organised with such precision that the patterns in which it encodes sensory data closely resemble the images formed on the relevant sense organs by the stimuli that they detect. And you are in no way accounting for why the choice of experience-type, in many cases, seems remarkably appropriate (pain for damage, pleasant feelings for the registering of beneficial situations, faint and fleeting images for memories, etcetera).

It is this latter observation, I think, that leads many respectable scientists and philosophers down the slippery slope to functionalism. They can't cope with the idea that pain experience might be an independent aspect of nature that was *adapted* to encode damage data (as it would have to be if it doesn't arise magically from the function itself as the functionalists propose). If pain were adapted to represent damage, it would have to be doing something that proved to be beneficial to an organism in circumstances where the organism was sustaining damage, which clearly requires that it have some sort of *physical influence*. How can one possibly factor an influence of pain into the laws of physics? And what about colour, sound, touch, taste and smell? Wouldn't all these other types of experience *also* need to be associated with a separate influence to explain how they acquired their function in human consciousness? At least functionalism doesn't require us to contemplate such a drastic scenario.

Nevertheless, functionalism is nothing like any scientific theory. In fact, it is so vague one can't even call it a theory. Wishful thinking would be a far more appropriate term. How could Nature possibly know what function a bit of a brain was performing? It could be considered to have *multiple* functions. As well as processing some visual information, it could also be holding up another bit of a brain, or stopping the processing of some other information. And even if Nature could detect a particular sensory-type function – visual processing, say – is it reasonable to believe Nature can then follow the cascade of relevant signals back to the sense organ (the retina in this case), work out how the image appears there, take into account all the transformations of that image that took place in the visual cortex, and then construct our subjective colour experience to perfectly represent that enhanced and corrected sensory image?

I find it incredible that respectable philosophers and scientists appear to think it can. Nature has never been known to work from the top down. The laws of physics determine the behaviour of the tiniest particles, and all else arises from their interactions (together with large-scale processes like natural selection). The neurons in a brain don't have any idea what function they are performing. They have just evolved to fire in certain ways in certain circumstances. Even the brain itself doesn't know what functions it is performing. It also just responds in particular ways to particular inputs. The fact that there is any knowledge in there at all is entirely due to the way some of those responses are represented in our consciousness – which is, of course, the big mystery.

This book will provide a relatively complete solution to this mystery. But it will not explain it by invoking that all-seeing and highly intelligent God-like Nature of the functionalists – the supernatural universe-wide entity that functionalism requires, with the power to see the functions of tiny parts of a brain and create a subjective experience in the twinkling of an eye that appropriately represents these functions (rather like George Berkeley imagined in the eighteenth century). It will instead explain it in the way that is suggested by our scientific explanations of other complex features of the human brain that happen to encode a similar amount of sensory information.

To the horror of many theoretical physicists, it will really identify pains, colours and other experiences as aspects of matter with distinct influences. And it will reveal why each of these influences proved to be beneficial to our ancestors in certain circumstances, and how they thus came to be adapted by the brain to their current functional roles. It will even detail a very plausible explanation for why the patterns of colour in our subjective visual experience have come to resemble the patterns formed by light rays impinging on our retinas, and for why the patterns of touch and feeling that we experience give us the sense that we extend throughout a human body. And rather surprisingly, it also provides a reason for how we know that those patterns of feeling represent the same object as the patterns of colour we call our body. In short, it will fully account *in this scientific way* for why we, as conscious minds, feel like a human being, when in actual fact we can only constitute a very tiny part of a human being's brain activity.

For reasons which will become obvious in chapter 7, I call this theory *Position Selecting Interactionism* (or *PSI-psychism*). Since it fully accounts for the organisation of our experiences as a product of natural selection, and doesn't invoke the all-seeing, benevolent Nature that functionalistic theories of consciousness demand, I have called the evolutionary process it envisages *The Blind Mindmaker*.

There are of course many different theories of consciousness in the literature. Due to the efforts of certain prominent philosophers, like Professor David Chalmers of New York University, it has in recent decades regained its rightful status as a worthy topic of academic debate. That status was somewhat lost during the mid-twentieth century due to the dominance of behaviourism – a tradition which sought to identify experiences with behaviours. Most now believe they are something quite distinct, and many have published their views on what that is. Hence you might be wondering why you should trust my proposal rather than the theories advocated by those other philosophers, many of whom occupy prestigious positions in world-renowned institutions. Why should you think my theory is more likely to be true than David Chalmers' theory, or the *Orchestrated Objective Reduction* hypothesis of Oxford mathematician Roger Penrose and American anaesthesiologist Stuart Hameroff, or Daniel Dennett's *Joycean Machine*, or Bernard Baars' *Global Workspace Theory*, or Johnjoe McFadden's *Cemi Field Theory,* or the views of theoretical physicist Henry Stapp?

Well, firstly you should take note of the fact that although those other theories of consciousness are promoted by scientists and philosophers who are leaders in their field, each is both *very different from* and often quite *incompatible* with the others. They cannot all be correct (or even *nearly* correct). If one happened to be correct, the others would consequently be totally wrong – which just goes to show that despite their reputations most, if not all, of these leading academics are wrong about consciousness. And secondly, unlike my proposal, none of their theories actually explain the *really mysterious* facts about our experiences: **what they are, where they come from, why they contain spatial patterns closely related to those formed by sensory stimuli, why they are all part of a single consciousness, and why that single consciousness understands what those patterns signify**.

Another reason you should doubt all those other proposals is that each, in one way or another, appears to rely upon functionalism to account for the quality of our experiences. The advocates of some of those theories may not admit this explicitly. But unless they can show that different qualities of experience have different effects that proved beneficial to our ancestors in appropriate circumstances, functionalism is exactly what they are implicitly assuming. As I have already mentioned, functionalism is such an unscientific hypothesis that it is almost certainly wrong, and it is so vague it cannot be considered a scientific theory. The only reason it is not completely ridiculed by respectable scientists is because it appeals to our intuitions (and because scientists can currently see no other way of explaining the amazing design-like perfection in our subjective representation of reality).

Now, you might think the fact that it appeals to our intuitions is in its favour. Most philosophers clearly do. However, what those philosophers are forgetting is that our intuitions are tools that our ancestors evolved to help them survive and compete as hunters and foragers in an often harsh environment. They have not evolved to help us solve problems like that of explaining consciousness, where knowing an accurate explanation does not improve one's chances of raising healthy offspring. With such problems intuitions are far more likely to make us prefer the simplest hypothesis, or the most popular hypothesis, or the one advocated by distinguished individuals (no matter how justifiable those views are). That's because when our ancestors happened to be genetically programmed to choose such courses of action in those circumstances, they gained more foraging time, became more popular, and rose in status, thereby giving their offspring better chances of survival and reproduction.

That, of course, doesn't mean intuitions are always wrong. But it does mean we cannot rely upon them. This is clear from the fact that after several centuries of scientific progress, during which careful observations have repeatedly refuted popular intuitions, our most accurate descriptions of reality have turned out to be highly *counterintuitive* ones. We should thus expect the same to be true of an accurate theory of consciousness. Hence our intuitions are not likely to lead us to such a theory. Instead, **we should judge how consciousness ought to be explained by looking at how science has accounted for other design-like representations of sensory data in the human brain**. These are all explained as products of natural selection operating upon structures built out of tiny particles according to the effects of these particles upon one another (effects that are fully governed by the laws of physics). My theory explains all the facts about human consciousness in exactly this way. That is why you can justifiably expect it to be correct.

Although the first edition of this book (December 2016) was the first published exposition of this theory, it was presented on four occasions prior to this at *The Science of Consciousness* international conference (formerly *Toward a Science of Consciousness*) run by The University of Arizona Centre for Consciousness Studies. On each of those occasions (2010, 2011, 2012 and 2016) it was discussed with leading academics, none of whom were able to identify any flaws in the theory. In 2011, the chair of my concurrent session felt the theory worthy of a further half-hour of question time. And following a chance meeting with Professor David Chalmers at Dallas Airport after the 2016 conference in Tucson, even that leading philosopher of mind has had a chance to read a paper on this theory.

In terms of getting philosophy journals to take this theory seriously, I have had less success. Judging from the positive comments that reviewers have made, and the dearth of serious criticisms in the comments that have been shared with me, I think this is far less to do with the merits of the theory itself than with the politics of the journal editors and referees (most of whom tend to be committed functionalists). My assessment here is greatly supported by the fact that following the publication of the first edition of *The Blind Mindmaker*, the *Journal of Consciousness Studies*, which had previously turned down a paper I had submitted, published a glowing five-page endorsement of this book (see *Journal of Consciousness Studies*, **24**, No. 7-8, 2017, pp. 233-7). This review was written by the journal's book reviews editor, professor Jonathan C. W. Edwards of *University College London*, who writes:

> There is something very refreshing about this book. It is free of the tired jargon of philosophy of mind. It sticks to a scientific agenda in a way that a lot of scientists would do well to emulate.

About that scientific agenda, Edwards writes:

> Morrison...sees rigorous science as something different from eliminative materialism, and I think he is right...the single-minded critical approach he takes is impressive and raises a number of fresh ways to look at the problem...Through much of the book Morrison rises admirably to the challenge of producing a specific testable model – what Popper called a dangerous hypothesis...his distinction between the 'what it is like' stream of consciousness and the wider category of 'thinking' is tied in to the idea that qualia arise locally, internally, and not as part of some global relation of organism to world. I see this careful adherence to causal locality in Morrison's approach as a major plus, and a refreshing change from views, often from professional neuroscientists, that seem to abandon the essential locality requirement of a scientific hypothesis...Locality is needed for testability, which is something Morrison very much

keeps in mind...In the latter part of Part 2 and in Part 3 he makes a bold attempt to bring value into the framework of physics...Such considerations naturally lead on to issues of ethics and the realm of religion. Most authors at this point tend to resort to naïve teleological arguments and hand-waving moralizing of the sort that Richard Dawkins likes to pounce on. But Morrison takes each step forward in a rational way and I think comes out on top having made it clear that there is something rather important that Dawkins sweeps under the carpet.

Apart from the inclusion of this endorsement and a few other small changes to the preface, this new edition is identical to the previous one. After almost a year of rigorous online debate, I feel as confident in the accuracy of the theory this book proposes as I did when I first published it. The need for a Darwinian account of all the design-like structure in our experiences remains as strong as ever, and I have so far not come across any alternative proposal capable of providing such an account.

One of the most intriguing things about this proposal is that it predicts certain otherwise unexpected experimental results. This is very unusual for a theory of consciousness. However, it is an expected requirement of all good theories in other scientific disciplines, since it allows incorrect views to be proven false – and thus progress to be made (a feature that is sorely lacking in consciousness studies). Moreover, the prediction in question would be fairly *easy* to test by experiment. Although a negative result in such a test would probably not cause me to abandon the entire theory (it is at present by far the only explanation that science supports), it would provide an important direction for further development. A positive result, on the other hand, would give us good reason to believe the theory is correct. Although technically it would only support one part of the theory, that part is clearly deduced from the rest of it. Hence, due to the fact that the prediction in question is fairly unlikely to be something I could have guessed, its confirmation would strongly support the theory as a whole. Whilst a positive result in such an experimental test never proves a theory correct, it does give one grounds to prefer the theory over others that don't make such predictions, and these grounds become stronger the more un-guessable the result of such an experiment happens to be. Hence a positive result in that proposed experiment ought indeed to inspire confidence in the theory itself.

The experiment is detailed on page 239. Hopefully someone in charge of a psychology lab who happens to be reading this book will soon be motivated to do this experiment and perhaps thereby give us solid grounds to denounce the functionalistic views on consciousness that are causing philosophy journals to reject carefully argued scientific theories of consciousness in favour of vague unscientific notions supported only by untrustworthy human intuitions. Until then, though, you will need to use your own judgement. Does Nature constantly conjure up complex, design-like representations of the world like an all-knowing, all-controlling, Berkeleyesque God, as functionalism requires? Or does she form such things out of the properties of tiny particles via the slow process of natural selection as this book claims? If you agree that science supports the latter view, you will probably find the argument of this book quite compelling. It may even change your worldview and open your mind to possibilities you had once dismissed as unlikely. And you will start to have great confidence that science has indeed revealed to you the true nature of things.

C. S. Morrison
January 2018

Beyond the sky,
My *skull*
must lie.
Somewhere out there
is my right eye.
My nasal cavity
yawns nearby.
And above,
or deep beneath,
My teeth!

C. S. Morrison (Beyond the Sky)

INTRODUCTION

The squares flew about madly as I watched in hopeful anticipation, not knowing what to expect or how long I would need to wait. A leaping blur of motion danced freely and haphazardly across the array of numbers; hopping rapidly and unpredictably from one point to another, and then jumping elsewhere almost faster than the eye could follow. It whipped across the screen throwing the already jumbled set of numbers into a turmoil. Sometimes it even seemed to bounce back from its landing point before bizarrely leaping out from some entirely different part of the screen. As the seconds ticked by, this strange rebounding behaviour grew more frequent. More and more often the motion seemed to be a vigorous ping-pong-like bouncing, rather than a swirl, and gradually the tumultuous swirling dance gave way to something more like a rapid flicker, shaking each of the numbers rather than throwing them around. But it was what had happened to the numbers themselves that I was really interested in, and my first inspection immediately brought a mixture of both delight and astonishment.

Each square contained a different pair of single-digit numbers chosen from the numbers 1 to 5. Twenty-five distinct pairs in all were present at every moment with no duplicates. At the start of the dance – a random-number-controlled iterative computer program – these had been placed in no particular order anywhere inside a five-by-five square grid. When the dance began, they were kicked around wildly, swapping positions with the pair on which they landed – though if you looked really closely you could sometimes catch the numbers in the act of changing, rather than the squares jumping. They even appeared occasionally to *roll* round to the new combination like the pictures on a fruit machine. And more and more often as the dance progressed the roll would go both forward and back (though the movement was too fast and the screen too flickery for the onlooker to remember whether the final number pair was actually identical to the one that had been there before or some other combination).

Even at the beginning it became obvious that some number pairs were sticking longer in certain places than other ones were. Like the sticky synthetic putty that children sometimes throw at a wall or ceiling, they would soon be whipped away again. But not long after that, they'd reappear close to where they had been before; and they were soon joined there by others like them. The (5,5) quickly picked up the (4,5); and then the (2,5) was cast down to join them on the bottom row. At the same time the top two rows were becoming dominated by pairs that had a 1 or a 2 as the second number. Within only a few minutes the pairs had been roughly sorted into rows in ascending order according to their second number, with one row occasionally breaking into a neighbouring one like the winners of a rugby line-up trying to carry the ball past the opposing team. A few seconds later those overlapping rows were untangled again, and a different two overlapped each other, while every-so-often the occasional adventurous pair made a run for an up-field position before being suddenly recalled like forwards who find themselves unexpectedly dispossessed by an opponent who carries the ball into the opposite half of the pitch.

Looking closely at the constantly flickering dance-floor it soon became apparent that the dance was slowing down. The pairs of numbers were changing places less and less frequently. And it suddenly dawned on the spectator that the numbers in each row had almost entirely sorted themselves out into a sequence – the same sequence of *first* numbers that was forming, or completely formed, in each of the other four rows. Towards the end of the dance, when only one or two number pairs were out of sequence, the flickering appeared to go up a gear. The wrongly placed pairs didn't just jump into position right away but insubordinately changed places with an adjacent number pair in the row above or below. Not long afterwards, however, without any warning they caved in and fell into line. And although the flickering did not die down, since each number pair still tried to swap positions with another every so often, no further swaps took place and a perfectly fixed and perfectly ordered arrangement of number pairs presented itself to the onlooker.

If you hadn't been a witness to the few minutes of chaotic swirling that had preceded this moment, you'd think that each number pair had been carefully placed in that sequence by the programmer. But that was not the case. They had found their way into that order by purely random swaps. And most interestingly, it had only taken the program a few thousand such swaps to accomplish this feat. The dance only involved one pre-programmed step, a step that was crucial in orchestrating its satisfying conclusion in anything like a reasonable amount of time: If after each swap the average distance between neighbouring pairs (when interpreted as coordinates on a Cartesian coordinate grid) was neither less than nor around the same size as its previous value, the swapped pairs were sent back to where they had come from.

As you will discover in chapter 8 of this book, a similar swirling dance, involving a great many more participants, but eked out at a snail's pace over millennia of evolution, appears to be the only scientifically justifiable way of explaining a very important aspect of the human mind – one that has been almost universally taken for granted by the many people who have attempted to account for this mysterious side of reality: It is the wonderful and extremely fortunate fact that we experience the world as a stream of images and patterns very similar (though by no means identical) to the ones formed on our sense organs by the various stimuli they have evolved to detect.

This book is about consciousness. More specifically, it is about *consciousnesses* – your consciousness and my consciousness, and the consciousnesses of other human beings, and whatever other consciousnesses may or may not exist. It is not concerned with consciousness as in 'the extent to which an organism with a nervous system is able to respond in a complex way to environmental stimuli'. That is what the *mass noun* 'consciousness' refers to. This book is about what the *count noun* consciousness denotes (and if you didn't think there was such a count noun, well you now know there is!).

A consciousness is simply a 'stream of experiences'. Your consciousness is the stream of experiences in which your knowledge of everything you think you know, and everything you remember or imagine, or intend to do, is represented. One could call it a 'mind'. But the word 'mind' suggests to me something capable of thinking and remembering. Although that is true of all the streams of experience we know about – it is true of your consciousness, and of my consciousness, and of the consciousnesses presumably possessed by all the many human beings we have encountered – it is nevertheless possible to imagine a consciousness that *can't* think, and which *doesn't* recall past experiences. A consciousness that just *experiences* things. And since our consciousness is a highly organised phenomenon that our brain has adapted in a rather perfect way to encode sensory information in highly appropriate types of experience (pain for damage, etc.), we should strongly expect there to exist consciousnesses that are *not* so organised – streams of experience that have *not* been adapted to encode information in a human brain.

The fact that we have never encountered such consciousnesses makes no difference. Unlike us, such consciousnesses will not be able to influence what an organism says, and they could not therefore advertise their presence in any currently detectable way. So the fact that we can't detect them counts for nothing. We must instead base our views concerning what range of forms consciousnesses might have on that of other natural information-carrying structures – brains, for example. Since these always range from highly complex examples (the human brain) to relatively simple ones (the nervous systems of insects), we should think it highly likely that an equally broad spectrum of different types of consciousness exist. We are only familiar with the very top end. Since we therefore have strong grounds to expect non-human-mind-like streams of experience to exist, we shall use the word 'consciousnesses', rather than 'minds', to refer generally to individual *streams of experience*.

Now, if you are a philosopher, you might be thinking that this definition isn't particularly good because I haven't defined what an experience is. However, the question of *what an experience is* happens to be a great deal easier to answer. Whilst we have access to only one kind of consciousness (the highly organised one that the human brain uses to encode sensory data), we are in contrast familiar with a wide variety of different kinds of experience. To define what an experience is, we need only point out a range of different examples of this entity and accept that 'experience' is the category of stuff to which these examples all belong (which is exactly how we commonly understand many other things – cats, dogs, lions, etcetera). Examples of experiences include colours, sounds, tastes, smells, pains, textures, all kinds of feeling and emotion, as well as occurrent memories and intentions (the memories and intentions that we are currently recalling or contemplating).

One thing we can say with confidence about all the things we call experiences is that they exist somewhere in our brain. We know this for a fact because they encode information that has been gathered and sent to our brain via our sense organs and the nerve fibres carrying their output signals. We know that this information has reached our brain because the information in our experiences is never purely the information that our sense organs gathered. The patterns of experience we call sights and sounds incorporate a lot of information that is not present in the patterns of light and acoustic pressure-waves that they represent. That information must therefore be getting supplied by the brain from the memories it stores of previous patterns of light and acoustic pressure-waves.

Colours, for example, encode information gathered by light-detecting cells on our retinas. But they do not encode *all and only* that information. Much of that raw data has been filtered out as somehow irrelevant for whatever task our visual experience performs, whilst other information, not from the retina, has been added. The most notable of that added information is the patterns of colour filling in the region of our visual experience that corresponds to the 'blind spot' on the retina where the presence of the optic nerve interrupts the array of light-detecting cells. To see this, close your right eye and focus your left on the + sign to the right of the black spot at the end of this paragraph. As you bring the page closer while looking at the +, you should find that at some point the black spot vanishes. The drop in light intensity caused by the black spot is not being detected by the retina. But the spot isn't just disappearing. It is being replaced by the same white colour as its surroundings. And since the same effect is apparent no matter what colour the surroundings are, extra information is clearly being added to compensate for the missing light intensities. The only place we know of where such sophisticated processing of visual data takes place is the visual cortex in our brain. Hence our visual experience almost certainly must lie somewhere in our brain.

●   +

Similarly, sounds encode variations in the frequency and intensity of the specific range of pressure waves that our ears detect – but only after our brain has analysed the auditory inputs and selected which signals out of that complex cacophony of incoming pressure waves are worth representing by distinct sound experiences. Moreover, as with our subjective visual experience, the sounds we hear also contain information that wasn't detected by the relevant sense organ (our ears). There are well-known auditory illusions showing that *visual* data – data from our eyes, not our ears – has a considerable impact upon the sound we hear. The famous McGurk effect, for example, is the observation that just looking at someone mouthing "Fah", while at the same time listening to a very clearly recorded 'Bah' sound being played back from a speaker, will make you hear a clear "Fah" sound instead (even though there is no change in the sound being played back).

But what about the things we feel? You may be rather surprised to learn that textures (tactile sensations), likewise, are not the actual impacts our touch sensors are making with surrounding objects. Just like sounds and colours, they also constitute something deep within our brain – a mysterious medium that some of the information coming from those touch sensors is getting *represented in* (after first being combined with relevant memory data). Our feelings of hardness and softness, hotness and coldness, roughness and smoothness are thus not properties of the objects we are touching, but patterns of feeling somewhere in our brain that are usually triggered by touch signals, and which have somehow come to have a form very similar to that of the surfaces we are making contact with. This obviously explains why we can remember, imagine and dream about touching things that are nowhere near us at the time. Those abilities are possible because, being deep within the brain, these patterns of feeling can also be triggered by memory signals initiated by another part of the brain rather than by a sensory signal. When we remember, imagine or dream, they are being triggered *purely* by such signals, with no signals coming from the sense organs being allowed to interfere.

This may seem obvious when you think about it like that, but it is extremely difficult to keep this brain-based nature of experience in mind. As soon as we stop thinking about where the information in our experiences comes from, we start to think that colours are physically present in the light our eyes detect or the things we happen to be looking at. We start to believe they are in the paint coating a surface, the ink on a printed page or poster, or the dye in our clothes and furniture. We applaud a good musician for far more than just the way our sound experience *changed*. And we reaccept the delusion that textures are the very contact we are making with the things our hands are touching.

We easily forget that when we see an object, we're not really experiencing that object at all. We are experiencing a pattern of colour experience that our brain is using to *represent* that object. The representation is fairly detailed and accurate, but it is still a representation. It is actually a representation *of* a representation because it is some kind of image – a 'mental image' – formed in the brain that represents the image formed by light rays focussed onto the retina! We only ever experience these *brain-based* images of what our eyes are looking at – not the actual objects themselves, nor even the light they project onto our retinas – though the clarity of these images, and an innate tendency to accept our sensory experiences as reality, makes this fact very easy to forget.

And it is even harder to remember that when you touch the objects that surround you, you are not even *feeling* those objects. You are experiencing a *pattern of feeling* that your brain has constructed to *represent* these objects. Indeed, when you experience your own body and limbs, and their relative positions in space, you are also merely experiencing a pattern of feeling that your brain has constructed to represent those things. In the medical profession it is called the 'body image', and people are well-known to suffer from disorders where their 'body image' is distorted so that it does not accurately represent the orientation, size or shape of the body.

Is there any difference between experiencing one's brain-based representation of the contact one is making with an object and experiencing the object itself? As you will see later in this book, there is at least one major difference. If you were experiencing the object itself, you would expect your experience to be occurring *at the same time as* your hand made contact with the surface of the object. You may be rather surprised to hear that this is not what happens. Careful experiments have consistently shown that our experience lags behind the events that are represented within it *by as much as half a second.* When you feel your fingers touch the pages of this book (or your kindle or tablet screen if you have an electronic copy), that contact actually took place half a second ago. It did *look* like it took place there and then. But that was only because your subjective visual image of that event, and the sound you heard at the same moment, were delayed too. In fact, all your sensory experience of that event occurred sometime after the event itself. That is inevitable because it takes a finite time for the nerve signals from your sense organs to travel all the way into your brain, and then through all the circuits that analyse them and construct the representation that you experience. But the delay is usually somewhat longer than is needed for this. For reasons that will become clear in chapter 10 of this book, your brain needs to wait long enough to receive any simultaneously-generated signals from peripheral parts of your body – your fingers and toes – before it constructs your experience of a particular event. Hence that experience usually always lags around half-a-second behind the external events that it represents.

But why does your brain *need* to construct this experiential – *subjective* – representation of reality? That is one of the biggest puzzles in neuroscience. At present, most scientists and philosophers would say we are *nowhere near* to answering this question. They will say that we don't actually know what an experience *is* yet. This is what Australian philosopher David Chalmers famously called the Hard Problem. He used this term because he is convinced that after so much scientific progress in understanding how the brain works and how the matter it is made of behaves, we have made relatively little progress in understanding what an experience is. We don't know what thing our brain is manipulating to change the sensory data from our visual cortex into a suitably organised pattern of colours, and to change the data in our somatosensory cortex into a perfectly timed and equally accurate experience of touch and feeling, and so on.

I disagree. Although we are far from identifying the *detailed mechanisms* required to input the data into our experience, I do think modern science now gives us enough clues to narrow down the nature of experience to a single type of physical substrate. And I also think that what we know about biology puts very stringent constraints upon what that entity was adapted to do and how it came to have such an accurate representation of reality encoded within it. In Part 2 of this book, I will show you why I think this. I will reveal to you what that substrate is, and I will demonstrate why identifying our experiences with that particular physical substrate allows a perfectly scientific explanation for their organisation and information-content. So why do so many philosophers and scientists think differently?

As you will see in chapter 2, the vast majority of the scientists and philosophers who have to date commented publicly on this issue defend very different – and very strange – views on consciousness. By 'strange', I don't mean that these views are unfamiliar. Indeed, the views most scientists and philosophers defend are the ones most people regard as *common sense.* What I mean is that these views are not in the least bit supported by our current scientific understanding of nature. In fact, they are in outright conflict with it. Why do so many scientists and philosophers subscribe to those unscientific views, when as I have already mentioned, there is a highly defensible position that fits perfectly well with what science has taught us about other things?

I suspect the problem is not that they are unaware of this scientific position – though they may not yet realise just how successful it has proven to be. It is more that the implications of that scientific explanation of consciousness are simply too bizarre, too counterintuitive, too revolutionary, for the average scientist or philosopher who values his reputation to stand up for.

Scientists and philosophers don't want to rock the boat too much, especially when it is likely to take in water in regions that are not their areas of expertise. Whenever that happens – whenever a proposed explanation for consciousness indicates that a popular assumption in another academic field is probably wrong – the experts in that field panic and vigorously pump that water out, shouting insults at the individual responsible, whom they rightly or wrongly deem to have no authority to make pronouncements that have such drastic implications. Instead of looking at the situation from the other person's point of view, they stick to the traditions and protocols that are sufficient for their particular field and completely ignore the bigger picture. Consequently, the boat may float on happily at anchor, keeping its occupants warm and dry, but the improvements in its design that are needed to steer it successfully across the uncharted ocean of subjective phenomena have so far not been successfully implemented.

As well as this reluctance to question time-honoured traditions and assumptions on the basis of what the bigger picture suggests is needed, scientists and philosophers are also very reluctant to embrace views that have potential *religious* implications. As you will see in Part 1 of this book, when we attempt to account for experiences and consciousnesses in the way that modern science tells us they *ought* to be accounted for, one very quickly discovers that the resultant hypothesis is likely to entail the existence of a consciousness that experiences everything in the whole universe. Moreover, it implies that this consciousness will be able to *act* on the basis of its experiences, and may even continue to remember the past.

Clearly, if there is a being with such powers, it is probably unreasonable to discount the possibility that it played a part in the evolution of the universe. Consequently, I suspect that scientists and philosophers who are committed to an atheistic worldview (probably the great majority of such intellectuals) are unduly reluctant to investigate this scientific explanation of consciousness for religious rather than scientific reasons. They assume that the existence of God is vanishingly improbable, and on that basis ignore views on consciousness that might predict the existence of a God.

As you can probably see, if that is true it is those scientists who are being irrational. If the theory of consciousness to which modern science points appears to entail the existence of a God, then God's existence ought to be regarded as *very likely*. The assumption that it is vanishingly improbable is an *error* – and therefore no reason to dismiss that theory of consciousness.

We will explore the theological implications of this theory of consciousness in Part 3. As you will discover in Part 2, neither that theory nor its derivation invoke the involvement of any supernatural power or process. They rely purely on principles and processes that have been established by science and shown to be effective by the experimental method. This is quite unlike all other theories of consciousness. Each of these, in one way or another, invokes a supernatural principle called 'functionalism' for which there is no analogue in empirical science.

We will discuss functionalism and examine some of those other views on consciousness in chapter 2. Before that, though, we need to go right back to basics. We need to make sure we fully appreciate what experiences are (or at least, what they *aren't*), and why their existence is so mysterious from a scientific point of view. We shall also answer the question of why this totally mysterious, and yet absolutely central, aspect of our nature appears to be rather badly neglected by science writers and popularisers. To do that, let us first look at the most familiar type of experience of all an experience so familiar that we don't really think of it as an experience at all. We think of it as a property of the things we see around us or the light those things reflect. Without it there'd be no rainbows, no glorious sunsets, no blue skies, there wouldn't even be any darkness or greyscale or snowy white. It is the experience we call 'colour'.

PART ONE

COLOUR AND CONSCIOUSNESS
WHAT WE ALREADY KNOW

I imagined the blue sky turn red,
So blue must be inside my head.
But if air that I see
Scatters blue light at me,
That blue cannot be where I said!

C. S. Morrison (The Blue Mistake)

CHAPTER ONE

The Confusion of Colour

Re-mystifying the Rainbow

Colours are deeply mysterious things. There is currently no scientific explanation for what they are or where exactly they come from, though that is not the impression you get from most science books and documentaries.

As a physics graduate involved in the education of young people, I am always deeply concerned when I hear scientists talking about the colours of the rainbow as though they are something we've explained. This happens a great deal – probably because our vivid colour experience is a much more beautiful and familiar thing to talk about and illustrate than the small portion of the electromagnetic spectrum that it usually represents. But it is only the latter that physics explains, not the former.

If one leaves out the fascinating but far-too-technical details provided by quantum theory, the latter consists merely of *electromagnetic waves* – imperceptibly tiny transparent wiggles in the strengths of electric and magnetic fields (which are invisible patterns of force[1] that affect the motion of charged particles). Different parts of that spectrum differ only in how vigorously these fields wiggle (the wave's frequency), which is actually totally dependent upon how an observer is moving. Just by moving towards a source of electromagnetic waves can make them wiggle more vigorously. The faster you go, the higher their frequency becomes (though you would need to be approaching the speed of light to notice any difference). Slow down, or start moving away, and they wiggle less. So different frequencies (or wavelengths) of electromagnetic radiation are really just the same thing seen from different perspectives. They are even, rather surprisingly, absorbed by atoms in the eye in chunks determined only by their frequency. And they all travel at *exactly the same speed*. They are thus rather dull and samey compared to the glorious pattern of distinct colours in which the detection of that radiation is represented in our visual experience. Their spectrum has none of the beauty of the rainbow.

Science writers don't like to appear dull and boring so they allow their readers to imagine all those beautiful colours zipping through the atmosphere mysteriously bound up in white sunlight, until refraction through a passing raindrop or prism splits it up and sets them free. Nothing could be further from the truth! A colour is a very different beast from the electromagnetic wavelength it is supposed to represent. The two don't even exist at the same time. But identifying colours with wavelengths of light in this way is

---

[1] Actually '*potential* force' is a better description. When a source of electromagnetic waves is extremely weak, the quantum mechanical description of these waves only specifies the changing *probability* that a given particle will feel a particular force in a particular direction.

bound to confuse the untrained reader into *thinking* they are the same thing.

In case you're wondering, 'white' light is not composed of colours at all. Until you see it, it isn't even white. It is composed of the mysterious but rather similar wiggles – called 'waves' – of electromagnetic fields that I've just described. The raindrop just causes those waves to travel in different directions depending upon how vigorously they are wiggling. After passing through the eye's lens they hit the retina where certain wiggles are absorbed by atoms in light-sensitive cells. There the light ends its journey. The colour that we misinterpret as being that light only comes into existence around *half a second later*[2] when the information carried by an electro-chemical nerve signal triggered by that absorbed wiggle is combined with information from other nerves and represented in our conscious experience.

Part 2 of this book is concerned with how and why that happens. As you will see, the seemingly harmless device of allowing the reader to think of wavelengths of light as colours often prevents him or her from realising the existence of an incredibly interesting and highly mysterious aspect of nature. That aspect of nature permeates our dreams and makes visible our memories. Out of it everything we see is actually constructed. It is the phenomenon of colour *experience* – what philosophers often refer to as colour *qualia*. Unlike the wavelengths of light that they have come to represent, the only examples of colour experience we

---

[2] Although the nerve signal travels from the eye to the brain much quicker than this, its information cannot be used to form our experience until information from sensors in peripheral parts of the body has had time to reach the brain. This is the only scientific way of explaining the fact that when you kick a ball you see and feel your toe touch it at exactly the same time despite the fact that it takes between a quarter and half a second for the nerve signals from your foot to reach your brain.

know of emerge in the dark recesses of the brain, deep beneath the skull; their spectrum is banded rather than continuous; and they include black, a colour that does not get used to represent light at all (or at least, it doesn't in *my* consciousness).

Why Colour Experience Remains Mysterious

Despite the contrary claims of some philosophers and scientists, I believe this aspect of nature *can be explained scientifically*. I think it is something we are able to fully account for in terms of the substances and processes we currently know to exist; and I demonstrate that in Part 2 of this book. There I construct a theory that explains our colour experience in a way that is as similar as possible to how science accounts for our retinal images – the patterns of changing intensity formed by particular frequencies of electromagnetic wave getting detected by the retinas of our eyes. Of all the things we think we know how to explain scientifically, those retinal images are obviously the things that our colour experience *most closely resembles*. You will hopefully agree with me that explaining a mysterious phenomenon in a way that is *most like how science explains the thing that is most like it* is the most justifiable approach – it is more likely than any other approach to hit upon the correct explanation for that mysterious phenomenon. In fact, it is the approach that scientists follow most of the time when they attempt to explain new observations. Nevertheless, the account that this scientifically-justifiable procedure appears to demand for colour experience has certain, rather startling, implications concerning our place in the universe that are likely to prove extremely controversial. As a result, it has been almost totally neglected by popular science writers.

Those writers must of course draw a line between what they consider to be the domain of science, and what they regard as best left to philosophers and theologians. As far as most are concerned, our colour experience is an example of the latter. However, in recent decades that line has been pushed further and further back, and with good reason. The inexorable advancement of science, and the increased confidence in its ability to unlock nature's secrets that each new technological spin-off has given us, lends the twenty-first century scientist a justified authority in the public eye that far outweighs that of the contemporary philosopher or theologian. Nowadays a popular science writer rarely fears criticism from philosophers or theologians when he or she ventures onto subjects that were once regarded as their areas of expertise. And indeed, it is philosophers and theologians who are often on the defensive. So why don't those writers attack the mystery of colour experience in the scientific way I have outlined above?

As I have said, such an approach does lead to an explanation that has extremely counterintuitive implications. But why should this put science writers off? The most accurate scientific theories we have so far discovered *all* have extremely counterintuitive implications that were highly controversial when they first came to light. Many of the things they predict just don't feel at all like common sense. They imply, for example, that particles of matter can be in two or more places at once, that widely separated particles remain instantaneously connected, that objects age differently according to how deep they are in a gravitational field or how much they are being accelerated or decelerated, that humans are very distant cousins of bananas, and so on. Yet they are still the theories that careful observations have shown to be our most accurate descriptions of reality. Hence those writers must be well aware that it is totally unreasonable to reject a theory on the grounds that its implications do not *feel* plausible. Provided these implications are not ruled out by observations, what we feel about them ought to be regarded as *completely irrelevant* from a scientific perspective. Judging from what science has revealed about the bits of reality that scientists can experiment upon, we ought to *expect* the implications of an accurate explanation for some other aspect of reality to feel strange and contrary to familiar experience and common sense.

So if science writers are not afraid of negative reactions from philosophers and theologians, and are quite used to expounding the merits of the complex and counterintuitive theories that the scientific method supports, why are they so reluctant to treat colour experience in that scientific way? As far as I can see, the problem is that science writers do fear something. They are extremely wary of the criticism that might come their way from others in their profession.

As you will see in this book, if they were to attempt to account for colour experience in the way that is most like how science accounts for the most-similar successfully-explained phenomenon (the retinal image), the resultant theory has very specific implications concerning the nature of matter. Modern experts in the scientific theories that describe matter (who will have their own favourite idea of what is going on) are bound to resist such claims, and the easiest way to do this is to highlight their counterintuitive nature. Naturally, popular science writers are keen to avoid such an obvious source of authoritative criticism, and they therefore tend to steer clear of philosophical views that have such counterintuitive implications.

The sad thing is that because of this you will rarely find a book that addresses the really important philosophical questions in the way modern science suggests they ought to be addressed.

The Colourful Scientific Approach

In this book I intend to break that mould. Throwing caution to the wind, I will be applying a genuinely scientific explanation to the subjects that have been avoided or mistreated by popular science writers. As I mentioned earlier, one of these is colour experience. But there are many others. You may even recognise some of them. They include consciousness, sounds, warmth, coldness, hardness, softness, pain, pleasure and many, many more.

Now you may recall from the introduction to this book that one of the reasons many scientists refuse to adopt this scientific approach could be the fact that it favours the view that there is a very real God. If so, you may be surprised to see that God is not on this list. The reason for this, however, is simple: God is not something we can assume to exist when seeking a *scientific* explanation for something – an explanation that we have objective grounds to believe is our most accurate description of the thing we're interested in. God is not a label for anything we observe. Nor is it justifiable from a scientific point of view to posit the existence of anything with the sort of powers God is usually reputed to have as a means of explaining something we observe. If we do that, not only will we be going against Occam's razor, the philosophical rule of thumb that says we should prefer the *simplest* of a set of alternative explanations (which would definitely involve a far *less* powerful being), but we will not be accounting for that observation in the most *likely* way – the way that is most like how the most-similar successfully-explained observation is accounted for.

Remember, to explain a new observation, a scientist usually looks for the most-similar successfully-explained observations, and then tries to adapt the explanation for these observations to fit the new one. In doing so, though, she doesn't usually invent entirely new mechanisms or substances. She tries to find ones that will work amongst those that are already known to science. Even when these aren't suitable, and a new mechanism must be invented, she isn't at liberty to choose any mechanism she likes (God is not an option). Instead, she ensures that the new mechanism works in as similar as possible a way to those that are already known about. In doing this, she minimises the role of intuitions in her choice of explanation – opting for a theory that can be objectively argued to be most likely. In this book we attempt to do likewise with colour experience and those other philosophical subjects.

So why mention God at all? I do so here mainly to give plenty of warning for readers who may have fixed ideas about the existence or non-existence of such a being, and who would be offended by a theory of consciousness that casts doubt upon any of those ideas. It is particularly aimed at readers who may be uncomfortable at the thought of God becoming a subject of serious scientific debate. Although it is rightly considered unreasonable to posit the existence of a God for the purpose of explaining some mysterious observation, this does *not* mean that it will never be reasonable to invoke some concept of God as part of a scientific explanation. That may seem like a contradiction, but it isn't. It would become reasonable to invoke God as part of an explanation for something if – and only if – two conditions are met: Firstly, there must be no more-justifiable explanation for the observation in question. And secondly, the existence of that God would have to be entailed by the most scientifically justifiable explanation for some *other* observations. In other words, the existence or likely existence of that God must emerge as a *predicted consequence* of a theory (or set of theories) that constitutes the most scientifically defensible explanation for the phenomena it explains – and which therefore does not invoke God in any part of that explanation.

That may seem like a tall order – and certainly, most science writers appear to have dismissed it out of hand. I do not. And the reason I do not is because the existence of a God does appear to be predicted by the scientific treatment of colour experience I am proposing. Of course, that would make no difference if there were no suitable observations that the existence of this God might reasonably be used to explain – in other words, observations that can't be explained by invoking some mechanism that occurs more commonly in successful scientific theories. However, I think such observations do exist. The problem is that the only examples of such observations I have been able to identify support certain views on God that will conflict with many people's beliefs.

To my mind this is inevitable. When God ceases to be a matter of faith and becomes a prediction of a scientific theory, that is exactly what we should expect to happen. However, the people whose faith is likely to be most seriously challenged by these observations are the majority of scientists and philosophers. They are the people who claim that belief in God is irrational. If God really is predicted by the most scientific explanation of colour experience we can come up with, then that God ceases to be an irrational postulate, and a search for possible evidence of that entity becomes a worthy scientific endeavour.

If you are a person who values the understanding of things that science provides, and who is eager to apply that understanding to the mysterious phenomena contemplated by philosophers and theologians whatever it may imply about human existence, then by all means read on. I must warn you, though, that everything I tell you about in this book will be something you will have strong scientific reasons to believe to be true. When you have understood these reasons, you will find it very difficult not to accept this book's claims; and this may cause you to question certain beliefs about the world and our place within it that you currently hold dear. I personally think this is a good thing. However, I have always been someone who wants to hold the view on reality that is most justified by our current state of knowledge. I recognise that others may prefer to hang onto the myths and half-truths they grew up with, regardless of how justifiable they are. After reading this book you might find that harder to do.

In this chapter, we have reminded ourselves that the colours we see don't originate from the light hitting our retinas. They are something deep within our brain getting used to *represent* that particular set of sensory stimuli. They represent it so well we tend to think that those colours *are* that detected light, and that tendency is encouraged by many science writers and popularisers. It conveniently hides the embarrassing lack of any accepted scientific explanation for colour experience, and removes the need to discuss the controversial views that such an explanation would demand. As we have seen, a scientific explanation for this phenomenon ought to explain it in a way that has much in common with the way our *retinal image* is accounted for (a view you'll soon discover to be quite controversial). The patterns in our colour experience can't be explained as *direct copies* of those on the retinal image because the information from different parts of the retina gets sent to different parts of the brain. Something must explain how it all gets put back together again – a process that ought to be somewhat similar to the evolution of the eye's lens, the process that caused scattered light to form patterns resembling the objects that scattered it. The part of our brain that builds our subjective visual image has to perform an information-gathering job that is *at least as impressive* as that performed by the eye's lens. But it doesn't form its images out of light. It makes them out of colour: a currently-unexplained aspect of the mysterious entity we call our *consciousness*.

CHAPTER TWO

What is Consciousness?

A Highly-Organised Part or Product of a Biological Organism

On a Sunday morning television debate about faith and science I once heard a Buddhist monk ask renowned evolutionary biologist Richard Dawkins a question that had obviously been bugging him for some time. He was not the only one with that question on his mind that day. The same question had been relentlessly tugging me onwards on my personal search for the most justifiable view of reality ever since my final year as a theoretical physics under-graduate. After listening to the brilliant archbishop of popular science convincingly demolish various arguments for faith that other members of the studio audience put to him, that orange-robed individual took the mike and calmly floated the one question Dawkins could not answer: "But professor…what is consciousness?"

27

Dawkins appeared flustered, and quite uncharacteristically could only manage the rather unsatisfactory admission "nobody knows what consciousness is" (or words to that effect). Of course, that is probably a true statement. But then, nobody really knows for sure what *anything* is. As Dawkins is very much aware, the explanations for things that science provides are always hypotheses that could potentially be disproven at some future time. Yet because they are derived from well-established theories (theories that yielded unexpected predictions that future observations happened to confirm and which have never yet been proven false), we have good reason to prefer them to other explanations. In view of this, it seems to me that we must have equally sound scientific reasons to prefer a certain explanation for consciousness over all the many others that have been put forward. And there is nothing to stop us obtaining that explanation by deriving it from established scientific theories in the same way scientists derive their explanations for entities that have a lot in common with human consciousness.

The main reason I found Dawkins' answer to the monk's question so unsatisfactory is because Dawkins is an expert on the one scientific theory from which we should expect a defensible answer to this question to emerge. Human consciousness (our subjective inner life), whatever else it is, **definitely constitutes a highly-organised part or product of a biological organism**. It contains information, for example, that has been carefully labelled with distinct types of experience according to which sense it was collected by. That information is often represented in images that resemble the patterns formed by the sensory stimuli themselves. And all our different types of experience appear to be getting used to encode information. None of them goes to waste. Moreover, experiences that happen to carry information about things that could be harmful to us tend to be unpleasant, whilst those encoding information about beneficial circumstances (ones that would have increased our ancestors' chances of passing on their genes to future generations) are usually felt to be relatively nice.

As such, its design-like structure ought to be explained as a product of natural selection. And we're not just talking about a by-product, here, like a creature's shadow or reflection. As we shall see in chapter 5, we are talking about something *incredibly complex* that has become *precisely tuned* to representing only certain, very specific, biologically-gathered information out of a vast, ever-present pool of such data. Everything else that carries out such a task in nature is very reasonably thought to be a piece of matter that gained its purposeful structure and biological function gradually over many generations of natural selection due to an advantage that each small step towards that structure gave the organism in which it arose. So the same ought to apply to human consciousness.

The implications of this very reasonable conclusion, though, are profound and highly controversial. Like it or not, it would inevitably mean that our consciousness (whatever it is) must somehow act upon our brain in a very real way that is dependent upon experiences (an inference that may not seem all that strange to you, but which fascinates the physicist in me). And far more controversially, for reasons we will come to shortly we should also expect it to be something that was adapted *by* the brain, rather than something that arises *from* it. I was kind of hoping Dawkins would point his listeners to those scientifically defensible views on consciousness, rather than dismissing the matter with an appeal to the ignorance of the human race.

There are, of course, a great many different views on consciousness in the philosophical literature; and Richard Dawkins is perhaps understandably reluctant to come out in favour of one view over another when no consensus currently exists. By pointing out that the design-like structure of human consciousness is most likely to be a product of positive natural selection, he would be arguing against the well-publicised views of fellow atheist and popular writer Daniel Dennett – a philosopher who believes in a *functionalistic* explanation for the organisation of our experiences (though many would say he simply ignores the existence of things like colour, sound, pain, etcetera, altogether[3]).

Feigning Functionalism

Functionalism is the view that consciousness, and the different types of experience it contains, arises from a brain *purely because of something the brain is doing at the time as part of the whole*

---

[3] It seems to me that he is simply identifying particular qualia (experience types) with particular brain-states defined according to their function (see his definition of colour in *Consciousness Explained* p.375-383, especially Otto's experience of pink on p.383 and his identification of qualia as 'dispositions to react' on p.398). In my opinion, his theory of consciousness is merely an attempt at specifying where the information in our experiences comes from. He is happy to account for *that* as a product of natural selection but makes no attempt to do the same for the organisation of the *experiences* – types of phenomenology – in which that information is encoded. Moreover, unless I've missed something, he doesn't even suggest a reason why a Joycean machine is so special that *its* operations are accompanied by experience, Why that particular program, out of all the other programs? Why should its serial nature and the fact that it decides what we say and think make its judgements any more deserving of phenomenology than those of any of the many other programs at work in Dennett's brain? Like every functionalistic theory, Dennett's implies the existence of extremely strange and unscientific fundamental laws to account for our experiences. One of these is stated in *Consciousness Explained* p.281 where he claims that anything is conscious if it possesses a Joycean machine as its control system. What I would like to know is: How on earth does nature know which sections of her vast and intricate networks of inter-swirling electrons, and atomic nuclei happen to constitute Joycean machines?

organism. In Dennett's view it happens when one part of the brain (a control program he calls a 'Joycean machine' responsible for determining the ordering of the outputs of many parallel processes and thereby the content of our speech and thought[4]) 'probes the narratives' (or 'multiple drafts') that other parts of the brain are constantly constructing. But he doesn't tell us *why* it happens, or why it feels the way it does. In fact, he makes no attempt to account for the different types of experience our consciousness consists of, invoking instead the increasingly popular but extremely strange claim that they are an illusion. He appears to be saying that things like colours, sounds, tastes, smells, and feelings of hardness, softness, hotness, coldness, and so on, are not something that exists within the brain.[5]

This unsubstantiated claim seems unlikely to me. After all, those things do obviously contain information that we know to be present within the brain because it is often subsequently used to determine what we say when we talk about our experiences. And even if they *were* illusions, like most philosophers I would still like to know why I experience them. What are those supposed illusions made of? Why do they only encode certain sorts of information in

---

[4] *Consciousness Explained*, p.281.

[5] *Consciousness Explained*, p.355. Here he specifically states that an image we experience is not re-created in a bitmap form out of anything in our brain. Our experience of a set of colours taking such a form in an experienced space is an illusion – *an illusion that doesn't even exist in the brain* according to Dennett! As this book will show, he has reached this position purely because he assumes there is no Cartesian Theatre – no place in the brain where all the information in our experiences is brought together. He mocks the concept of the information in the brain being re-presented for the enjoyment of some ghostlike observer. But as you will see in chapters 7-11, that concept is a straw man. Although our consciousness is indeed a place where it all comes together, as those chapters will show, it is not a ghostlike observer but a piece of matter playing a constantly active role in determining behaviour. And every pixel of its stream of experience is a location where that matter can act upon the brain in a distinct way – the quality we experience that 'pixel' to have being used by the brain to determine how likely that action is to take place.

seemingly very appropriate ways? And why do the same aspects of my experience consistently encode the *same* sorts of data (pains for damage, colours for visual data, sounds for hearing, etcetera)?

As we shall see in chapter 6, based upon how science currently explains aspects of our biology that contain the high degree of perfection evident in the information-content and organisation of our experiences (all of which are justifiably thought to be products of natural selection), there are no grounds for believing that any form of functionalism will turn out to be the correct explanation of consciousness. So why do so many scientists and philosophers subscribe to such a view?

I suspect the real reason is that at present it is felt to be the safe option. No-one is going to think you're weird if you say that pain is caused by damage itself. Since it always accompanies damage in our experience, that seems a perfectly reasonable claim to make. Likewise, you are not likely to suffer harsh criticism for saying that colours arise from the processing of visual information because most people can't imagine visual information being represented in anything *but* colours. On the other hand, if you were to argue that the association of pain with damage and colour with vision in us humans is merely a product of natural selection, your fellow scientists and philosophers are bound to point out that this would mean that pain and colour *won't always have represented damage and light in the consciousnesses of our distant ancestors.* When people find out that you believe this, there's a chance they might think you're barmy and not read your books. And that possibility is only going to become more likely when they realise that this perfectly scientific view has even weirder implications: As you will see in chapter 4, it strongly suggests that there must exist other consciousnesses in nature that are not connected with brains, but which still experience colours, sounds, feelings and such like.

This conclusion – known as *panpsychism* – is often claimed to be implausible. But provided you are not imagining these non-brain-based consciousnesses as being capable of thinking about their experiences and remembering their past experiences (tasks that require the storage and accessing of memories), there is in fact no reason to think their existence is unlikely. Indeed, due to the fact that a version of this position is entailed by an evolutionary explanation for the information-content of our experiences (as you will discover in chapter 6) it ought to be considered far *more* likely to a scientifically-trained mind than the claim that consciousnesses like ours arise perfectly formed whenever a brain starts to do something like probing its narratives. Since all properties of biological matter are well-known to be formed out of the properties of tiny particles, properties that are capable of combining to form our experiences ought to be widely assumed to be present in such particles too (a panpsychistic view known as 'micropsychism').

Rather than admit this, though, and risk harmful criticism from academic peers who choose to stick to the safe zone of intuitive functionalistic views, most philosophers and scientists who don't like the unscientific nature of functionalism adopt one of two other positions that I believe are a hindrance to scientific progress: They either deny that consciousness is something that *needs* to be explained (a position known as 'eliminativism'), or they claim that our lack of progress at explaining it is evidence that we are truly *incapable* of explaining it (a view aptly termed 'mysterianism').

Mindless Materialism and Lazy Mysterianism

As far as the first of these positions is concerned, the very fact that our consciousness is a highly stable and organised phenomenon,

33

exhaustively encoding extremely-specific brain-based information in sensory-image-like patterns, means that it is something unique in neuroscience – something *unlike anything we've ever seen on brain scans.* As such, it is definitely something that needs to be explained. It isn't just the presence of sensory data. The mysterian claim that we are incapable of explaining it is in my view hardly justified when one considers the tremendous progress that science has made over the last few centuries. We have explained so many other strange things (the paths of the planets across the sky, the origin of species, spectral lines, reproduction, the outbreak of diseases, the constancy of the speed of light). These were explained by theories that made unexpected predictions that subsequent experiments happened to verify. And those successful theories have often emerged from sudden bursts of inspiration at times when no progress appeared to be getting made.

Although mysterians point to our lack of scientific progress in the case of consciousness as evidence of its supposed inexplic-ability, they fail to mention that at many other times in the history of science a period of zero progress in the explanation of something has been ended suddenly by a theory that not only explained the phenomenon in question but made predictions that could be experimentally tested. Indeed, it was the fact that experiments verified some of the theory's predictions that persuaded scientists that progress had been made. It allowed scientists to abandon the theories that were too vague to be testable and focus on improving the hypotheses that did accurately predict some unexpected experimental results.

The main reason there are currently so many different views on consciousness is simply the fact that one cannot test the predictions about consciousness that such theories make. The private nature of experience makes it difficult to verify peoples' claims about their experiences and impossible to test hypotheses about the existence of experience in anything other than the human brain. It seems philosophers can say whatever they like about consciousness and never be proven wrong.

On the other hand, the one thing we do know for certain about current theories of consciousness is that if one *could* test such theories, many are *bound* to prove false. That's because each theory of consciousness currently makes claims that are incompatible with those made by other theories. Some say consciousness does nothing to the brain, others that it plays an important role. Some claim it emerges only from complex information-processing, others that it is abundant in even the simplest of living things. Some claim it to be located in a specific region of neural tissue, others have it widely spread out. Some claim that it has something to do with the strange behaviour described by quantum mechanics, others that it is a purely *classical* – i.e. *non-quantum-mechanical* – phenomenon. Consequently, they can't all be right. If one theory were right, others would have to be wrong. But there often appears to be no experiment we could do that will conclusively demonstrate which are the wrong ones.

What I think philosophers are forgetting, though, is that this does not mean we can't reject a theory of consciousness on *other* defensible scientific grounds. In proposing explanations for physical, chemical and biological phenomena scientists do this all the time. It is only when no reasonable grounds to reject a theory can be found that they insist on experimentally testing its predictions. As I have already indicated, I believe the unscientific nature of functionalism (which will be further demonstrated in chapter 6 of this book) gives us extremely good grounds to reject the many theories of consciousness that invoke it *even in the absence of contrary experimental evidence.*

The Ethical Responsibility of the Scientist

Since Richard Dawkins is a public figure dedicated to popularising scientific ideas and overturning naïve intuitions, I was rather hoping he would at least take some kind of stand against those 'safe' functionalistic intuitions that are holding back justifiable scientific thought about the origin of our subjective experiences. Due to the private, unverifiable nature of the claims people make about their experiences, and the impossibility of testing hypotheses about the existence of experience in other things, it is unlikely that experiments will ever be able to rule out those unscientific views. Consequently, no real scientific progress on this issue is likely to be made until respected scientists like Dawkins leave the safety of functionalistic thought, eliminativism and mysterianism, and promote the scientifically-defensible views on consciousness that are implied by its organised structure and biological context in spite of their counterintuitive implications.

Another reason I found Dawkins' answer to the monk's query so unsatisfactory, though, is because Dawkins often claims to be fairly sure that there isn't a God. As we shall now see, the question of whether or not a God is likely to exist turns out to depend an awful lot upon what the best explanation for consciousness is. And the explanation that I think is by far the most consistent with current science happens to be highly *supportive* of the case for God. Not just any God, mind you; but one with certain features that are widely attributed to God by followers of the world's main monotheistic religions. And intriguingly, some of those features could make that God capable of causing beneficial changes in the genetic code at a rate greater than would be expected from chance alone, giving that scientifically-predicted being the power to control the course of evolution.

CHAPTER THREE

Why it is Rational for a Scientist to believe in a God

The Problem with God

So what is a God? Obviously we're talking about a very powerful being who can accomplish extraordinary feats such as creating universes. That goes without saying. But what other attributes must the theistic (continually active) sort of God typical of the world's religions possess?

The one thing almost all theists agree upon is the idea that God is a person. But what is a person? Those theists almost certainly do not mean their God has a human-, alien- or animal-like body. What they do mean is that God has (or is) a *consciousness* or *mind*, and usually a very intelligent one. Like us, a God has experiences containing the information necessary for the requisite creative activities, is capable of thought and memory, has the ability to cause events within the universe in response to those thoughts and memories, and has the power to choose which events to bring about.

One of the main reasons atheists currently assume that it isn't rational to believe in such a being is the fact that in humans these faculties are enabled by a complex nervous system, and we have good reason to think that this would be the case wherever else they may occur. Thus in order to have these faculties, it seems that a being must first possess a brain – and a very large one at that if it is to know and remember pretty much everything. As well as rather hampering any plans such a being may have of being everywhere at once, a brain is an extremely complex structure. If the reason for positing the existence of God is to provide an explanation for some of the remaining mysteries of the universe – the origin of life, the fine-tuning of the laws of physics, the evolution of intelligence, etcetera – proposing the existence of something that requires a brain for that purpose is not particularly justifiable. One can easily come up with a more reasonable hypothesis – one that doesn't involve assuming the existence of an entity that is far more complex and organised than the most complex and organised structure that is known to have evolved. One could, for example, just say these things came about by pure chance, or that they are the consequence of a hitherto unknown fundamental law. Although unlikely, these options are more justifiable than a cosmic brain.

Of course, most theists would respond that the God they believe in doesn't need a brain in order to have experiences and thoughts, just as He (or She or It) can supposedly act without having a body. Atheists will then confidently contend that proposing a *disembodied* or *non-incarnate* mind as a potential explanation isn't any better because the existence of such an entity isn't consistent with what science has told us about the universe. In this, however, they would be wrong.

Non-incarnate Consciousnesses

As we shall see later in this book, current science actually *supports* the view that the ability to experience certain things (things like colours, sounds, feelings, scents, flavours, meanings and patterns of such things) is *not limited to brains or even bodies.* The common idea that it is so limited is an illusion – a very *powerful* illusion – arising from the way our experiences are organised. We don't just have experiences. We have experiences that very accurately reflect patterns of sensory stimuli, such as light hitting the retinas of our eyes – and not only the stimuli that are currently being detected, but those our brain is recalling and imagining too. Since a particular colour (lemon yellow, for example) is usually triggered by our eye's detection of light scattered from a particular material (such as a lemon or lemon-coloured paint or dye), people almost always think that a colour they see is a property of an external substance or surface. But it isn't. It isn't even a property of light.

As we discovered in chapter 1, the colours in which we see the shapes of external objects can only be properties of something deep inside our heads that our brain is using to *encode* that external information. And from what science has so far revealed about information-carrying structures in biological organisms, **this neurological use of colour should be expected to constitute a product of Darwinian evolution**. In other words, colours (whatever they are) ought to have been *gradually* adapted to this use over many generations by the slow process of natural selection!

That is what current science tells us; and it obviously means that at some point in the past they *didn't* encode visual information (or indeed any other information about external objects). Although they must still have been generated by brain activity at that time, the fact that we should expect them to have existed in a form that didn't encode specific information makes it quite possible that, like heat and many other by-products of brain activity, they could be something that occurs *in other structures too*. And I don't mean in the sense in which the 'lemon yellow' we experience is (wrongly) believed to occur within the surface of a lemon or some other 'lemon-coloured' object. I mean that colours like lemon yellow could occur in *other minds* – minds that happen to form within structures that aren't brains, and whose colour experiences consequently do not represent external objects, bitter tasting fruit or anything else. If the way our experiences are organised to represent things is a product of natural selection (as its design-like perfection strongly suggests), there is therefore a good chance that consciousnesses (minds) *are not limited to brains* – though any that occur out-with a brain shouldn't have organised experiences like thoughts and perceptions.

If what we mean by 'experience a colour' is 'detect a specific wavelength of reflected or emitted light, or the reflective property of a particular surface', then of course a brain is required. It is needed to analyse the signals from the light detectors on a retina, and represent the results of that analysis in a suitable form within the colour part of an experience. But since all I mean is literally 'have a colour experience' (which could be a nondescript blob of blue in a meaningless and formless dream, for example), none of that gathering or processing of information is implied. Consequently, unless it is the processing of information *itself* that causes the colour (a bizarre theory invoking the position known as 'functionalism' that will be rejected later in this book on the grounds that it is both unscientific and unsatisfactory) we therefore have no reason to think a brain is needed.

Why Science Supports Simple Minds

At this stage, you might be somewhat puzzled by my conclusion that we have absolutely no grounds to believe that a brain is necessary for the existence of an experience. Perhaps you are under the impression that a working brain is what *has* the experience. Hence, in chapter 5, I have provided lots of evidence that whatever our minds are they cannot be identified with the whole brain, or even with a large part of it. The vast majority of what goes on in our brain is *sub*conscious. And although one cannot entirely rule out the possibility that all this subconscious processing somehow causes the existence of our conscious mind, that again is an assumption – an extremely common assumption – that we have no scientific grounds to think true.

Nothing in science gives us any reason to believe that complex information-processing activity produces experience (colours, feelings, etcetera). In fact, the popular idea that the complexity of the brain somehow causes a mind to pop into existence is an idea that flies in the face of evolutionary theory and every other scientific discipline. Every other part of a human being is formed out of the properties and interactions of tiny particles of matter, and fashioned by the slow process of natural selection, so we should expect that to be the case with consciousness too. No part appears suddenly as if by magic, as would a mind that emerges from the complexity of a brain. Apart from the unscientific nature of such a postulate, it would be impossible to account for the contents of such a mind in any reasonable scientific way. Where would it get its experiences from? What could they possibly be made of? How could they come to be so perfectly organised to encode sensory information, memories, emotions and intentions, as they are in us humans? The idea that a consciousness only ever occurs in a complex brain offers no scientifically-justifiable answers to these questions.

To account for the existence of our highly-organised type of experience in a genuinely *scientific* way, other things *must* have experiences – particularly things that could end up incorporated into the structure of a human brain. And even the simplest such things must be able to act in a way that's guided by their experiences. If they didn't do anything at all to their environment they couldn't have had the beneficial effect upon brain activity that allowed brains to adapt them in the first place.

However, that does not mean these things (whatever they are) *understand* their environment, or *think* about what to do like we do. In most cases, that guiding cannot involve any understanding at all of what is being experienced because understanding requires experiences to be organised a certain way (current experiences calling up appropriate memories, for example), and such organisation has to be a product of many generations of brain-centred evolution. Prior to their adaptation by the brain, the effect of those simple experiencing entities cannot be guided by something that requires generations of brain-centred evolution to come into being. Instead it must be a case of those entities – whatever they are – *responding in some instantaneous and simple way to the basic qualities of the experience itself* (the colours, sounds, feelings, etcetera that it consists of).

Those responses must be different for different types of experience; otherwise it would be impossible to explain how different types of experience became adapted to different purposes (colours for vision, sounds for hearing, and so on). And in the case of at least one of those simple experiencing entities, they must obviously have had a beneficial effect upon the activity in some part of a brain. The entity responsible for that beneficial effect has to be something capable of getting captured or generated by a brain structure that can manipulate its form. After all, our brains clearly determine what experiences we have. The capturing or generating of that experiencing entity must have improved the way that brain structure worked. And due to further slight improvements caused by random changes in that brain structure, that entity must have gradually evolved the wonderfully rich organisation and information content typical of what we call 'human consciousness' as nature's way of *maximising that benefit*.

In that genuinely scientific explanation for our experiences (which I will expand upon in Part 2 of this book) only a tiny fraction of those experiencing entities ever have *meaningful* experiences like thoughts and intentions and mental images that they understand to be providing knowledge about the world around them. These are the ones that happen to be adapted to perform the very specific task that our own consciousness performs in the brain of an intelligent organism. The rest just have experiences. However, there is one important exception.

The Possibility that the Universe has a Consciousness

For reasons that will be given in chapter 12, the universe *as a whole* turns out to be one of those simple experiencing entities, and the content of its experiences just happens to be everything that exists (and probably also everything that has ever existed in the past). Due to the completeness of the information represented in those universe-wide experiences, there is good reason to conclude that they are meaningful ones. If the history of everything is always represented in the experiences of that universe-wide being, it would automatically know where things came from, and how one thing relates to another. It would not need a brain to supply that knowledge.

The question then becomes: with all things and their recent history already represented in its experience, and continually informing its actions, would such a being not be able to act intelligently? Since I can see no reason why it shouldn't be able to, I am confident that the existence of a brain-free, intelligent, universe-wide agent is actually predicted by current science.

Of course, for you to properly appreciate why I am so confident of this, I will need to convince you that there is something that the many scientists who are not so confident of this have failed to consider which is important enough to radically alter their worldview. It may therefore be of some comfort to know that I am not the only scientifically-trained philosopher to have reached the conclusion that consciousness (mind) is not something that only ever occurs in a brain. In the early twentieth century, this was a fairly popular position, though it is today advocated only by the occasional brave philosopher like Galen Strawson of the University of Texas (formerly of Reading and Oxford) who calls it 'the most parsimonious, plausible, and indeed 'hard-nosed' position that any physicalist who is remotely realistic about the nature of reality can take up in the present state of our knowledge.'[6]

In the next chapter, I shall introduce you to two eminent scientific thinkers who arrived at exactly the same conclusion, but via two radically different lines of thought. The first – an Englishman – was one of the highest authorities in astrophysics in the early twentieth century. He became famous for carrying out the first test of General Relativity (Einstein's extremely successful theory of gravity). And the second – an American – is renowned as one of the founders of the science of psychology.

---

[6] Strawson, G (2006a), p.29

CHAPTER FOUR

The Mental Substratum

The Nature of the Physical World

The great British astrophysicist Sir Arthur Eddington, famous for first observing the minuscule gravitational bending of a beam of light predicted by General Relativity, once stated

> It is difficult for the matter-of-fact physicist to accept the view that the substratum of everything is of mental character. But no one can deny that mind is the first and most direct thing in our experience, and all else is remote inference.[7]

---

[7] Eddington, A. S. (1928), *The Nature of the Physical World*, ch. 13.

He makes this observation in the thirteenth chapter of his 1928 popular book on fundamental physics *The Nature of the Physical World* (adapted from the Gifford lectures he delivered the previous year at the University of Edinburgh). He reached his belief in this 'mental substratum' simply by recognising that scientists only ever detect the effects of things upon their surroundings, and that their theories are merely models of these effects. They don't tell us what the things that produce these effects actually are – only what they are likely to *do* in a given set of circumstances. Yet unless we, as consciousnesses, constitute *immaterial souls* (a view known as 'dualism' that was justifiably out of fashion by Eddington's time and which we have no scientific reason to think true), we must be composed of some of the matter – the substratum – out of which our brain and body are made. Hence a part of that substratum is definitely of mental character – the part that is us (your consciousness and my consciousness). And since we have no scientific knowledge of what the rest of it ultimately constitutes – we know only what it *does* – we have every reason to expect that it too is of mental character.

It is important to emphasise that by 'mental character', here, Eddington did not mean his substratum was ghostly and insubstantial. Our experiences, judging from their content, are not ghostly, insubstantial things at all, but things that can be precisely controlled by brain activity to such an extent that they are able to carry stable, high-resolution, movie-like images of our environment. As such, they must be fully governed by natural laws. Although Eddington doesn't go into great detail about what his substratum is made of, he no doubt felt that its mental constituents interacted with each other in a very real way governed by some suitable interpretation of the known laws of physics. Moreover, some of their effects upon one another should actually be expected to consist of feelings of hardness, akin to those in which contact with rigid solid surfaces is represented in our experiences, and we don't tend to think of these feelings as insubstantial. In fact, they are where our very idea of substance comes from. Hence the view that the substratum of everything is of mental character is not a commitment to a ghostly, unscientific view of reality. On the contrary, it is a position that holds the promise of reconciling the existence of our experiences with the law-like structure of the universe that science has so far revealed.

The Requirements of an Evolutionary Explanation

Another advocate of this view was the nineteenth century American psychologist William James who offered a different argument in its favour. He rightly pointed out that unless some kind of consciousness existed in matter prior to the evolution of life, it is impossible to explain how a highly-organised example of such an entity came about as a product of the sort of continuous evolution known to account for all other facts about biological organisms that science has successfully explained. In his prestigious philosophical work *The Principles of Psychology* (1890), he wrote:

> Consciousness, however small, is an illegitimate birth in any philosophy that starts without it, and yet professes to explain all facts by continuous evolution.[8]

Many philosophers have objected to this claim by pointing out that lots of novel properties emerge only in complex structures, so

---

[8] James, W. (1890), *The Principles of Psychology: Vol. 1*, ch. 6.

why not consciousness? However, the point James was making is that if consciousness is not in matter from the very start, one cannot explain the facts about human consciousness *as a product of continuous evolution*. In other words, one cannot identify any circumstances permitted by the known laws of physics in which non-conscious elementary particles and forces would come together to form a consciousness.

That is not the case with other so-called 'emergent properties'. The facts about 'liquidity', for example (one of the favourites of philosophers who believe in a magically emerging consciousness), can easily be explained as a consequence of continuous evolution without needing to insist that liquidity was present in matter from the start. And the same is true of all other properties that are not experiences or aspects of consciousness. But it is *not* true of human consciousness, or any of the experiences it may contain. Consciousnesses and experiences simply cannot be formed out of elementary particles if the properties of these particles are exactly as most physicists currently understand them to be; and our consciousness could not therefore have come about by continuous evolution (the combining of these particles by natural processes).

The Task Ahead

To understand why James thought it so important that the facts about human consciousness *ought* to be explained by continuous evolution, we need to see how satisfactory an explanation has been achieved by those philosophers who think differently. We should also note that only a minority of philosophers nowadays agree with James and Eddington. As we shall soon see, though, that is not because any evidence against their position has come to light since

Eddington's time. Rather, it is due to a false confidence that modern philosophers have in the claims about consciousness that come from matter-of-fact physicists and biologists, very few of whom make any sustained attempt to overcome their common-sense beliefs about their consciousness.

As most philosophers, psychologists and neuroscientists are aware, many of the things we think about our experiences are not actually justified by the evidence available to us. In fact, some are even *refuted* by it – though even these delusory beliefs are very hard to escape from. You might be surprised to learn that they include such common physical and biological notions as the idea that colours come from light, and sounds from pressure waves travelling through the air, that a pain in one's foot is really located in one's foot, that a surface feels hard because it stops one's hand or other body part deforming it, that information guiding an organism inevitably gives rise to experiences, that you are a brain, or a whole human being, or even some relatively large part of a human brain's activity, and many more. Before we can form justifiable ideas about our consciousness, we need to recognise such delusory beliefs, understand why they can't be right, and reject them.

I have included chapter 5 for this purpose. As well as exposing these common misconceptions, this chapter also explains why, contrary to the conclusions of many modern neuroscientists and philosophers, human consciousness is likely to be 'a place in the brain where it all comes together' (a *'Cartesian Theatre'* in the derisory words of Daniel Dennett) – and a very small one at that. Only this can account for the fact that no-one ever detects neuronal structures in their experiences, even after brain damage or a bump on the head, and it is strongly favoured by the highly-coordinated way in which our experience changes from moment to moment.

The reason most scientists and philosophers nowadays reject this view is because they think that evidence from brain scans, and the power of many different types of drug and brain damage to alter consciousness, rules it out. Hence, in chapter 5, I also show why the widely-distributed activity that brain scans reveal to be connected with consciousness, and the well-known effects of drugs and brain damage, are in fact perfectly consistent with this view. Ironically, they actually turn out to be *more* consistent with this view (the view that the seat of consciousness is highly localised in a very specific part of the brain) than with the opposite view that they are currently used to justify.

If you are happy to take my word for this, though, you can skip forward to chapter 6 where we begin to develop the explanation for consciousness that fulfils James' and Eddington's criteria, and compare it with the popular alternative hypotheses. As you will discover, it is not only *far more scientific* than those other proposals, but it actually turns out to support our sense that we have some form of free will – a central assumption underpinning our criminal justice systems that has been largely denied in recent times by the proponents of those alternative views. If there were no free will, nobody could really be guilty of committing a crime. They couldn't have chosen *not* to commit it. And nobody – not even God – would be worthy of any praise (since they couldn't have done anything other than what they did). Any evidence in favour of free will would thus be widely welcomed by the judiciary and clergy, and no doubt by people of all religious faiths. As you will discover in Part 3, the type of free will implied by this scientific theory of consciousness plays an important role in the theological views to which it leads.

CHAPTER FIVE

Why You are likely to be something very very small

The Evidence of Dreams

REM sleep means *Rapid Eye-Movement* sleep. It is a stage in our nightly slumber that occurs in between waking and deep sleep when, if woken suddenly, a person is likely to report that they were dreaming. As the name suggests, it is easily recognised by the fact that during this dreaming stage of sleep a person's eyes move frequently, just as they do when the person is awake and attending to his or her surroundings. As we all know, when dreaming, that is exactly what we *feel* we are doing. Or to be perfectly accurate I should say, when we *remember* a dream, that is exactly what we feel we *were* doing.

There is in fact no way to tell whether we were actually conscious during REM sleep or whether we just think we were later on. The dream we think we remember could merely be a memory that we became conscious of when we woke up. On the other hand, the same could just as easily be said of *all* reports about our conscious experiences. Those reports must be constructed *after* the experience they are referring to, so how can we tell whether they were real experiences or just memories? The answer is we can't. Nevertheless, we rightly *assume* that they were real experiences because we know we are experiencing something similar at the moment we make the report. It is that present experience that gives us reason to trust our memory of a past experience – or at least, it gives us no reason to *doubt* the accuracy of that memory. And the same applies to dream memories too. Nothing we know of says that conscious experience only starts when we become fully awake, so the fact that we feel as though it began before then, and the fact that we have reason to trust those feelings, is justifiably assumed to mean that it did.

Since our eyes were closed at that time, though, they were incapable of obtaining relevant information from our environment. So why do they move? For some reason, during REM sleep instructions generated by the dream appear to be getting sent to the sleeper's eyes, regardless of their shuttered state, making them aim at different points in space – points where the dream suggests there might be interesting objects or relevant visual information.

One thing this tells us is that our conscious experience (which we are now justifiably assuming to include dreams) is closely associated with the brain's attention-focussing processes. In other words, it is somehow involved in the calculations that determine what our eyes (at least) are to be aimed at next.

Over the next six chapters we will be identifying the explanation for conscious experience that is most suggested by modern science. We will be examining how science explains things that have much in common with our consciousness, and accounting for consciousness in a way that is as similar as possible to those explanations. Interestingly, as we shall discover in chapter 8, the close association we have just observed between our experiences and those attention-focussing processes is one of the things that this scientific theory of consciousness *predicts*. Another is that conscious experience does not require the processing of *sensory* information. That is of course something else that our experience of dreams demonstrates. However, the part of this theory that predicts it says some surprising things about what a consciousness is that are quite contrary to what many philosophers nowadays believe.

As we shall see in chapter 7, it indicates that we are not something extending out into all the different sensory regions of the brain, but something confined to a *very small* region of tissue, and which therefore depends upon *very little* brain activity. Instead of extending out into those different brain areas, our consciousness gets fed the information those areas contain when we are awake in much the same way it gets fed the information from the parts of our brain responsible for our dreams when we are asleep.

The Moving Mind Mentality

Although the view that our consciousness is generated by a fixed region of the brain that gets fed the outputs of other regions may seem a *logical* conclusion to many readers, it is currently not the most popular philosophical position. Most philosophers nowadays appear convinced that our consciousness is not located in *any* specific part of the brain. They think it somehow emerges and vanishes in many different regions, summarising the relevant information that each contains like a reporter for a news channel.

I will be arguing against this view. To me, the idea that consciousness pops up in different regions of the brain is quite inconsistent with the empirical evidence obtained from verbal reports and brain scans. The patterns of activity that brain scanners detect never exactly (or even closely) correspond to the detailed structure of an experience that the subject in the scanner may report having at the time. Yet the view that consciousness pops up in different regions of the brain is motivated purely by the fact that this non-experience-like activity pops up in different regions of the brain of a conscious subject. If it were really true, one would expect to find some subjects reporting experiences that don't seem like anything at all, or that feel rather like tangles of neural fibres or lumpy regions of cortex. Such experiences ought to be brought about occasionally when those constantly-emerging-and-vanishing consciousnesses accidentally emerge in the wrong place (as they surely must do now and again with all that flitting around!).

This moving mind model completely fails to explain why we feel as though we are experiencing a lot of different sensory data at the same time, and why it all feels connected up correctly to form patterns that look (and sound and feel) incredibly like objects in our environment or parts of our body. And more seriously, it prevents that organisation and information-content of our experiences being explained in anything like the way similar products of the human brain are accounted for.

For reasons to be given shortly, the common idea that our consciousness reaches out into different regions of the brain when experiencing different types of information is as ridiculous as the ancient notion that sight involves our eyes sending out rays into our environment, and our current everyday misconception that we feel our fingers and toes because our consciousness extends throughout our body. Although the latter may seem like common sense, it is firmly ruled out by our understanding of the nervous system, and the many distortions of the aptly-termed 'body image' that neuroscientists have documented. In the case of both vision and touch, science has shown that information from outside the brain gets *fed into consciousness* rather than consciousness 'reaching out'. Information generated by sensors throughout our body gets gathered by the nervous system and *brought to consciousness*. And as you will see in a moment or two, the same must be happening with information generated by different neural structures *within the brain itself.*

Rather than being a reporter popping up all over the brain whenever something interesting or relevant is detected, consciousness turns out to be more like the manager in the newsroom who decides where next to position his reporters for the best chance of the best story. In a real newsroom, it would never be beneficial for such a task to be automated. If it were, all the news channels would send their reporters to exactly the same places – the ones associated with the stories their computers ranked highest in order of public interest. Due to the finite number of reporters on each channel's payroll, this means they would all neglect the same stories, too (the ones their computers did not rank so highly). After all, if they chose to report on these stories instead, they are likely to attract fewer viewers and become less competitive. On the other hand, they are also all much more likely to miss out on an exclusive, and their coverage of the news would be rather limited in breadth. Allowing their reporters' destinations to be decided by the imperfect judgement of a human being introduces a certain amount of variety into the news coverage that not only gives each channel the possibility of an exclusive, but greatly increases the number of stories that get reported on (when the coverage of all the channels is considered together). The greater knowledge of world affairs provided by that increased breadth of reporting improves the ability of all the channels to guess where the next big story is going to come from in time to have their reporters on the scene.

As you will see in chapter 7, the advantage of consciousness to the brain is rather similar to this superiority of the human manager over an automated manager in a newsroom. But we are jumping ahead. Before you can see this, you must fully understand what consciousness is, and why it cannot be the sort of inter-cortical reporter that it is so often assumed to constitute.

What it is like to be…a certain (tiny) part of a Human Brain

Look around you and consider what you see. You may think you are seeing various external objects – this book, the chair you're sitting on, the walls of a room – but that is not the case. You're only seeing *images* of those external objects, not the objects themselves – images generated somewhere deep within your brain. Now you might protest that the verb 'to see' actually means something like 'to experience current images of', making it perfectly reasonable to say 'I see these objects'. But that would be missing the point. As soon as you realise your sight involves experiencing an image – a pattern of colours and brightness representing something – you are faced with the question of where that image lies and what it is made of.

'In the brain' is the obvious answer to the first question, and almost certainly an accurate one as we saw in chapter 1. But *where* in the brain? And what are the colours that the image is made of? What part of your brain takes on the form of this book as it appears to you, for example, or the words on this page that you happen to be looking at; and then changes to some other form when you look at something else? The obvious answer is, of course, the activity on the retinas of your eyes. But that answer is wrong. Your visual experience can't possibly be the images on your retinas because it frequently incorporates optical illusions – effects not present in those retinal images. In the Introduction chapter, we saw that each retinal image has a blind spot where the intensities and frequencies of incoming light rays are not recorded due to the absence of light detectors at the place where the optic nerve is located. Yet in the image we see (even with one eye shut), that blind spot appears to be 'filled in'. We can usually only detect it in circumstances that trick the brain into applying the wrong type of 'fill'.

Since some philosophers (notably Daniel Dennett) dispute the idea that the blind spot is 'filled in', a less controversial example is the phenomenon of colour constancy. It is a well-known fact that the perceived colour of an object depends on the frequencies and intensities of the light from other objects, as well as on that of the light forming the retinal image of that object. This is one way the brain ensures that objects have much the same colour in poor light as they do in bright light (Why it needs to ensure this is explained in chapter 9). If the colour of an object were simply the frequency profile of the light coming from it, as is often naïvely assumed (even in many science documentaries and popular books), that would not be the case. They would have very different colours because the frequency profile of the light coming from them in those different circumstances is very different.

Hence your visual experience is not the image on your retina. It is definitely generated deep within your brain. The blue that appears to belong to the beautiful expanse of a clear midday sky is actually something inside your head, as is the pattern of green you see when you look at a healthy lawn, and the shimmering red glow of a sunset. Indeed, your visual experience of everything you've ever seen was always something that occurred deep inside your head. There are many other optical illusions that demonstrate this, but to my mind the most obvious evidence of it is the fact that we have visual images in our dreams when our eyes are shut. Those images are obviously nothing to do with activity on our retinas; and we have no reason to think that whatever brain region generates those images doesn't also generate the retinal-image-like patterns of colour and tone that we experience when awake. After all, it must be *perfectly set up* to generate such patterns.

But what then are the colours and tones out of which those patterns are constructed? Nobody knows. As we saw in chapter 1, they are a complete mystery to science. Although many science books claim to explain colours, all these books actually account for are the frequencies of light rays hitting our retinas. The claim that these are colours is completely misleading, for as we have noted, the colours we see can only be something generated deep within the dark recesses of our brain where those light rays do not penetrate. They must be something quite different from light – some as-yet-unidentified medium that our brain is using to *represent* those light frequencies and encode their spatial patterns (the retinal image) to form the images we see.

This may come as quite a surprise to many readers if my own memories of science education are anything to go by. Rarely do science writers and educators give you even the slightest hint that there is anything mysterious about colours. One comes away with the impression that colours are somehow in the light our eyes detect or in the pigments that cells in the retina use to detect different frequencies of light. You rarely hear any scientist announce that they are something completely mysterious that the brain is using to *represent* the frequencies and spatial patterns of that detected light. Yet that is definitely what they are.

And colours aren't the only mysterious medium our brain is using to represent information. *All* our different types of sensation fall into that category. However, we are so used to thinking of them as properties of the things they represent, rather than of the unknown part of the brain to which they really belong, that we rarely notice this. That scientifically-misleading way of thinking is no clearer than in the case of the feelings we call hotness and coldness, hardness and softness, wetness, dryness, and such like. Do you ever think the coldness of ice is something *in your brain?*

We often assume our feelings of touch are the actual pressures (and flow of heat) exerted by objects against our skin – the weight of this book pressing down on the hand you're holding it with, for instance, or the resistance of your seat to gravity's downward pull on your body. But they are not. The fact that we can have dreams in which we feel surfaces made of materials that are nowhere near us at the time (and if you haven't had such dreams I can assure you I have) shows us that the brain can generate the feelings of objects without detecting the physical pressures and heat-flow that such feelings usually represent. Not only can it create the feelings of objects, it can create the feelings of our limbs and body as well.

Amputees, for example, can often still feel a limb they no longer have. This phenomenon is usually called a 'phantom limb'. It occurs because the part of the brain that generated the feeling of the limb that was amputated is still there. If it happens to receive signals from nerves in the stump or some other part of the amputee's body, the feeling of the limb comes back (though usually not the ability to adjust its perceived orientation). Hence, patterns of feeling, just like the images we see, are generated somewhere deep within our brain and not in the parts of our body making contact with the external world. When you press down on a hard surface, the resultant feeling of hardness is not the actual pressure you are exerting but something your brain is producing somewhere inside itself as a means of *representing* that pressure!

This is confirmed by the fact that just as there are optical illusions, there are also *tactile* illusions. A person can be made to have touch sensations that are quite unlike the pattern of impacts that brought them about. There are even illusions in which the type of feeling that arises is dependent upon *how many* impacts take place in a certain fraction of a second. In these experiments the brain must actually be counting the impacts *before* it supplies the experience! But wait a minute. Doesn't that mean it would have to send the experience *backwards in time* so that it would begin at the same time as our perceptions of simultaneous events and stimuli?

Fortunately for physics, the answer is *no* (though I'm surprised at how often I find philosophers defending this suggestion). When one examines the scientific implications of the synchronised nature of our experiences in the light of what we know about the nervous system, how the brain achieves this feat isn't actually as mysterious as it at first seems. It is still far from being something that science can explain; but it needn't involve any time travelling.

What the subjective synchrony of simultaneous stimuli tells us

Tactile illusions where the experience depends upon sequences of touch stimuli are possible because of the surprising fact that our conscious experience lags around half a second behind the reality it represents. Yep! What you are seeing right now actually took place half a second ago! Although that may be hard at first to swallow, it is a conclusion that many experiments now support; and since it takes between a quarter of a second and half a second for some nerve signals to reach the brain, some such delay is clearly to be expected. A delay of around half a second allows time for signals from touch sensors in peripheral parts of our body (our toes) to reach the brain *before* the form of our experience gets determined.

Without that delay our experience would in fact be rather chaotic. Due to the different lengths of the relevant nerves, signals from touch sensors in our hands arrive at our brain about a quarter of a second *after* signals from touch sensors in our nose that are triggered at the same moment. As a result, if there were no delay in the construction of our experience, when you touch your nose you'd feel your nose getting touched a significant fraction of a second before you felt a similar pressure in your fingertip. That would be really weird, wouldn't it? Fortunately for us, the brain has evolved to delay the construction of our experience until all the possible nerve signals have time to reach it. It then constructs the experience in a way that ensures simultaneous sensory stimuli are almost always *felt* to be simultaneous. How it does this, though, is still a mystery because nobody knows for sure what a consciousness is, or – more controversially, as we shall now see – where in the brain it is located.

Over many years of research on brain-damaged patients, scientists have gradually developed a detailed map of what different bits of our brain do; and it turns out that different sensory information gets processed in quite separate – and often quite large – areas of brain tissue. However, that must not be taken to mean that our consciousness somehow extends over these regions. We have already noted that our brain must be receiving and storing information from our sense of touch for as much as half a second without us experiencing any of it. So there must be room in the brain for that information to be stored subconsciously. We have also seen that the brain must then bring all that stored information together and *construct* the detailed and mostly accurate experiences we have – a process that almost certainly requires much more subconscious neural activity. Hence, much of what goes on in our brain takes place *outside* our consciousness. The obvious synchronisation in our experiences of touch thus clearly demonstrates that we are not a whole brain – and as we shall now see, probably not even a large part of one.

Since the brain also synchronises our experiences of stimuli from *different* senses in such a precise manner – we see and hear our finger touching our nose at the same time as we feel the touch – this strongly suggests to me that our consciousness is in fact a single place where all that information comes together, rather than being distributed throughout the brain as most philosophers currently assume. How else could the brain achieve such a perfectly synchronised and interconnected representation of our separately processed sensory stimuli? If different aspects of our experience (such as colour and sound) were in fact located in different regions of our brain, we would expect to see regular mismatches between them, as in a badly dubbed movie, rather than the smooth transitions and precise associations that our audio-visual experience usually consists of. The fact that we don't generally experience such mismatches strongly suggests that those different aspects of our experience are part of a unified whole; and as we shall now see, this hypothesis is further supported by the fact that we don't normally have any experiences that are not encoding biologically-gathered data.

What the information-content of our experience indicates

If part of our experience were located in one part of the brain, and another part in an entirely separate region, one would expect to occasionally encounter experiences arising from the *intervening* brain regions. That's because it is hard to see why whatever condition makes the information in these two separate regions appear in the same consciousness couldn't accidentally be satisfied by the intervening brain structures. We'd then get a glimpse of their *normally subconscious* information-content: Duplicates of our visual images, for example, at an earlier stage in their processing – perhaps revealing an empty blind spot region or a lack of depth – or else discords caused by an experience of recently arrived auditory signals at the same time as those from half a second before. This clearly appears not to occur. Moreover, we don't have any experiences that we do not regard as representative of something that is, or was, or could be, *a sensory perception of internal or external stimuli or a state of mind.* We don't normally have strange, unidentifiable experiences that could be merely *random brain events,* as we should surely expect to have if one part of our consciousness arises in one part of the brain and others in separate parts linked by intervening brain structures exposed to all sorts of surrounding activity. Hence, the subjective evidence strongly suggests that we are indeed a place where all the information in our experiences is brought together – a view that is strongly supported by the explanation for consciousness that we will be deriving from science and rational principles in chapter 7.

Instead of originating from distinct regions of the brain, our different experiences would therefore need to be *distinct facets* of a *single, highly localised, but as-yet-unidentified medium.* It must be a medium that can be finely and instantaneously manipulated by neural signals, but only by those carrying the fully synchronised sensory data that the brain has decided to represent within it. As we have just seen, that is one reason we should not expect it to be something extending throughout a large region of the brain where all sorts of neural signals could affect it. However, as well as having such specific and finely-tuned inputs, it must also have an *output effect* on the brain that was somehow dependent upon these inputs. That is simply because if it didn't affect brain activity in a way that was dependent upon its inputs, those inputs couldn't possibly have evolved to control its form (and therefore our experience) in such a precise, sense-dependent way.

Such complex, design-like perfection in a biological organism can only be *scientifically* explained as a product of positive natural selection. It can only be accounted for, in a way that's consistent with established science, as the result of gradual changes driven by an advantage that small steps toward that design-like organisation gave our ancestors in their daily battle to survive and raise healthy offspring. And it is very unlikely that beneficial changes in the medium responsible for our ancestors' experiences would have arisen often enough to allow those experiences to evolve their perfect representation of sensory data if each such change didn't affect their prospects in a way that was always dependent upon the *change in experience* that resulted, and not on any side-effects.

We will be returning to these observations in Part 2 of this book. For now though, the relevant fact is that such perfection in the way our experiences represent sensory information is less likely to be possible by this process *the bigger or more distributed the part of the brain they constitute happens to be.* That is because the bigger it gets, the more likely it is that steps toward that perfect structure will *detrimentally affect another brain process*, thereby preventing them from being selected. This rarely-noted fact gives us further strong grounds to expect that this 'direct correlate' of our experiences is something quite small and highly localised – something that can easily undergo beneficial changes in structure *without negatively affecting the function of other parts of the brain.*

Now, I should point out that this view is currently a minority one amongst philosophers. That is largely because of the fact that brain scans of conscious subjects show activity correlated with conscious experience occurring (not surprisingly) in *many separate brain regions*. This is often taken as showing that 'there is no one place where it all comes together'. The highly coordinated and relatively seamless structure of our experiences seems no longer to matter.

However, in view of the complexity of the brain and the relatively low resolution of such scans, this conclusion is to my mind very premature. It is quite possible to conceive of a highly-localised consciousness whose effect upon brain activity *at the level detectable by brain scans* would still be widely and randomly distributed. This would create the illusion that there is no place from which all that activity emerges, when in actual fact there is. And it is also possible to envisage how data from widely separate regions of the brain could be brought together *without* causing a constant bright-spot on such scans, as I shall now explain.

How the Illusion of a Distributed Consciousness Could Arise

Neurons (nerve cells) are the cells in the brain responsible for its information-processing capability; and there are around a hundred billion of them in the brain of a healthy adult. Each has branching parts that allow it to potentially make contact with *tens of thousands* of other neurons. They work by firing off a chain of electrical pulses called 'action potentials', the frequency of which depends (in a complex manner that isn't yet fully understood) on the total strength of the inputs arising from the action potentials that other neurons generate. As with any other complex array of wires and switches, what they do depends upon how they are connected up. Due to their complex treelike structures, each one can potentially receive simultaneous inputs from *tens of thousands* of other neurons situated anywhere in the brain, and it can send its output signal to any number of target neurons that need not lie in its immediate vicinity. This makes it easy for a small part of the brain to receive inputs from many very-distant brain regions; and if its operation didn't result in a lot of nearby neurons firing, that region would not 'light up' in a brain scan.

The regions that do 'light up' are naturally those involved in *processing* the incoming sensory data and working out how it should all be combined and synchronised *before* we experience it. As we saw earlier, there is a lot of subconscious combining and synchronising taking place behind every experience we have. We only ever experience a minuscule fraction of the information being processed by our brain at the time, which is another reason we should expect that we constitute something very small. Each part of that processing will naturally cause regions of the brain to 'light up' in brain scans; and if the output of those regions is only used for the task our consciousness performs, they will light up in a way that is *perfectly correlated with conscious experience*. Yet we have no reason to suppose that any of these bright areas will actually be where some part of our experience resides. We only ever experience the *end-product* of all that processing; and what we (the consciousness) contribute in response may well involve very few *nearby* neurons firing off their signals. Hence, the observation that there are many areas of activity correlated with consciousness in brain scans does not at all rule out the very reasonable conclusion that our experience is part of a single, highly-localised medium in a very small part of the brain – **a conclusion strongly supported by its unity, the limited amount of information it encodes, and its highly synchronised and well-organised structure**.

Whilst the well-documented effects upon consciousness resulting from drugs and many distinct cases of brain damage are regularly touted as evidence that our experience somehow arises from many separate areas of the brain, there is in fact no reason to accept them as such. That is because drugs and brain damage could quite easily be affecting our experience *indirectly* by altering the ways in which images and other sensory and memory patterns are combined *before* we experience them. Remember, we are only aware of the final combination. Any change in the way it was put together would therefore naturally result in a change in our experience further down the line. In fact, given that drugs aren't carefully designed to generate particular types of hallucination or alteration of consciousness, my claim that they only affect the combining of memories, emotions and sensory data *upstream* from consciousness is more likely. That is because, were they to affect the part of our brain activity that constitutes our experience, one would not expect anything enjoyable or meaningful to result.

But why am I arguing for this minority view on consciousness? Well the reason is that, unlike the currently-popular 'roaming mind' type versions of functionalism, the view that our consciousness is a single, very small and highly-localised, as-yet-unidentified medium actually allows a *scientific explanation* for its existence and design-like structure. It allows us to explain its existence and design-like structure in much the same way science currently accounts for the existence and structure of similarly complex, information-carrying media in natural biological systems.

If this claim is true – and I shall show you why I think it is in Part 2 – that is a stunning achievement. If the assumption that our consciousness is a single, highly-localised part of the brain is the only way to explain its organisation scientifically, we should strongly expect that essential assumption to be correct. So why, you might wonder, don't more scientists and philosophers argue in its favour?

As you will discover in chapter 12, that scientific explanation appears to predict that there will be a consciousness associated with the universe itself – a consciousness that not only experiences and remembers everything, but which has the freedom to act anywhere in space and time on the basis of its experiences and memories. In short, it appears to entail the existence of a God. It also has some rather discomforting implications about what we as consciousnesses actually are, and it even suggests that our very notion of matter must radically change. Since one doesn't have to derive much of the theory in order to appreciate that it is likely to entail these things, it is very probably the sensational nature and political sensitivity of this fact that has caused this scientific explanation of consciousness to be so completely overlooked by scientists and philosophers.

But so that you can examine this claim for yourself, we must now turn our attention to the nuts and bolts of that explanation. We need to derive the basic details of this theory of consciousness by considering how science explains similarly-organised structures in the human brain, and then attempting to explain the facts about our experience in as similar a manner as possible. As far as I can see, that is the only approach that we have any reason to expect to be successful. We can expect it to be successful because similar things in similar circumstances are more likely than other things to have similar explanations. As you will discover, when we follow that approach it is not long before things start to fall into place in a remarkably beautiful manner – a strong indication that we are going in the right direction.

PART TWO

THE SCIENTIFIC
SOLUTION
TO THE
MIND-BODY PROBLEM

Behind the sight of blueness, the physical event
is as likely to suit vision as the one behind a scent.
If this were not the case, it would be a *surprise* –
A fundamental law of Nature would seem made for *eyes*!

The most we should expect is that the processing of sight
might result in slightly *more* events of colour or black or white,
and the processing of smell in more of odour than of hue.
But we shouldn't expect a perfect neat division between the two.

The fact that such a perfect separation was created
suggests our ancestors' genes were better propagated
when events with similar qualia became more and more confined
to bring data from but *one* of their senses consciously to mind.

To explain the gain in reproductive fitness this imparted,
it seems necessary to postulate an influence exerted,
by a mind that's *free and whole*, upon *attention*-shifting actions,
that's affected by the way that soul *experiences* its options.

C. S. Morrison (The Advantage of Colours, v.12-15)

CHAPTER SIX

Why a Consciousness *Must* Affect Brain Activity

Are we Epiphenomena?

Fix your eyes on a part of this page where there are no printed words, and after five seconds say the name of the colour that you see there.

If you followed this instruction you probably spoke or mouthed, or said to yourself, the word "white". But was that *you* speaking, or was it just your brain? Was the word "white" that got formed by your mouth or mind a few seconds ago something that your *consciousness* caused to be so formed at that moment, or was it simply the inevitable end-product of a chain of events that began with the light from the inky part of the page stimulating cells on your retina, and ended with your lip movements or the neural firings that generated your inner voice? Did the part of your brain that constitutes your experiences play any part at all?

The initial stimulation of those retinal cells sent signals into your visual cortex (the part of your brain that analyses the visual information), and there the patterns of light intensity were identified as similar to ones already stored in your memory. Through a complex process involving the language region of your brain, the accessing of these memories caused a plan of action to be formed and executed, moving your gaze to the inkless region and preparing your brain to trigger the production of a single word from a range of alternative colour words (though in this case probably very few) according to what signal next arrived from the visual cortex. But did the arrival of that signal *automatically* trigger the option "white"? Or was there an intermediate step whereby your consciousness, which obviously did receive that information, *freely chose* to say "white" rather than one of the other alternatives, and thereby determined what action resulted?

This is the age-old problem of free will. Do we really have a choice over what we say and do? Does our consciousness, in this case, have any influence over our speech that might make our production of the word "white" actually determined by our private colour experience, rather than by just the effect that the neural structures generating that colour experience have upon our brain? And if so, is it possible for that influence to be something that we actually have some control over, as we frequently imagine it to be? If the circumstances in which we chose to say "white" were set up in exactly the same way (with all our brain structures doing precisely what they were doing at the time), could we really have chosen *not* to say it?

Now, you might think the answer is yes, because one could easily have lied and said a different colour (and perhaps you did).

Likewise, you could have refused to follow the instruction in the first place (as I'm sure a lot of readers do). But many scientists would nowadays argue that your decision to lie, or to not cooperate, at that moment was actually made by a *non*-conscious part of your brain (or at least a part that is not *your* consciousness). After all, the idea of taking that rebellious course of action would presumably have crossed your mind before you did it, and the structures that subconsciously constructed that idea could equally well have initiated the action. Indeed, there is now a growing body of experimental evidence showing that the brain prepares itself for an action before you become conscious of choosing to perform it. Consequently, many scientists would probably attribute the making of that choice to the non-conscious part of your brain that fed you the idea. They would argue that you only *felt* as though you made it because your brain *made* you feel that way – and there is in fact a considerable amount of evidence that our brains can make us feel like we chose to do something we did not actually choose to do.

The existence of a part of our brain that determines how we feel about something was discovered by neuroscientist Michael Gazzaniga, and it has been given a fairly revealing name. It is called *The Interpreter*.[9] And the interpretations it comes up with, though often accurate, are created entirely subconsciously. We do not experience their construction, or the elimination of alternative possibilities that this Interpreter must be performing. The interpretation we experience cannot therefore be influenced by any free will we may have – which suggests that we are thinking what our brain *wants* us to think rather than what we choose to think.

---

[9] Gazzaniga (2012), pp.82-83. His evidence is from split-brain patients (patients who've had the corpus callosum – the nerve fibres joining the two hemispheres of the brain – severed for medical reasons). By getting their right hemisphere to respond to a stimulus unseen by their left, he found that the latter routinely *made up* an explanation for the response, which the patient clearly felt to be the truth.

Discoveries like the existence of this Interpreter (which renders our feelings of free will untrustworthy) have led many scientists and philosophers to conclude that our consciousness has no effect upon our brain over and above the effect of the structures that determine its experiences. They call it an *epiphenomenon* – by which they mean something that's caused by structures around it but which has absolutely no effect at all upon anything. They often use examples like a shadow or a reflection, or the steam whistle on a steam locomotive, to illustrate this concept. As you'll probably have noticed, though, these examples aren't very good because all these things (even shadows) do affect their environment. The truth is, there are *no* examples of true epiphenomena. But then, how could there be? Things that have absolutely no effect upon their environment couldn't possibly be detected by scientific instruments. We couldn't ever *know* of their existence…unless of course they are a part of us. Those scientists and philosophers think our consciousness and its experiences are the one set of true epiphenomena we *can* know about.

Other scientists and philosophers, however, are not so sure – and with very good reason. Although true epiphenomena are unknown to science, scientists do know of things that are *almost* true epiphenomena. Successful scientific theories do predict things that have so little influence upon their surroundings that it is extremely difficult to detect them. These things are thus very close to being epiphenomena; and crucially none of them is predicted to have anything like the sort of complex, biologically-determined structure that human consciousness shows. Those approximations of true epiphenomena (such as the tiny uncharged particles called neutrinos predicted by nuclear physics) all have very simple physical structures and tend merely to radiate outwards from a source. Human consciousness is completely different. Its sense-dependent organisation is reminiscent of the design-like structure inherent in fully functional and highly evolved parts of a brain. Its information-content is completely free from the random distortions and deletions that affect the information-content of shadows and reflections and other traditional illustrations of epiphenomena. And distinct parts of it (distinct ranges of experience) just happen to always encode functionally-distinct information (colours for vision, sounds for hearing, pains for damage, etcetera).

For reasons that will be made crystal clear in this chapter, this almost certainly means that its structure is a product of positive natural selection (i.e. Darwinian evolution). It evolved because small steps towards its current form increased our ancestors' chances of passing on their genes to future generations. And for that to be the case, it must be doing something to the brain. That is because a feature of an organism cannot be shaped by natural selection in a way that makes it perfectly designed for the function it performs unless its performance of that function has a beneficial impact on the organism's reproductive fitness (through improving such things as its health, attractiveness to potential mates, un-attractiveness to predators, life-preserving behaviour, or ability to raise offspring or protect relatives). Since consciousness is located within the brain, the only way it can do this is by influencing the brain's activity in some way. In fact, it must act upon the brain in ways that vary according to the different types of experience it happens to be having. Otherwise slight improvements in the way experiences represent information could not possibly have accumulated by natural selection to form the perfect experience of humanness that we modern human consciousnesses enjoy. Most interestingly, though, the fact that our nasty experiences tend to carry information about detrimental circumstances (pain for damage, for example) strongly suggests that its influence is actually dependent upon *the nature of the experience itself* rather than just the structures giving rise to the experience.

Although that on its own doesn't mean we have free will, it does mean that when someone says "white" their utterance could be getting caused by their *actual colour experience* rather than just the structures that give rise to it. And as you will discover over the next six chapters, when we try to explain in as scientific a manner as possible how this situation could have come about, the theory that emerges does indeed predict that we have a form of free will. It entails that we do in fact have some control over our speech and actions. That does not mean that we, *as whole human beings*, do and say things for the reasons we think we do and say them. Gazzaniga's experiments clearly showed that this was not always the case. However, it may mean that we, *as consciousnesses*, do. We may be *choosing* to do and say them for *precisely* these reasons (reasons that our brain presented us with at the moment we made the choice) regardless of whether these were the real reasons our brain was trying to get us to make that choice.

Fundamental Laws and Functionalism

To fully develop this explanation of consciousness would require a lot of very technical discussion. However, it is possible to understand what it involves without going into the technical details. Over the rest of this chapter, and the five that follow it, I shall derive that theory and show you how it accounts for all the main features of our conscious experiences. You will discover how it accounts for their information-content and image-forming nature; how it explains their link with attention; how the subjective separation of our senses can be accounted for (colours for vision, sounds for hearing, pains for damage, etc.), how it solves an infamous difficulty known as the 'binding problem', and how it explains the fact that unpleasant experiences tend to indicate detrimental circumstances, and pleasant experiences beneficial ones. You will also learn why such a theory ought to be considered more scientific than all other proposals.

The key observation is the fact that *all* aspects of our conscious experience have been adapted to encode biologically-gathered information (though when we are asleep they are not always used for this purpose). When awake, we tend not to have any experiences that are definitely not being used to represent features of our body, its environment, and its beliefs and intentions. Moreover, as the restriction of colours to visual information, sounds to hearing, and so on, reveals, the different aspects of our consciousness that we call 'colours', 'sounds', 'feelings', and such like, have clearly been adapted to represent distinct categories of information in a rather beautiful and perfect way.

Now, it has become common in recent times for philosophers to invoke functionalism to account for this beautifully perfect organisation and information-content. Remember, functionalism, roughly speaking, is the idea that the processing of visual information (in a certain not-well-understood way) *inevitably* results in colour experience, auditory information in sound experience, damage information in pains, and so on. It is as though there is a *fundamental law of nature* that supplies the 'right' experience whenever the associated biological function is being realised.

By 'fundamental law', here, I mean a principle or process that is *not a consequence of other principles or processes as far as we know*, rather than a principle that is universally applicable (as some physicists understand it). Defined like this, fundamental laws can be regarded as part of the very fabric of which the universe is made. Functionalists seem to be attributing all the design-like organisation of our experiences to a principle (or set of principles) that is not a consequence of any other principles – a fundamental law of nature. They seem to be assuming that the apparent coincidence of colour experience with visual processing, for example, is built into the very fabric of the universe.

As an example of a fundamental law of nature, though, this one seems to me to be extremely strange and out of place. Compared to the fundamental laws of physics – the only fundamental laws of nature we know about – it seems to have rather a lot to do. Since the neural signals carrying visual information within the brain are much the same as those carrying auditory data, it must somehow recognise that the former originated from a retina and the latter from vibrations of tiny hair-like cells in an inner ear. It must similarly distinguish damage signals from those triggered by temperature and touch sensors, and smell signals from those triggered by taste buds on the tongue. And it must somehow exclude from the experience that results all the images and patterns generated by the many stages in the processing of those streams of sensory information that occur before the stage at which we experience them. Moreover, unless a modified copy of the sensory image is reconstructed at that final stage, it must also correctly transform those outputs into such an image *in consciousness.*

A fundamental law that does all this seems, to my scientifically trained mind, to be more like a magic spell than a law of physics. The fundamental laws of physics all apply to entities (called 'quantum particles' or 'fields') that exist at the *very bottom level* of reality.[10] They don't describe retinas or visual systems or other

---

[10] There is an exception: the equations of General Relativity – Einstein's theory of gravity. However, the fact that gravity is not observed at the level of

parts of a brain or organism. They describe the tiniest components from which all such things are made. They make precise predictions about the interactions of these tiny entities that, with some suitable statistical assumptions, fully 'explain' the behaviour (though not the origin) of large-scale complex objects like living organisms. Although the laws of physics don't account for the *origin* of such large-scale structures, even that is not explained by invoking fundamental laws like functionalism. It is explained by the gradual process of evolution – a natural process triggered and sustained by an exceptional combination of environmental conditions (such as those that occur on planet earth).

Fundamental laws are only involved in that explanation by the fact that they endow the tiniest constituents of matter with properties that allow them to combine to form the complex molecules and environmental processes that make evolution possible. This is *nothing like* functionalism. As we have seen, functionalism demands the existence of fundamental laws applying exclusively to brains or whole organisms rather than elementary particles. These supposedly endow very specific brain states with the ability to produce minds that *automatically* have highly appropriate forms of experience – No evolution necessary!

The Structure of Matter

Even less like functionalism is the fact that the fundamental laws of physics don't actually apply to individual instances of the things that they describe. The behaviour of these tiniest components of

---

elementary particles is mainly because gravity is so weak a force that its effects can't currently be detected at that level. No physicist argues, for example, that the earth's gravity is definitely not a cumulative consequence of undetectable distortions of space-time caused by the masses of tiny quantum particles.

matter is in most circumstances **intrinsically random** or **'indeterminate'**. It is as though individual particles are *freely choosing* where they appear. The fundamental laws of physics do not tell you where a particular particle will be found at a particular moment in a given experiment (even when you know everything about how the experiment was set up). Instead, they make **precise predictions about the *distribution* of the energies and positions of particles that are observed when the same measurement is repeated a large number of times in an identical way, and they specify how these distributions change in different circumstances**. In other words, they tell you how *likely* it is that the particle will be found at a given place and time, or with a certain energy or momentum or angular momentum (spin), etcetera, and they tell you how that likelihood changes as time passes. **The way in which that likelihood varies across all the possible values of something you want to measure (such as the particle's position) is called a 'probability distribution'**, and this is usually the only theoretically predictable aspect of these variable properties that can be observed in carefully controlled experiments.

It is probably worth reading the previous paragraph again if you are unfamiliar with this fact because an awareness of the random behaviour of individual quantum particles, and the fact that physical theories merely tell you their *probability* of being in a particular place or state, is essential for understanding the theory of consciousness that chapter 7 proposes. When thinking about these particles, though, it is important to remember the lesson that Eddington taught us in chapter 4. Our measuring devices merely detect the effects that are exerted upon them. They tell us nothing about the things that exert these effects (other than that they exert these effects). What we call 'particles' could easily be just the effects of some deeper level of reality – which is, of course, exactly what their unpredictable nature and probabilistic behaviour suggests they are.

Although the way in which those probabilities change with time often depends upon the information those entities carry, it never depends upon how that information was gathered. Two streams of photons (particles of light) that are set up to have exactly the same polarisation (a property that allows them to pass through certain materials according to which way round the material is oriented) will behave in the same way no matter what method was used to set up their polarisation state. Likewise, two streams of free electrons that are accelerated to the same energy level will have the same effects on a given material even if different methods were used to accelerate them. Moreover, the *type of particle* in every case is completely independent of the information it happens to be carrying. Physicists interested in using such particles to perform computations will tell you that the same computations can be performed using photons, electrons, atoms, or whatever quantum particles they prefer. Their choices are purely determined by the practicalities of how easy it is to confine and manipulate the quantum states of different particles. Not by the type of information they want to encode. The type of particle being used doesn't suddenly change when they decide to encode different information in an existing quantum system. This is quite unlike functionalism, where the type of experience one has (whether it is a colour, sound, pain, and so on) is supposed to depend upon which sensory apparatus gathered the information it contains (whether it was a retina, inner ear, damage sensor, etc.) – and thus on what type of information is being encoded.

The thing that is *most* contrary to functionalism, though, is the fact that **everything we have successfully explained at a higher level than these fundamental particles has been accounted for**

as a product of the nuclear, chemical, biological and mechanical processes that the probabilistic laws governing those particles allow (combined, of course, with the initial conditions and subsequent evolution of the universe). In other words, all examples of *complex* organisation that science has accounted for have been explained as the result of *processes* rather than fundamental laws. That includes the organisation of the human brain and all the non-mysterious information-carrying structures associated with it.

To my mind this strongly suggests we should *not* be invoking fundamental laws like functionalism to account for the beautifully perfect organisation of our experiences. Just as the quote from William James in chapter 4 implies, we should be explaining that design-like structure as *a product of continuous evolution* in the same way science accounts for other parts of our biology that show a similar degree of perfection.

This means, of course, that we should be explaining it as the work of *natural selection* – Darwinian 'survival of the fittest'. We should expect the design-like organisation of our experiences to constitute the end-result of a series of gradual changes driven by an advantage that greater organisation within a conscious region of the brain gave to our ancestors in their daily struggle to survive and raise healthy offspring. And we should be explaining the existence of that conscious region of the brain, in the spirit of James and Eddington, as a consequence of the fact that consciousnesses – streams of experience – are a part of what matter *really is made of*. Consciousnesses ought not to be assumed to emerge from nothing. Like everything else, they ought to be formed out of the properties of elementary particles; and that would only be possible if some basic kind of consciousness were present at that elementary level in nature.

Elementary Consciousnesses

The reasoning behind this last assertion is simply the observation that the things that a consciousness is known to consist of – experiences – cannot exist without some consciousness to experience them. For a complex consciousness to be formed out of elementary experiences, there must be some kind of consciousness to *have* these elementary experiences. Now, philosophers often argue that the notion of a complex consciousness being formed out of simpler consciousnesses is not a very intelligible one. It isn't obvious what it means. Nevertheless, even if this indicates that such a situation isn't possible, as those philosophers no doubt suspect, this would still be no reason to believe in a magical emergence of consciousnesses at the level of brains – consciousnesses that, unlike everything else we know of, aren't formed out of properties of elementary particles. That is because there is an obvious alternative possibility that still allows our consciousness to be composed of elementary properties, just as a scientist should expect: The experience of a simple elementary consciousness contained within a brain could simply have *gotten more complex.*

It is important to remember that we will definitely need to assume the existence of *some* consciousness in the distant past that didn't contain biologically-gathered information if we are to explain the design-like organisation of our experiences in a scientific way. That is because the perfect nature of that organisation, and its obvious biological context, clearly demands that it be explained as a product of *positive natural selection* – i.e. Darwinian evolution – which would be impossible without the prior existence of such primitive consciousnesses. If there were no such consciousnesses, experiences could not have existed in a disorganised form in the brains of our ancestors, and could not therefore have had the beneficial and detrimental effects that allow particular design-like arrangements of matter (and hence experience) to gradually emerge over many generations.

To explain the information-content and organisation of our experiences in a genuinely scientific way, natural selection has to have adapted a *pre-existent* form of consciousness to a role in determining an organism's behaviour, just as it adapted the nerve-cells that became the brain and retina, or the reptilian jaw bones that became the mammalian middle ear. Primitive, unorganised consciousnesses arising naturally in some biological material must, via random mutations, have found their way into a part of the brain in our ancestors where whatever natural effect they have on their surroundings had a beneficial influence upon the operation of that part of the brain. The information-content and organisation of the experiences of those adapted consciousnesses must then have *gradually evolved a humanlike form* (a form reflecting the patterns of sensory stimulation occurring on those ancestors' sense organs, or being recalled or imagined by their brains). It must have developed that form as a way of *improving the efficiency* with which those consciousnesses performed their acquired biological function. That is the only way of explaining the features of human consciousness that is *remotely* like our successful scientific explanations of the most-similar explained phenomena, so our methodology demands that we adopt this position regardless of what we may privately think of its implications.

An important consequence of this is that whatever consciousnesses (minds) are, they must have an effect upon their environment that is dependent upon the experiences they are having at the time. And not just upon the *type* of experience. The fact that complex retinal images have come to be fairly accurately represented within the colour aspect of our experience means that the effect of a consciousness must depend upon *whole patterns* of experience, rather than on just the types of experience making up these patterns. Furthermore, since consciousnesses ought to exist at an elementary level in matter, as we have just deduced, we should expect to find an effect with those same properties *in the interactions of the fundamental particles out of which all matter is composed.*

Remember, as William James rightly pointed out, 'consciousness is an illegitimate birth in any theory that starts without it and yet professes to explain all facts by continuous evolution'. Some kinds of consciousness are therefore likely to be present in the substratum out of which all things are made (just as Arthur Eddington concluded). And we have no reason to doubt that these consciousnesses exert an influence upon their surroundings akin to the one we must be exerting upon our brain in response to our changing patterns of experience – the one that enabled human consciousness to evolve its current design-like organisation through the gradual process of natural selection. Since the gradual adaptation of that influence must *account* for the organisation of our experiences, the existence of that influence *cannot require an organised experience to come about first.* In fact, that influence needs to arise from consciousnesses whose experiences are *not* organised in any functionally-specific way, and these include the ones that we can infer to exist at an elementary level in matter.

However, if that is true, we ought to be able to identify what consciousnesses are. That is because the interactions between the simplest sorts of elementary particles that play a part in brain activity (electrons) are extremely well understood. They are described by a physical theory called Quantum Electrodynamics, which makes predictions that have been experimentally verified to an astonishingly high degree of precision. If there were some other effect acting upon those particles that the theory of Quantum Electrodynamics happened not to be taking into account, such a precise match between theory and experiment would simply not be possible. Yet all the influences known to be involved in the brain's processing of information are ones that result from- or affect-electrons (they are either electrical, magnetic or chemical in nature). So the same presumably applies to the influence of a consciousness. A consciousness must have some effect upon electrons. Bearing in mind our recent conclusion, that we have no reason to expect consciousnesses to be *limited* to brains, we can therefore be fairly confident that the effect of a consciousness (on electrons) has already been described by physics. Physicists have accurately measured and modelled it. Their model of the behaviour of electrons is so accurate that it must be taking this influence into account. They have simply not *recognised* that it is the missing influence of a consciousness that evolutionary theory clearly demands. In the next chapter, we shall correct this oversight.

Before we do so, though, let us briefly remind ourselves of the argument that has led us to this position. Remember, we are committed to explaining human consciousness in the way that is as similar as possible to how science accounts for the most-similar successfully-explained phenomenon. Whether or not we feel satisfied with the conclusions that result from this procedure is irrelevant because as far as accounting for consciousness is concerned we have no good reason to trust our intuitions. They evolved to improve our ancestors' chances of survival and reproduction – not to solve difficult philosophical problems. Since their track record on consciousness is not good, our feelings about a theory of consciousness are a far poorer indication of its chances of being correct than is the extent to which it is similar to the scientific explanation for the most-similar phenomenon that has been successfully explained. Remember, the more similar two phenomena are, the more likely they are to have similar explanations.[11] Hence, the sensible way to proceed is to first identify the explained phenomena that have *the greatest number of features in common* with consciousness, extract those that have *the least number of different features*, see how they are explained, and then determine the simplest assumptions that will allow the facts about consciousness to be accounted for *by the most-similar processes*. It doesn't matter whether we like the resultant theory. What matters is that we have followed this fully justifiable method of inference *correctly*. The steps we have taken in this chapter were as follows:

(1)   We noted that our experiences have a design-like structure typical of complex products of positive natural selection; and they are clearly produced by a biological organism's brain and used to encode sensory and other information.

(2)   This makes them most similar to the structures in a brain that have evolved by natural selection to encode such data.

---

[11] You might be thinking "my reflection and I are very similar but nevertheless have very different explanations – the first being a product of light rays, and the second natural selection". However, you and your reflection are actually very *different* things. When we assess how similar two phenomena are, we need to look at all the ways in which they *differ* from one another, as well as all the things they have in common. Although my reflection shares a similar form with the pattern of light my body scatters in a particular direction, it is nevertheless *purely* made of light, whereas my body is made of flesh and bone dressed in man-made fabrics. The flesh is made up of cells, and these cells each contain a complex array of biological machinery, including DNA, which is shared by a whole host of other objects called organisms. The similarities between me and my reflection are thus dwarfed by the number of things I have in common with every other living organism on earth. And, of course, its explanation is similar to that of another living organism rather than a reflection, as the far greater proportion of common features in the former rightly suggests.

(3)   To invoke that process requires, firstly, the existence of consciousnesses with *unorganised* experiences; and secondly, that consciousnesses *affect other things* in a variable way that is *dependent* upon their experiences.

(4)   Consciousnesses (whether organised or unorganised) ought, like everything else, to be formed out of suitable properties of elementary particles. Since a consciousness consists of experiences, this will only be possible if elementary particles can somehow give rise to experiences – a requirement that demands (or at least *strongly favours*) the existence of consciousnesses at that elementary level.

(5)   Since step (3) requires that our consciousness, and the unorganised consciousnesses from which it evolved, have an experience-dependent influence upon their surroundings, we have no reason to doubt that other consciousnesses, including those that arise at an elementary level, also exert such an influence.

(6)   We should therefore expect to find such an effect in the interactions of elementary particles.

As I have already mentioned, provided this argument is logically consistent, whether or not you or I like its conclusion is irrelevant. Our intuitions are not a reliable guide to accurate views on nature. What's important is that the conclusion we have reached allows us to explain all the other facts about human consciousness *in the way that is most like how the most-similar successfully-explained phenomenon has been accounted for*. As you will see over the next five chapters, that is indeed what it allows us to do.

CHAPTER SEVEN

Solving the Hard Problem

A Scientific Identity Theory

So what is a consciousness? Intriguingly, in fundamental physics there is only one effect that *could* be dependent upon a pattern of experience. And even more intriguingly, it appears to involve a *free choice*. We actually already encountered it in chapter 6 (p.80). It is the ability of a quantum particle or system to *freely choose its position or configuration* (or some other indeterminate aspect of its state) so that when one measures that property the result is essentially unpredictable. One can usually never say beforehand precisely what such a measurement will show.

Although random, this effect could nevertheless still be dependent upon a pattern of experience. That is because when the same measurement is performed on *a large number of identically prepared examples of such a system* (the same types of quantum particle generated in exactly the same way and passing through precisely the same experimental apparatus) the random results of those measurements always conform to a perfectly predictable probability distribution. Nobody knows why this happens. But judging from *other* statistical distributions – such as that which we might obtain by rolling a weighted dice (or die) many times and counting how often each number comes up – that calculable pattern of probabilities must have some underlying cause. In the case of the weighted dice, the cause is the internal weight distribution (i.e. the *density* profile) within an otherwise regular and rigid solid shape. Making the dice denser behind one of its faces makes it more likely to land with that face downwards by a certain amount, thereby increasing how often the number on the opposite face gets thrown, and no doubt also making it somewhat more likely to show one of the four adjoining faces than the weighted one. In the case of a quantum particle or system, nobody knows what directly underlies the probability distribution for each possible measurement.

However, that mysterious entity does have a name, and its required features are ones that a pattern of experience could quite conceivably provide. For example, just like our sound experience, it appears to be *wavelike* in nature. Another unusual feature is that it often requires to be widely spread-out across space, and yet every part of it must make an instantaneous contribution to the probability of each possible result that some measurement of the system could yield. In the same way, our consciousness appears to be spatially spread-out – How else could its colour aspect form spatial images very like those on our retinas? – And yet it must do something to the brain that's affected at each moment by its *whole pattern of experience*. If it did not, the presence of sensory images in that pattern of experience would be impossible to explain as a product of positive natural selection (and as we saw in the previous chapter, there is no other scientifically justifiable way to explain this feature).

That unknown physical entity – the thing that determines the form of quantum probability distributions – is called the *wave function* of a quantum system after the wavelike nature of the mathematical solutions that describe it. Since nobody knows what this so-called 'wave function' is, though, it is perfectly reasonable to suppose that it constitutes an experience or *combination* of experiences. In fact, that is the only means of incorporating things like colours, sounds, flavours, scents, pains, and all the other feelings we have – hardness, softness, hotness, coldness, joy, sorrow, certainty, doubt, etcetera – into our understanding of the universe in a manner that is consistent with current science. All other proposals suffer from the fact that they either invoke functionalism (supposed fundamental laws that sound more like magic spells than the fundamental laws of physics, and are never precisely defined by their adherents), or they require bizarre interactions to take place in the brain that are not known, or even envisaged, by physicists – interactions involving ghostly souls whose own structure and organisation is left completely unexplained.

By proposing that the experience of a consciousness is the wave function of a quantum particle or system, the existence and information-content of our consciousness can be accounted for *purely in terms of the processes and substances that our scientific theories currently require.* **A consciousness becomes the hitherto unidentified entity that freely determines the outcomes of individual measurements of indeterminate (uncertain) aspects of such a system**. For example, it is what determines where an individual quantum particle shows up when one tries to pinpoint its location (which, as I mentioned earlier, is something that appears to be chosen randomly – as though the particle had a completely free choice of location). **The spaces that a consciousness feels or sees or imagines become the sets of possible measurement outcomes that it chooses *from*.**[12] Its experience is the system's wave function, the form of which is fully determined by the system's environment – which explains how our experience can be fully determined by processes in our brain. And **the *effect* of experiences, so vital for a Darwinian explanation of the design-like structure of human consciousness, can be identified as the ability of the wave function to determine how likely each possible measurement outcome is.**

In this way, consciousnesses and experiences can be incorporated into our understanding of the universe *without any strange new laws and substances being needed*. All we need to do is show how some aspect of our brain activity came to depend upon the outcomes of measurements performed upon an individual quantum system, and explain why the structures confining that system would subsequently evolve in a way that resulted in its wave function containing precisely the sorts of information and organisation that are evident in our experiences. We would then be able to identify the aspect of that wave function encoding our visual information as *colour* experience, the aspect encoding auditory data as *sound* experience, and so on. Whilst these aspects must have distinct effects, it's worth noting that nothing requires these effects to be as distinct as the experiences that cause them. In fact, the physics demands that they are all *probabilistic* in nature.

---

[12] It's worth noting that in the case of our visual experience, at least, these would almost certainly have to be *positions* in the brain. If they were the potential outcomes of any other measurement, it would be exceedingly difficult to explain how they came to be organised so accurately into patterns so similar to those formed by the positions of stimuli being detected by the associated sense organ.

A View that Modern Physics Supports

Whilst some physicists have cast doubt on the possibility of quantum indeterminism playing a role in brain function, as this theory requires, recent studies do indicate that natural selection has adapted this fundamental effect to an information-processing role in other organisms, and even in the human sense of smell.[13] Moreover, it has recently become apparent that human decision-making often follows the sort of logic one would expect from a quantum-mechanically controlled system.[14] Of course, that does not mean those decisions definitely originate from such a system. However, it does indicate that the sort of decision-making that such a system produces proved to be highly beneficial to the human species. And this gives us good reason to believe that if the brain *were* able to adapt such a system for this purpose it would do so (and may therefore have already done so).

The reason physicists have cast doubt on this possibility is that any interactions with surrounding matter can 'collapse the wave function' of such a system – which simply means cause it to have definite values of properties like position and energy, instead of the indeterminate (uncertain) ones that a quantum system usually possesses. If that happened too quickly, it would prevent the brain making use of its quantum randomness and probabilistic behaviour in the way we will be proposing in this chapter; and the warmer and busier the environment surrounding the quantum system is, the sooner that collapse would take place. A higher temperature in physics means more movement. Hence, more frequent interactions. For this reason, the tepid and constantly active environment of the brain is rightly thought to rule out large-scale quantum effects.

---

[13] See e.g. Al-Khalili & McFadden (2014), pp. 161-9
[14] Aerts (2009)

However, in the position advocated here the quantum system involved *need not be anything larger than a single particle* (an atom or molecule, for example). Remember, it is perfectly reasonable to expect our experience to be located in a *very small* region of the brain, as its highly coordinated inputs, seamless structure, and limited information-content suggests (Read chapter 5 again if you find this difficult to believe). A very small quantum system – such as a single particle – could easily be shielded from its environment by some suitable biological structure long enough for its quantum properties to be utilised. The shielding would prevent the interactions that collapse its fragile quantum state. And when that was the case, even if it were something as small (i.e. light) as a single atom, its wave function would spread out to fill the volume of space in which that particle was confined and become highly sensitive to its surroundings, making it quite possible for these to input sensory data into its structure.

Although we would then be essentially a single particle, we must bear in mind that this does not mean we are a tiny spherical ball of mass or electric charge. As Eddington made clear, that is only what the *effect* of a single particle appears like to a physicist measuring it. It is not what the thing *causing* that effect is like. Quantum theory strongly suggests that the thing causing that effect is *widely spread out*, just like our experience seems to be.

It is also important to remember that the wave function of a quantum system is the only thing known to physics that our experiences *could* possibly be. Assuming they are not that well-known possibility is the same as committing oneself to the view that they are something *entirely unphysical*. It is the same as claiming that they are an emergent property that is *not formed out of the properties and interactions of known elementary particles*. No such property is known to science; though this fact does not stop philosophers suggesting physical properties that supposedly illustrate this concept.

They often claim, for example, that experiences emerge from brain activity in the same way water emerges from the chemical reaction of hydrogen and oxygen gas. Don't believe it! This claim is highly misleading. The difference between the physical properties of those gases and the physical properties of water is *nothing like* the difference those philosophers presuppose between brain activity and experiences. Although water does have very different physical properties from those gases, these properties are *fully explained by the way hydrogen and oxygen atoms interact*. In contrast, the components of brain activity as they are currently described by science come nowhere near to explaining the properties of our experiences. Taking into account our scientific knowledge of the properties of hydrogen and oxygen atoms, the physical properties of water are not at all mysterious or unexpected. It is only its *subjective* property of wetness that remains strange and unexplained. But wetness is not really a property of water at all! It is an experience that our brain is using to *represent* our body's contact with liquid material. Like all our experiences, it is therefore something in our head that still needs to be accounted for.

If one genuinely wishes to defend the view that experiences like wetness can only ever emerge from the activity of a brain, one must at least specify what properties or constituents of brain activity they are formed *out of*. What material (or immaterial) structures other than quantum reality could possibly combine to form them? Moreover, in view of the fact that the only scientific means of accounting for their organisation (natural selection) demands that they *affect* brain activity, the assumption that they are not the wave function of a quantum system ought to be backed up with evidence of the *entirely new influence* which that assumption entails – evidence that is nowhere to be found.

Which is more reasonable: identifying experience as something we know (the wave function of a quantum system), or claiming that it is something entirely unknown that must nevertheless affect ordinary matter in a way we ought to be able to detect but never have? As you will soon see, the known possibility has certain properties that allow us to *fully explain* why the brain adapted it, and how it came to encode just the sort of information we find in our experiences. First though, we need to ascertain what sort of quantum system we are most likely to be.

What Human Consciousness Most Probably Constitutes

Theoretically there is no limit to the size of a quantum system. They can range from the lightest elementary particles to the very universe itself, depending on which interpretation of quantum mechanics you subscribe to. Nevertheless, the system that we constitute must possess certain tell-tale properties. Its wave function must be able to exclusively encode *images and patterns* rather similar to those formed by light hitting our retinas and surfaces making contact with our skin. And we have very good reason to believe that this would only be possible if the system in question is a *single particle*.[15] That is because for a single quantum

---

[15] Remember, that does not mean a tiny ball of mass and/or charge, etc. That is only how the *effect* of a single particle on a measuring device appears to the physicist measuring it. The thing that causes that effect – the true nature of the quantum particle – is almost certainly something widely spread out (as the wave function that describes it suggests). Moreover, its form is completely determined by its environment, just as our experience is determined by our brain. Since the wave function can also be extremely complex – its complexity increasing with the complexity of the particle it describes (we could easily be some kind of

particle (and only for a single particle) the wave function is defined in a *three-dimensional space* – the sort of space we feel we occupy and think we see. For any other system the wave function is defined in a space consisting of many more than three dimensions; and as I shall now explain, if we were such a system we ought to experience all those many dimensions. The mathematical space in which the wave function of our quantum system is defined ought to *resemble* the space we experience.

Now, I have to be a little more specific at this point. The mathematical space I'm talking about is what's called the *'configuration space'* of the quantum system. That just means the set of all possible arrangements of its constituent particles in normal 3-d space. Since each particle can potentially be located at any point in 3-d space, each of these possible arrangements is mathematically represented by a point in an abstract space that has three separate dimensions *for every particle the system contains* (which, for any system larger than a single particle, is not something you can picture in your head – a fact that turns out to be quite significant, as we shall now see).

The way in which all the many spatial relationships on our retinal images are so clearly represented in our visual experience, and the fact that we have feelings that accurately represent the positions of our limbs and other body parts, strongly suggests that we are experiencing *some* spatial aspect of whatever quantum system we constitute. The measurement outcomes we are choosing from in this theory must therefore be the positions of the system's

---

complex molecule) – the view that we are a single particle is not in the least bit incompatible with the way our experience feels. Indeed, it is far *more* compatible with that than the view that we are a set of neurons or neural activity. We certainly do not feel anything remotely like the squishy tangles of vast numbers of interconnecting cells that form our nervous tissue, or the rapid electrochemical signals chaotically pulsing through it. At least a wave function *could* change in the dramatic ways in which our experience constantly changes.

particles, and hence the possible *configurations* of the system. For our experience to actually *be* the system's wave function, though, it must *fully determine how likely we are to select each possible arrangement of those particles*. And it could only do that if the space we experience is the system's whole *configuration space*. Only that will make our consciousness free to select particular configurations of this system in such a way that our experiences *fully determine the probabilities of those choices* according to established quantum rules. If some of the possible configurations were not represented in the spaces we choose from, then it is hard to see how we could possibly be taking into account the *probabilities* of those outcomes when we make our choices.

Remember, in this theory the spaces we experience can only be explained as *sets of possible outcomes* of some measurement that could be performed on the quantum system we constitute. In other words, they represent *all the possible values* which some variable property of that system could be found to have when the brain measures it. Our consciousness *freely chooses what the outcome of that measurement is going to be* by somehow selecting one or more points within those spaces. And the effect of our experiences is to make some points (and hence some measurement outcomes) *more likely to be selected than others*. Since our experienced spaces are probably real spaces in the brain (judging from the information that has come to be encoded within them), the measurement outcomes we are choosing from would have to be the *potential positions* of the particles our quantum system consists of.

The reason our quantum system is unlikely to consist of anything more than a single particle is because if it did we would need to be choosing *more than one position* in our experience at each moment in time. If we were a pair of particles, we'd have to be selecting *two* positions; if three particles, *three* positions; and so on. And crucially, we couldn't always be choosing positions that were near to each other. In fact, our experience (as the system's wave function) would have to be able to make some combinations of positions far more likely to be selected than others, *even when one or more of the positions are the same*. It is extremely difficult to imagine how our experiences could possibly be doing this. On the other hand, it is relatively easy to imagine how they might be determining the probability of us selecting a *single point* in our experiences. The relative brightness of the colour, loudness of sound, or intensity of feeling coming from each point could quite conceivably be doing this. Hence, we should strongly expect that our consciousness is indeed selecting *single subjective points.*

On its own, this observation doesn't mean that our quantum system is definitely a single particle. But it does mean that **each and every possible arrangement of its particles** must be **represented (in a suitable type of experience) by a** *distinct* **subjective location – a distinct** *point* **in our experience.** In other words, each point in our subjective representation of space must correspond to a distinct point in the mathematical *configuration space* of our quantum system, and vice versa. And this means that the latter *must have the same number of dimensions as the former.*

Now remember, that mathematical configuration space requires *three separate dimensions for each particle the quantum system contains.* Hence, if the wave function that forms our experience according to this theory were anything other than that of a single particle, the theory predicts that the spaces of our experience (our visual field and the felt-space in which our tactile stimuli are represented) would seem much more than three-dimensional. As they clearly don't seem that way, a single particle is the only reasonable possibility. **The possible configurations we are choosing from can only be the potential** *positions* **of that one**

particle within a region of real 3-d space somewhere inside our brain. And fascinatingly, there is a very obvious purpose for which a brain might adapt position measurements of a single quantum particle, as we shall now see.

Why Our Experiences Encode Sensory Information

If a neural structure confining such a particle were able to repeatedly measure its position, each time allowing it to return to its isolated quantum state, the results of those measurements could be used by an organism to randomly select between a large number of potential courses of action. The advantage of this is that it would introduce a *random* element into the organism's behaviour. Now, random behaviour would generally be bad for a creature. However, provided the options from which this system selected were constantly being restricted to ones calculated to have a high chance of being *the most appropriate* course of action the creature could undertake at the present moment, the result might in fact be highly beneficial. It could, for example, make it difficult for predators to predict what the creature will do next. It would also make it much easier for a group of such creatures to scan their environment for potential threats and opportunities (as they wouldn't all be looking at the same things at the same time). Due to the constantly restricted choice of outputs, the randomness resulting from such a system wouldn't affect those creatures' prospects in any *detrimental* way. That is because they'd never be able to opt for actions that didn't have a high chance of being the most appropriate thing to do in each situation they encountered.

But how does this explain why our experiences (supposedly the wave function of such a system) happen to be so full of sensory-image-like patterns? Well one of the requirements of such a system is that the set of behaviour options from which it chooses would have to be quite flexible. It would need to *change* from moment to moment in order to ensure that only the most promising courses of action were included. In other words, the brain would have to restrict this choice of behaviour options in a *controllable way* – a way that made it possible to choose from a different set of behaviours at different times. And the simplest means of doing this would be to have *all* potential courses of action hard-wired into the system so that each is chosen by a particular position of the quantum particle, and then use *targeted changes in the particle's wave function* to control which can be selected at each moment in time.

The brain could alter that wave function in a way that favoured certain choices of behaviour and made other choices much less likely. Remember, that wave function is really describing a spread of *probability*. Its size (amplitude) at each position in space tells you how likely it is that the particle will be found in the vicinity of that position. By altering it in a certain way the brain could ensure that an appearance of the quantum particle at a position where it triggers a typically appropriate behaviour is always made *much more probable*.[16] The reason this helps us understand why our

---

[16] Remember, the form of that wave function determines how *likely* each potential position of the quantum particle is (and therefore the chance of each potential behaviour being chosen). The quantum particle is unlikely to be found at positions where its wave function (technically the 'squared amplitude' of its wave function) is small, and much more likely to turn up in those where its wave function is big. A typically beneficial behaviour could thus be made more likely by having it selected by appearances of the particle at a position where its wave function has a high amplitude (i.e. squared amplitude). Although evolution could instead have simply allowed a *greater number* of potential positions of the particle to trigger that behaviour, once more and more possible behaviours were added to the system this solution would become less and less feasible. It simply wouldn't be possible to move detectors triggering other behaviours out of the way to make room for those triggering the more beneficial behaviour.

experiences contain sensory information is that the patterns formed by sensory stimuli interacting with our ancestors' sense organs would have provided natural selection with **a ready-made means of controlling these probabilities.**[17]

For organisms in general, the things they ought to look at first when exploring their environment tend to be *closer* objects. And these tend to be the objects that reflect more light in the organism's direction, make stronger auditory vibrations or nasally detected molecular signatures, and most importantly, those exerting pressure and heat (particularly *damaging* pressure and heat) against the organism's skin. If they don't assess the threat posed by these objects first, they may not succeed in doing so in time to prevent these objects reducing their chances of survival and reproduction.

To ensure that these objects are always prioritised, the easiest way – the way that is easiest for natural selection to discover – is obviously to let the size (amplitude) of the wave function at a position where an appearance of the quantum particle triggers a given course of action be determined by *the intensity of the sensory stimuli* **associated with that course of action**. Then whenever the intensity of those sensory stimuli increased, the amplitude of the wave function at the appropriate position would also increase. Since this would make the quantum particle *more likely to turn up at that position*, the action associated with that increased sensory stimuli would become *much more probable*.

Consequently, increasing the amplitude of the wave function would eventually become the only available means of increasing the probability of a particular behaviour.

[17] It's worth noting that the information from those sensory images may already be available in the appropriate region of the brain. That's because we can expect it to have been used for a similar purpose in the calculation by which a previously deterministic system chose the creature's focus of attention before the output of that system came to be affected by the position of a quantum particle.

Let us assume for argument's sake that the actions this system chooses between are shifts in attention, which we can crudely define as *changes in the direction in which a creature is pointing its sense organs* – an assumption we shall fully justify in the next chapter. Each point in space that a creature could look at or listen to or think about would then constitute a different potential focus of its attention that could be selected by a particular position of this quantum particle. And, for the reasons I have just outlined, the sensory stimuli coming from that point in space would be used to determine the size (amplitude) of the *wave function* for that particular measurement outcome. In other words, **the relative *intensity* of those sensory stimuli would be adapted to control the relative *likelihood* of the quantum particle showing up at that position and thereby triggering that particular shift in attention.** The more intense those sensory stimuli are, the greater that amplitude becomes, and the higher the probability of the quantum particle turning up at that position. If that were the case, the action of examining – attending to – immediately threatening objects would be made *much more likely* than other such actions because the greater intensity of the sensory stimuli they produce would, through its effect upon the wave function, *greatly increase the probability of that action.*

Since the form of that wave function is the form of the organism's experience, according to this theory, this very simple initial proposal would clearly explain why our experience has come to contain sensory information. It would explain, for example, why the intensity of colour experience[18] that we call 'brightness' appears to change in much the same way as the

---

[18] Note that we have not yet explained why it is colour experience rather than some other modality for visual information – a topic that will be dealt with in chapter 5. All this really accounts for is why intensity of experience is connected to the intensity of a sensory stimulus. But that is an important first step.

intensity of light that our eyes are detecting. And a similar story would apply to the intensities of all our other types of experience. The only extra thing we need to postulate in order to accomplish this is that the intensity of our experience is directly proportional to the *amplitude* of our quantum particle's wave function. However, if you recall that in this theory we (as consciousnesses) are freely choosing the position of this particle by selecting different locations in our experience, that extra postulate makes perfect sense. It is quite reasonable to think that a very bright colour at some location in our visual field could be making us *more likely to choose that location* over the many others that are evident in our visual experience. Its increased brightness would thus be making our quantum particle *more likely to be found at the associated position in space,* which is exactly what increasing the amplitude of the wave function of a quantum particle does.

The proposal that our consciousness is the wave function of a quantum particle adapted to introduce randomness into our behaviour in a non-detrimental way thus offers a logical reason for why our experiences have come to be so full of sensory information. However, this proposal doesn't yet explain why they form *images and patterns very like those in which that information is first detected by our senses.* Since we have so far not identified any constraint over *which* potential positions of the quantum particle trigger *which* courses of action, the fact that we can expect sensory information to be inputted into its wave function (and hence our experience) doesn't account for why that information has come to be encoded in patterns that are similar to those sensory images, rather than in some other – non-image-like – form.

To account for this extremely prominent feature of our experiences we would at least need to find some reason why sensory stimuli coming from (or associated with) *adjacent* positions in space (positions that were next to each other) would be adapted to determine the amplitude of the wave function for *adjacent positions of the quantum particle*. Only then would intense bursts of light coming from neighbouring points in space be represented by intense flashes of experience at neighbouring locations in the *subjective space* that the consciousness of that particle experiences.

You may have noticed that I am here assuming that neighbouring positions and directions in our visual experience, or the felt-space we think of as our body, constitute neighbouring positions and directions in the *brain-space* over which the wave function of our quantum particle extends. However, as no obvious alternative possibility for this essential mapping between experienced space and physical space suggests itself, this simplest possibility seems a very reasonable assumption to make.

You may also have noticed that this use of the amplitude of the wave function to control the probabilities of each of these possible courses of action (which is an essential requirement of this theory) does not appear to be the *only* means of controlling these probabilities. It seems that natural selection could instead have used *more* potential positions of the quantum particle (larger regions of the brain-space in which it could appear) to trigger shifts in attention to the sources of stronger sensory stimuli, and *fewer* potential positions (smaller regions of brain-space) to select sources of weaker stimuli. In fact, this is a simpler solution, so we should expect natural selection to discover it first. Hence, in order to account for our subjective sensory images in the way I have proposed here, we also need to identify a reason why natural selection preferred the use of *a very small region of potential positions* to select each potential focus of an organism's attention, and *changes in the wave function* to control its probability.

Why each point in our Experiences represents a point in Space

Another obstacle for this theory is that if each object we could look at – or indeed each *point in space* on which our attention could be focused – represents a possible course of action for that system to choose from, one might rightly wonder how it came to choose between so many possible courses of action in the first place. This is a very good question because until the right sensory signals evolved to adjust the wave function in an appropriate way (see p.103), each of these possibilities would have had a more-or-less *equal* chance of being selected (or at least a probability unrelated to its chance of being the most appropriate choice). The creature would have had just as much chance of choosing a typically *in*appropriate course of action as it would a course of action that had often proven beneficial. Such a situation would give rise to the sort of random behaviour that would be *bad* for a creature, and it would consequently be eliminated by natural selection. In fact, it would never evolve in the first place.

There is, however, an intriguing solution to this dilemma, and that is the possibility that the system started out choosing from *only a very small set* of possible actions that were each calculated by the brain to have *the highest or very close to the highest* chance of being the most appropriate choice. This situation *would* be beneficial because it would not really matter which of these more-or-less equally promising options the brain selected. The resultant choice would almost always be just as good as a choice made by a deterministic system (one that used a calculation rather than a quantum particle to decide between these options). However, the randomness that the quantum particle introduces would greatly improve the creature's ability to avoid predators and detect opportunities – particularly if it were a member of a group that could alert each other. That is because it would ensure that the members of such a group did not all explore the same options at the same time, which would enable them to spot predators and opportunities sooner than would otherwise be the case.

Imagine what would happen if creatures always attended to the option that their brains calculated to have the greatest chance of being the most appropriate source of data. More often than not they would find themselves looking at surrounding objects in the same order (noisiest to quietest, for example). To spot a quiet, camouflaged predator, they'd need to wait until at least one of their number had examined all the objects that its brain calculated to be more likely to constitute the most appropriate focus of attention (all the noisier ones, for example), and this would take time – time that could cost them dearly. **If instead their focus of attention were chosen randomly from a set of quite appropriate-looking possibilities, each is more likely to aim its sense organs at a different object**. Although the quiet, camouflaged predator may not feature as one of these objects, the simple fact that each creature's senses were being oriented to receive information from a different direction would greatly reduce the time that would be required before one of their brains picked up some hint of that impending danger. And as soon as that happened, all the others could be immediately alerted via an appropriate signal.

As a result, **a creature using a quantum particle to choose between a very narrow range of very-favourable-looking courses of action is indeed something we can expect to evolve**. However, due to the uncertainties in the brain's assessment of which actions are likely to be most favourable, such creatures would clearly gain an extra advantage over their competitors if their quantum particle happened to choose between *more* options – options that might include attending to quieter and less-salient objects like the predator mentioned earlier – provided one very important criterion was met: The addition of each new option to the system *must not reduce the chance of it selecting a typically more favourable option by too great an extent.*

What this means is that we can expect more and more possible courses of action to be gradually added to such a system, but only when the detectors[19] that select them are triggered by the

---

[19] It's worth noting that it is unlikely to be the number or position of the detectors that *directly interact* with the quantum particle that varies with genetic mutations. It is more likely to be the external structures that utilise the output of the system to trigger shifts in attention. The quantum particle is likely to be confined in a medium (probably within a single neuron) uniformly packed with structures that detect its position. Assuming that each of these structures produces the same type of signal, and only one can be triggered at any moment in time, an output registering the position of that particle could result if those signals were able to affect connecting neurons via *three independent paths* whose lengths depend upon the location of the detector that was triggered. If each of the connecting neurons were only able to fire when the three parts of the signal arrived simultaneously, genetically-caused variations in the lengths of the pathways connecting each neuron to the one housing the quantum particle would change which potential position of the particle was registered by that neuron. It's also worth noting that adding further connecting structures to such neurons would allow them to be triggered by more than one position of the quantum particle – thus crudely varying the probability of the course of action they trigger. Once a means of adjusting the amplitude of the wave function for each potential position of the particle had evolved, we should expect these extra connecting structures to gradually disappear. The ability to favour a particular behaviour by adjusting the amplitude of the wave function would make it no longer necessary for many positions of the quantum particle to trigger the same behaviour option. Likewise, if two or more of these neurons happened to be triggered by the same position of the quantum particle, one would expect natural selection to favour future mutations that caused these neurons to be triggered by *different* positions, thus allowing more behaviour options to be added to the system. Once natural selection had thereby maximised the system's efficiency, each of those connected neurons would register a single distinct position of the quantum particle, and the resultant output would trigger the processes that focused the creature's attention upon the associated position in space. Remember, random mutations could easily cause further changes in the lengths of the pathways connecting each of these neurons to the one housing the quantum particle, thereby changing which position of the quantum particle happens to trigger it. It is this that allows the future evolution of the image-forming condition (see chapter 8).

appearance of the quantum particle *in only a very small region of space* (thereby leaving most of the space over which its wave function has a non-negligible amplitude to trigger the typically more-favourable courses of action).

Eventually, however, due to the sheer number of possibilities that would come to be added through genetic mutations, the space available for triggering the more-favourable-looking courses of action would become infringed to the extent that it reduced the probability of those actions getting selected *below* its optimum value. Since this would prove detrimental to the creatures concerned, **the only way in which further possibilities could be added would be to increase the size (amplitude) of the wave function for the potential positions of the particle that selected those more-favourable-looking options**. However, if the amplitude of that wave function could be increased appropriately, only a very *small* (point-like) region of potential positions would be needed for *every* course of action that was included – *even for the more-favourable-looking ones*. This would maximise the space available for further additions to the system, allowing all potential measurement outcomes (each distinct position in which the quantum particle could be detected) to become wired up to select a separate course of action. As we saw earlier, **the intensity of the sensory stimuli associated with each possible course of action would provide *a readily available guide* that the brain could use to set that amplitude to an appropriate value**. It would be readily available because natural selection would almost certainly have utilised the same information for the deterministic system from which this quantum-particle-controlled system evolved.

Not only do these considerations provide a good explanation for how sensory information came to be incorporated into the wave function of that particle (and thus into our experience), but they also explain why point-like locations in our experience appear to represent point-like locations in the external space that our senses tell us about. That is because, for reasons that will be given in chapter 8, each of the possible courses of action that this system chooses between must involve the orienting of our senses towards a particular point in space. And as we have just seen, that course of action will have come to be selected by *only a very small (point-like) region of potential positions of our quantum particle*. Since in this theory that point-like region corresponds to a similarly point-like location *in the experience of the consciousness* that chooses the position of this quantum particle – in other words, *our* consciousness – the theory clearly predicts the emergence of **a one-to-one correspondence between** *locations in our experience* **(subjective locations) and** *locations in the external space* **that our senses tell us about** (where 'external' means 'outside the conscious part of our brain' rather than 'outside the body'). As you will see in chapter 10, that one-to-one correspondence is a very real aspect of our consciousness that is essential for explaining how our experiences allow us to understand the world around us.

Now, we realised earlier that the sensory stimuli coming from these external locations constitute a ready-made means of setting the wave function's amplitude at the corresponding internal positions (the potential positions of our quantum particle) to an appropriate value. And we noted that in this theory the wave function's amplitude is mainly determined by *the intensity of our experience*.[20] Since no other convenient means of prioritising those

---

[20] Remember, we are the thing that freely chooses which position this particle turns up in. The intensity of our experiences makes us more likely to choose one position over another. Although, for reasons given in chapters 9 and 11, it cannot be the *only* thing that does this, it does feel as though it is probably the most *important* factor. After all, our most urgent information (damage signals)

different sources of data is available, natural selection is bound to adapt that mechanism as soon as random mutations allow. As a result, **this theory also accurately predicts that the intensity of our experience at each subjective location will come to be mainly determined by the intensity of the sensory stimuli coming from the corresponding location in space.** I say 'mainly' here because, for reasons that will be given in chapters 8 and 10, the intensity of connected memories, ideas and emotions must also be playing a part. Nevertheless, the vividness and light-dependent variations in brightness across our subjective visual field when we look around us clearly testifies to the accuracy of this prediction.

And let's not forget that due to the inevitable uncertainty in the brain's calculations, it would be most beneficial if *all possible* courses of action of the type that this system chooses between were potentially selectable by it at each moment in time. As you will discover in chapter 8, these turn out to be shifts in our attention to particular points in space. We can therefore reasonably expect this system to evolve until *the maximum number* of these potential courses of action had been added – as many distinct shifts in attention as possible – the total being limited only by the availability of the brain space needed for the neural apparatus responsible for triggering them. As a result, this theory really does account for the information-content of our consciousness. The very fact that all the points in space we could look at, or otherwise attend to, will come to be represented by locations in our experience, and the very fact that setting the likelihood of looking at them will involve adjustments to that experience brought about by all the sensory information and memories associated with them, *guarantees* that all the observed data will be present.

---

do seem to be represented in the most *intense* types of experience.

As I mentioned earlier, though, it doesn't yet account for why that information is represented in the form of *sensory-image-like patterns*. It doesn't yet tell us why the intensities of sensory stimuli at *adjacent* positions on our sense organs have come to affect the amplitude of the wave function (the probability) for *adjacent* positions of the quantum particle (which we experience as adjacent locations in our experiences). The occurrence of this *image-forming condition* is slightly more difficult to explain than the presence and quantity of that information. Nevertheless, without that piece of the puzzle the theory would clearly fail to account for why that information is actually represented in patterns similar to those detected by our eyes, ears and other senses.

Fortunately, therefore, there is a way in which this system *could* evolve to have that image-forming condition. As we shall see in chapter 8, the circumstances under which that can happen are entailed by the only explanation this theory offers for an entirely separate aspect of our experience. And, once in place, they make the evolution of patterns of experience that closely resemble the associated patterns of sensory stimuli a seemingly inevitable product of natural selection. Indeed, the resultant story has a lot in common with the evolutionary explanations by which biologists currently account for the existence of those original sensory patterns, as I shall now demonstrate.

Why our Experiences form Sensory Images

The existence of the *visual* image we experience is the example we shall focus upon. However, it should be noted that a very similar story applies to the patterns of feeling we imagine to be our body and the contact it is making with external surfaces, and even to the patterns of sound that give us our sense of the direction of the sound sources.

Our subjective visual image is explained by this theory in a way very similar to the way in which modern evolutionary theory explains the sharpness of the *retinal* image that it resembles. Due to the existence of optical illusions and the filling in of our blind spot (ch.5, p.57, see also p.7), we know that our visual experience definitely is *not* that retinal image. So the question is, why does it have such a similar form? As you will now see, its similarity to the retinal image turns out to be because the structures that create it were formed in an analogous way to utilise the same information deep within the brain.

Remember, that *retinal* image is the pattern formed by the light falling onto the retinas of our eyes. Evolutionary theory currently indicates that it came about by natural selection because of the development of a transparent layer to protect the light-sensitive cells of a primitive fish-like creature.[21] These cells were originally only capable of detecting changes in the level of illumination in its environment (such as the shadow of an approaching predator). However, certain variations in the shape and density of that transparent layer and the distance between it and the light sensitive cells happened to make light rays from nearby points (or regions) on an object consistently detected by nearby cells, and those from widely spaced points by cells that were further apart. These particular variations helped creatures that inherited them make beneficial decisions more often than their competitors because it allowed their brains to gauge the size and direction of objects that could constitute potential threats, food sources, or mating opportunities. Consequently, it improved their ability to reproduce and outbreed members of their species that had variations

---

[21] Dawkins, R (1995) *River out of Eden* (London: Phoenix), p. 93

generating less-informative retinal images. This happened repeatedly in subsequent generations as random mutations caused further variations in the shape and density of that transparent layer. The system only stopped evolving in this way when light rays from adjacent points (or regions) on the light sources and reflectors were always detected by adjacent cells, and light rays from the same point by the same cell. This happened when the transparent layer reached a lens-shape capable of focussing perfect images of those objects onto the area of light-sensitive cells (the retina).

In the theory of consciousness we are considering, the *subjective* visual image (the retinal-image-*like* pattern of colours we experience) is accounted for in the following way: In some population of our distant ancestors, random variations accrued in the positions of the detectors involved in measuring the position of a quantum particle that had become adapted to direct their attention. Each of these detectors directed the creature's attention to a particular point (or region) in space whenever the quantum particle showed up in its vicinity, and certain variations in their distribution improved the system's ability to direct attention in a beneficial way. For reasons we need not go into right now (they are covered in chapter 8), this happened precisely when detectors that directed attention to *nearby* points in space happened to be *closer together*, and those that directed attention to points that were further apart happened to also be further apart. Eventually, after many generations, **the distribution of detectors became perfectly correlated with the distribution of the spatial points to which they directed the creature's attention**. (Note the similarity here with the evolutionary explanation for the *retinal* image).

Assuming for simplicity that this quantum particle only ever experienced different tones (brightnesses) of a single colour, it is easy to see that this would explain the subjective visual image.

That is because, as we discovered earlier in this chapter, the size (amplitude) of the particle's wave function at the location of each detector (and thus the probability of finding the particle there) will have come to be determined by the intensity of the light coming from the point in space to which that detector directs the creature's attention. **Since the distribution of these detectors becomes identical to the distribution of the associated spatial points or directions, the variation in the amplitude of that wave function over the brain-space in which the quantum particle is confined will become very similar to the distribution of light intensity over the retina** – with one interesting difference: Since the space to which attention gets directed is three-dimensional, unlike that retinal image, the final form of the wave function will include a representation of depth as well, which the retinal image lacks.

Finally, we must remember that according to this theory the amplitude of that wave function at each location in that brain-space is *the brightness of the colour* that the consciousness of the particle experiences at a correspondingly-placed location in its subjective field of experience. **The variation in that subjective brightness will thus very closely resemble the variation of light intensity across the retina, thereby forming the subjective visual image.**

As you can see, this explanation is very similar to the evolutionary explanation for the *retinal* image that our subjective visual experience so closely resembles. Since it ignores the multi-coloured nature of that visual experience (a topic we shall deal with in chapter 9), as well as the many other types of experience we have, it is far from a complete account. However, I think it suffices to show that this theory of consciousness[22] permits exactly

---

[22] The justifiability of this theory of consciousness is in my opinion a good reason to take the interpretation of quantum mechanics that it demands extremely seriously. It seems to entail that our distinct modalities of experience (colour, sound, feeling, flavour, scent) are each the effect upon the wave

the sort of explanation a scientist should *expect* to apply to our subjective images. And as far as I am aware, it is the only theory that does so. It is for this reason that I think it is correct.

Answering Initial Objections

Of course, if you followed the development of this explanation closely you will have noticed that it contains a few gaps. I have

---

function of our quantum particle that arises from the potential for a distinct type of interaction, and that the distinct forms of experience within each modality are the effect of independent *ways* in which the associated interaction can occur. If these interactions can be identified by comparing the subjective structure of each modality of our experience with the structure of known physical potentials, this may hold the key to ascertaining what sort of particle we must constitute (and perhaps neuroscientific verification of this theory).

Although we are only a single particle according to this theory, the form of our experience must be the cumulative effect upon that particle's wave function of the billions of quantum particles in its environment (since potentials in physics ultimately arise from particles). To account for the 3N-dimensional configuration space of the N-particle wave function describing the system that includes ourselves and all those other particles, each particle must both affect and have its experience affected by every other particle in a prescribed way (depending upon what type of particle it is). The location of that effect is freely chosen by the particle's consciousness but statistically dependent upon the form of its own experience (which, as stated previously, is determined by the effects of all the other particles in its environment). Since each of those N particles experiences a three-dimensional subjective space containing the effects of the N-1 other particles, and positions its own effect upon each of those particles under the influence of all those other effects, the result is a 3N-dimensional statistical pattern of subjective influence and response. Although the location of each particle's effect upon another's experience will thus be always randomly changing, there are usually so many identical particles that the constantly shifting nature of their identical effects is unnoticeable. All each particle experiences is the large-scale patterns formed by the differing densities of these identical effects in different regions of its subjective fields; and these patterns are determined by the controllable wave functions of these particles rather than by their random choices. This is why they are able to evolve, in suitable circumstances, to carry biological data and to encode high-resolution images of an organism's surroundings.

assumed a few things without justification. I have assumed, for example, that there is something that would make it beneficial for nearby positions of the quantum particle to trigger shifts in attention to nearby points in space. And I have assumed that the courses of action selected by this system *are* shifts in attention. I have even assumed the existence of something that would make it advantageous for visual information to be exclusively encoded in colour experience. That is not because the reasoning needed to justify these assumptions is not forthcoming. It is merely because to include it in this chapter would perhaps obscure the beautiful analogy I have tried to show between the evolutionary explanation for our retinal images and the evolutionary explanation for the subjective visual image that this theory offers. Hence, in the next four chapters I shall fill in those gaps. As you will discover, the mechanisms needed simply fall out of the theory in a remarkably straightforward manner. That, in my view, gives us further reasons to believe the theory is essentially correct.

As with every scientific theory that has ever been proposed, though, there are certain gaps that *cannot* yet be filled in. These concern the specific identity of the quantum particle we constitute, and the specific neuronal structures needed to confine it and cool it down and manipulate the form of its wave function in the very precise manner proposed in this chapter. Admittedly, this is a significant weakness in the theory, and anonymous critics have pounced on this as though it provides sufficient reason to doubt that this proposal is correct. Hence, let me briefly explain why it does not.

The first reason is historical. When Charles Darwin came up with his theory of evolution by natural selection he was proposing a process that required a sophisticated mechanism: the mechanism by which random changes in an organism's features can be passed on from one generation to the next. He had no good idea of how nature accomplished that feat and received considerable criticism as a result. Nevertheless, he stuck with his theory due to its logical scientific nature, and later scientists have proved him essentially correct. The existence of a mechanism of inheritance could therefore be regarded as a *prediction* of Darwin's theory – one that was eventually confirmed (first indirectly by the rediscovery of Gregor Mendel's inheritance laws, and later by Crick and Watson's work on DNA). I think the same should apply to the mechanisms required for my theory of consciousness.

I'd also like to point out that most – if not all – accepted scientific theories have rather similar gaps. Yet despite this, they are regarded as successful. Papers on quantum theory are not turned down because the author hasn't identified the mechanism that makes quantum probabilities conform to the square of the wave function. When quantum entanglement is invoked to account for certain observations, referees don't criticise the author for failing to explain the mechanism by which this instantaneous action at a distance occurs. And accepted neuroscientific explanations of subjective reports (what people say they are experiencing) don't get criticised on the basis of the fact that their authors never explain the mechanism that translates the proposed neural activity into the reported experience.

My third reason for believing that this lack of a specific mechanism is not as serious a weakness as has been made out is that the idea of cooling a particle down to near absolute zero, manipulating the form of its wave function, and then measuring its position, is a perfectly conceivable one. It is something physicists involved in the modern drive to develop workable 'quantum computers' (computers that use quantum processes to speed up calculations) are doing all the time. To my mind, if humans can do it, nature can do it a whole lot better – especially if it is something small. She doesn't require brains cooled to near absolute zero to maintain a spread-out quantum state because she has an immense variety of complex molecular structures available to try out instead. Sooner or later she is bound to find something that does the same job in a very small space within the brain. And I suspect she is perfectly capable of coming up with one that has a random effect upon its environment caused by interactions that are dependent upon the position of a single particle, regularly released and recaptured by that structure, whose probability of being at any location just happens to be determined by external influences.

And the final and most important point I'd like to make on this issue is that all other theories of consciousness are equally lacking in specific mechanisms to at least as great a degree as this one is. This applies even to those that identify an influence or emergence of consciousness with some kind of brain event or structure (the consciousness-caused collapse of a brain-wide quantum state in Stapp's theory, for example, or the gravitationally-induced collapse of the quantum states of intra-cellular structures called microtubules in Penrose and Hameroff's proposal). None of the papers on these theories suggest specific mechanisms that account for the perfect retinal-image-like organisation of the colour experiences that form our subjective visual image, or the equally amazing body-like organisation of the experiences in which our current touch and proprioceptive data is subjectively encoded. My theory at least identifies what the mechanism that it needs for this ought to do. I think it even gives sufficient detail to allow neuroscientists to begin looking for the necessary structures.

Of course, the proponents of those other theories may claim that they don't need a mechanism for this because they are functionalists. They believe that this human-body-like organisation *just happens.* Nature simply makes it so. But as I have mentioned before, such claims *do* require a mechanism. They require an exceedingly powerful and rather over-worked *Nature* that somehow *recognises* the occurrence of whatever functional criterion is believed to make a pattern of sensory data conscious, *traces the origin* of that pattern of sensory data back to the sense organ from which it originated, *sees* what the original patterns were like, and then *uses* this information to *reinterpret* the sensory data encoded in neural synapses (connections) into a suitable form of experience. And, of course, it must be doing this over and over again at each moment in time for every single conscious organism, and for each of its different senses. I think you'll agree that such a mechanism is pretty much ruled out by what science has shown us so far. So surely those theories that invoke it ought to be ruled out too.

The theory we've been considering in this chapter explains these facts as products of natural selection, just as science says they ought to be explained. And for this reason, it is far more likely to be correct than those other views. As you will see in the next chapter, our current inability to fill in the specific neuro-physical details does not prevent us from working out precisely how natural selection could have formed the main features of our subjective experiences once the proposed system had come about. In particular, it reveals obvious selection pressures that would act upon the proposed system, causing it to evolve exactly as laid out in this chapter, into a form that reconfigures the synaptically-encoded visual information into a perfect spatial image closely resembling the patterns on our retina. As I have maintained throughout this book, it is only when a theory of consciousness can explain our subjective images *in this scientific way* – the way science explains the most similar explained phenomena – that we have any reason to think it could be correct.

CHAPTER EIGHT

The Spotlight on Attention

Amazing Characteristics of Our Colour Experience

Staring intently at my laptop screen as I re-write this paragraph for the umpteenth time, I am amazed at how clear and steady my subjective visual image is. It is so reliably put together in a way that combines relevant retinal information with gap-filling memories that it hardly wobbles even when I nod or shake my head vigorously. As I read the words I've just typed, I am astounded at how perfectly formed their letters are. The Times New Roman font is exceptionally well reconstructed out of my black colour experience. The letters of each word I choose to examine are all in sharp focus and crystal clear against the translucent gentle glow of their uniform bluey-white surroundings. The tops and bottoms of the small letters all line up neatly in my internal visual space, and every other letter seems exactly the right size, and appropriately placed relative to its neighbours. The image is so crisp and undistorted I can actually make out its thinnest lines, the dots on the i's and j's, and even the sharp stylistic points where the lines terminate.

Living in the modern world, we tend to take such clarity and resolution for granted as we encounter it every day in the innumerable photographs, videos and printed images we are constantly bombarded with. We forget that every one of these reproductions required a sophisticated image-forming medium – a good quality, perfectly smooth photo-paper or camera film, or a highly-ordered LCD display intricately programmed to decode and re-present digital or analogue information from scanned, recorded or broadcasted images in forms that closely resemble the original objects. They are not something we would normally expect to find within a bumpy and wobbly jelly-like mass of tangled neural fibres such as that which lies beneath our skulls. Yet such images obviously are formed within that jelly-like mass, as our experience of them reveals. The information content of those visual images clearly shows that they are *not* formed on the retina at the back of our eyes, but somewhere deep inside our brain.

Now, I should point out that the superb clarity and high resolution of our subjective visual image only actually applies to a *small central portion* of that image. On my laptop screen, I can only make out the dots on the i's and j's when I'm looking directly at a word that contains them. I have to actually shift my gaze in order to read any of the other words. However, these observations do not constitute reasonable grounds to claim (as some philosophers have) that such an image doesn't exist in my brain. That high-resolution central region obviously *does* exist, and the rest of it *seems* to be there. As far as I can see, this *seeming* simply cannot be explained unless the way it seemed to me was actually a pattern that my colour experience formed for at least part of the time I was examining these words. The very occurrence of this seeming tells me that whatever my peripheral colour experiences constitute, they have indeed been formed into a background image perfectly aligned with the high-resolution central portion of my visual field that contained the word I was examining.

The theory developed in the previous chapter showed how such an image could come about despite the brain's wobbly jelly-like consistency and uneven texture. Interestingly, as we look in more detail at that process we discover that the proposed image could not have been created by natural selection *without* the sort of high-resolution foreground and lower quality background that a careful analysis of our visual experience reveals. It is discoveries like this that give me a *not unjustifiable* sense that this theory really is on the right lines.

Why Consciousness is Linked with Attention

Perhaps the most obvious reason to think this theory is correct is the fact that it fully explains why the information most evident in our experience at each moment in time is the small part of our sensory or memory data that our brain happens to be paying attention to. In the above example that was the word I was looking at on my laptop screen; but at other times it could be a sound I'm listening to, or something I'm feeling or thinking about. As you will see in this chapter, this theory provides a very simple explanation for why the thing we are looking at or listening to or thinking about at each particular moment appears to stand out, whilst at the same time seeming not to lose its link with other things around it. We seem to remain aware of those other things, but only as related patterns of background colour or sound or feeling until they themselves jump out at us when our attention shifts.

Neuroscientists already know what this shifting attention is. It is a mechanism the brain has evolved in order to cope with the vast amount of sensory information it receives at each moment of time. Due to the fact that we only have one set of sense organs, it is impossible to direct them at the same moment towards every interesting source of sensory information. Hence the brain must prioritise. Attention is simply the brain directing its information-gathering resources to the source of data that it calculates to be the one most likely to offer the most appropriate information at that moment in time – the information most conducive to making beneficial choices of behaviour.[23] It is important to note that often those choices of behaviour include where next to shift its attention, and that these choices will usually be the ones it makes *most frequently*.

Although neuroscientists know what attention is, few have any defensible idea of why its focus seems so evident in our experience, or why we feel as though we also sense the presence of an unattended background. Philosophers often suggest that this is because the neural processes that direct an organism's attention are the *cause* of consciousness. But as we discussed in chapter 6, such functionalistic views are neither satisfactory nor justifiable in the light of what science has revealed. We have no scientific reason to

---

[23] Admittedly that may be a memory or thought, rather than a source of sensory data. However, even when that is the case, our senses must be directed *somewhere* while our brain analyses that thought or memory – preferably towards the object the brain needs to identify or assess next, or at least to a location from which it is likely to be easiest to shift attention to such an object (if it is yet to be identified). Hence there will still be a most appropriate position to which the sense organs ought to be directed for greatest data-gathering efficiency.

expect our consciousness to be generated by our brain's performance of a particular function; and we have many scientific reasons to expect it to be something (the wave function of a quantum particle) that was instead adapted to the associated role in the brain through the gradual process of natural selection as chapter 7 proposes.

So the question is: Is there some reason why a confined quantum particle would be adapted to choose between different potential foci of attention, rather than between some other set of behaviour options (such as what to eat for one's next meal, or where to go on vacation)?

As it turns out, the answer is yes. The key property of the proposed decision-making system is that its output is random. The position the quantum particle turns up at each time a measurement is made is never predictable. And as any wandering drunk knows, random behaviour is not generally conducive to survival. It does not normally increase one's chances of procreation or raising healthy offspring. As we realised in chapter 7, the only way such a decision-making system could possibly be adapted to a beneficial role is if it was adapted to choose between behaviour options that the brain had already calculated to have the highest (or very close to the highest) chance of being the most appropriate choice the creature could make. **Only when it doesn't really matter which option is chosen could pure randomness have a beneficial influence on the creature's survival chances** (through making its behaviour difficult for its predators to predict, and through improving the efficiency with which groups of such creatures explore their environment).

Of course, due to the effect of the wave function the output of the proposed system is not *purely* random. The quantum particle turns up in the vicinity of some locations less often than it does in others. And as we saw in the previous chapter, this effect could allow behaviour choices that were not as likely to be the most beneficial to get included in the system's output. However, that could only happen gradually. When it was first adapted, the random output of this system means it could only have been used to choose between options that had a very high chance of being the most appropriate choice.

Even then, though, there is a circumstance that would prevent such a system being of any benefit to a creature. That circumstance is the presence of another system making random choices that affect how likely the first system's options are to be the most appropriate choice. Say, one system randomly choosing the focus of attention whilst another randomly decides what activity to do next (a choice that will inevitably affect the priorities for the attention-focussing system). In that circumstance, even if the options from which the first system chooses were determined by the output of the second system, there'd be no advantage for the organism in having that later choice made by another quantum particle. That's because it wouldn't matter if the later choice were made by a fully deterministic process. The behaviour that results would be *just as unpredictable* due to the effect of the earlier choice (the random one) upon the options from which the second system (the deterministic one) selected. And if there were no benefit to the organism from replacing a fully deterministic process with a quantum-particle-controlled one, whose output will not always be the one the deterministic system would calculate to be most appropriate, we should not expect that replacement to occur.[24]

---

[24] The only advantage of the quantum-particle-controlled system is that it introduces unpredictability into a creature's behaviour. When the creature's behaviour would otherwise be deterministic, this advantage would easily exceed the slight cost incurred by the fact that the random choice will sometimes select

What this means is that we should expect only *one* decision-making process to have adapted the proposed random-output system. Moreover, in view of the considerable *benefits* of randomness in choices where each option is more-or-less just as likely as all the others to be the most appropriate choice, we should expect that process to be **the one that makes behaviour-altering choices of this nature** *most frequently*. As we noted earlier, that most-frequent behaviour-altering process is the one that chooses what a creature *attends to* at each moment in time.

Now it should be noted that this does not mean that *every* shift in our attention will have come to be controlled by such a system. It is now well established that the focussing of our attention involves many competing processes, some of which (such as those triggered by unexpected movements) are clearly automatic reflexes brought about by deterministic circuits that have evolved to ensure evasive courses of action are implemented in time to avoid collision or capture. What it does mean is that we should expect the proposed quantum system to be adapted to control *one* of those competing processes. Moreover, since the data used by this system represents the state of our body and its environment around half a second ago (see chapter 5), we should expect that system to be choosing between sources of data that have been detectable for at least that long – and not one that controls emergency responses to impending threats, or any other immediate data-gathering tasks. This is, of course, perfectly consistent with the fact that unexpected changes in experience – sudden movements or highly unusual shapes – tend to 'catch our eye' immediately. We only seem to choose our focus once the unexpected patterns have been assessed.

---

slightly less-favourable-looking courses of action. However, if the creature's behaviour were already unpredictable, this cost would *not* be compensated.

The Salience of the Attended Object

Whilst that explains why there is a connection between our experiences and the neural process that shifts our attention, it doesn't yet account for why the object we are looking at, listening to, or remembering appears to be more salient in our experience than the things that surround it. To see why that happens we need to remember back to the previous chapter where I explained how sensory information became encoded in our experiences in the first place. The reason was that variations in the intensity of the stimuli detected by our senses turned out to be a convenient means of adjusting the quantum particle's wave function so as to favour attention being focussed on sources of data that were most likely to be most appropriate. In particular, increases in the intensity of visual stimuli were adapted to increase the amplitude of the wave function (the probability) for the positions of the quantum particle that directed attention to those stimuli. This resulted in intensity of light being represented by the intensity of some suitable aspect of our experience (in this case the brightness of a colour – though we haven't yet ruled out other aspects of our experience like the loudness of a sound or the hotness of a feeling of warmth).

We can understand why those increases in the amplitude of the wave function produced increases in the intensity of our experience in the following way: Recall that the amplitude of the wave function in quantum physics is what determines the *probability* of the quantum particle showing up at each of its potential positions. The larger the amplitude at a particular position, the more likely it is that the quantum particle will be found there when a measurement of its position is made. But now remember that according to our current theory its position is actually being *freely chosen* at that moment *by our consciousness.*

The amplitude of the wave function must therefore be affecting that conscious choice in a way that makes our consciousness more likely to select a location where that amplitude is high. This is where the intensity of our experience comes in. The intensity of an experience (such as the brightness of a colour) is directly connected with the amplitude of the wave function simply because it does exactly the same thing. Intense experience *makes our consciousness more likely to choose the position where the intense experience is located* when it next decides where the quantum particle we constitute will be found. As we shall now see, the salience of the object in our attention is probably doing that too.

Like brightness, the *salience* of the part of our experience representing the object we are currently attending to appears to make us focus subjectively on that part of our experience in preference to other parts. Consequently, we have reason to believe that it is another example of an instance where the amplitude of the wave function has been increased to favour certain positions of our quantum particle. All we therefore need to do in order to explain this so-called 'spotlight' of attention is to identify a reason why positions of the quantum particle directing attention to locations on or nearby the currently attended object would *need* to be favoured. What benefit would increasing the probability that attention will remain on the current object have given to our ancestors?

Although you might think there'd be no benefit in this whatsoever because attention is already focussed upon that object, we have to take into account the fact that, as far as this system is concerned, the focus of attention is not actually an object but a point in space. The purpose of this system is to choose the point that our sense organs are to be aimed at next. Only that will allow us to account for the very high spatial resolution of our visual images in the way proposed in chapter 7. Hence the point in space that they are currently aimed at is our current focus of attention, not the object on which that point lies; and the salient region of our experience representing that object will inevitably include a lot of locations representing positions in space that we have not actually focussed attention upon. To explain its salience we need to identify something that makes it more advantageous for us to attend to one of these positions next as opposed to attending to some other point in space. And just such an advantage becomes apparent when one asks the question: What is the most *efficient* way for such a creature to gather information from its environment?

If one's attention simply jumped from one point to *any* other (as would happen according to this theory if all parts of our experience were equally salient), the process of gathering inform-ation would become considerably inefficient. Apart from the fact that our eye and neck muscles would become quite exhausted as our gaze constantly swivelled through relatively large angles in response to the brain's instructions, the brain itself would take a lot longer to identify and respond to the most urgent stimuli. That's because those things are often things that are moving or things that are close. To identify moving objects and determine whether they are approaching (a potential threat) or receding (less urgent), as well as how distant they are and how fast they're moving, the brain must acquire several images of the same part of its visual field. If we were randomly shifting attention all the time between widely spaced locations, it would take longer to obtain those images than it would if our gaze paused long enough at each position for those images to be immediately gathered. Although that would reduce the speed at which our gaze could shift to other parts of our visual field, the advantage gained from being able to immediately identify or form a reasonable assessment of each object we look at would far outweigh this slight disadvantage because it would allow the brain to calculate where next our attention should shift for the best chance of obtaining the most beneficial data.

Although we often feel we chose to look at certain things, our attention does also appear to shift unconsciously on a regular basis. Hence as well as responding to the random outputs of the proposed quantum system, our attention must also be shifted *determinist-ically* on many occasions to the locations the brain identifies as potentially important sources of data. The reason we sense these brain-chosen foci is because our brain then increases the amplitude of the wave function of our quantum particle for positions that direct our attention *to the vicinity of these locations*. It does this **so that the quantum system is less likely to cause attention to shift elsewhere before sufficient data has been gathered**. That increase in the amplitude of the wave function is what we perceive as the increased salience of the object we are attending to.

Of course, one might wonder why the brain doesn't just *remove the possibility* of that quantum system shifting attention away from the chosen region before the necessary information is gathered. However, there is a simple answer to that one. Were it to do this, it would be removing the one thing that makes this system advantageous. No matter how good the brain's calculation is, there will always be times when it gets it wrong. By allowing that limited amount of randomness, which would inevitably cause some members of a group of creatures to attend to things that were different from what the majority were attending to at the time, it allows hidden threats or opportunities to be spotted more easily.

Hence the salience of an attended object is evidence of a mechanism that increases the amplitude of the wave function of our particle in a way that favours attention being kept on or nearby that object. The trade-off with the need to keep attention shifting is what determines how salient that region is, and thus accounts for why we still sense the presence of a rich background experience to which we can direct our attention next if we so choose.

How the Image-forming Condition Evolved

One really interesting consequence of this logical explanation of our attention spotlight is that it provides the most important ingredient that was missing from our explanation for the image-forming nature of our experiences. As I explained in chapter 7, the fact that our subjective visual experience resembles the images on our retinas is a consequence of three things. The first is the fact that the proposed attention-focussing system would evolve until every tiny region of potential positions of the quantum particle directed a creature's attention to a different point in space. The second is the fact that the intensity of reflected or emitted light proved to be a good rough guide to the urgency of particular sources of data in a creature's environment. And the third is that for some unexplained reason our ancestors' chances of survival increased when nearby positions of the quantum particle happened to always direct their attention to *nearby* locations in space (and widely separate positions to widely separate locations). The necessity of the attention-spotlight mechanism we have just discussed provides that unexplained reason.

The story goes as follows: Due to random mutations, a primitive mechanism emerged that happened to increase the amplitude of the wave function for positions of the quantum particle that directed a creature's attention back to the currently attended object. For the reasons we have just discussed, this proved to be beneficial. However, as the number of detectors shifting attention to other locations in space grew in a disorganised fashion, the resultant close-packing of detectors[25] would make those increases in the wave function's amplitude begin to favour positions that directed attention to *other* locations *as well as* those that kept it in the vicinity of the currently attended object. Whenever the positions in space favoured by this effect happened to be *near* each other, there would have been no great disadvantage for the creature (because its gaze would not tend to shift far away from its current focus before sufficient data was gathered). However, when the positions thus favoured to receive the creature's attention happened to be far apart, the resultant shifts in attention would frequently move its gaze away from the object to which it was currently attending *before its brain had had time to obtain sufficient data about that object.* As this would reduce its ability to assess its environment efficiently, creatures in whom nearby positions of the quantum particle triggered shifts in attention to nearby regions of space more and more often would always have an advantage over their competitors.

---

[25] As mentioned in footnote 19 (p.108), it isn't likely to be the structures that interact directly with our particle that change in number or distribution. These are likely to be uniformly distributed (and relatively close-packed) throughout the space in which the quantum particle is confined. Rather, it is the number of neurons making connections with the one housing this quantum particle. These are the detectors I'm referring to here because I envisage each of them as being triggered by a particular position of the quantum particle through a signal that reaches all those neurons via at least three independent paths (see footnote 19). Due to the differing path lengths, the three parts of the signal arrive simultaneously at very few of those neurons triggering them to fire their own signals. It is these neurons that actually register when the particle is detected at that position. Initially each one of these neurons might have responded to signals from a large number of different positions. But gradually, those other positions would have been adapted to trigger *different* neurons, and variations in the amplitude of the wave function used to adjust the probability of these outcomes. In those circumstances, an increase in the amplitude of the wave function for positions triggering shifts in attention to the currently attended stimulus would have proven beneficial. And, since increasing its amplitude at neighbouring positions as well could not have been avoided, the system evolved so that neighbouring positions always directed attention to neighbouring points in space.

As a result of this, there was considerable pressure for the system to evolve until adjacent positions of the quantum particle *always* shifted attention to adjacent positions in space. And as we saw in chapter 7, this is the condition that allows the retina-dependent variations in the wave function's amplitude to have the same form as the retinal image, thereby bringing that image into the experience of the quantum particle.

The Blind Mindmaker Game

When I first discovered this explanation for our subjective images, I found its simplicity and scientific nature so compelling that it inspired me to develop a computer model to illustrate and test the principle behind it. For me, that was no easy task, as I am not a whiz-kid with computers. Consequently, I had to limit myself to modelling a greatly simplified version of the proposed attention-focussing system – one in which the fully-evolved visual images would have the exceedingly myopic resolution of no more than twenty-five square pixels (the most complex sufficiently symmetric model that I could program into an Excel spreadsheet!).

Nevertheless, it was with some trepidation that I first pressed the F9 key to start the iterating process. As a maths teacher, I was well aware of the fact that the number of different arrangements of twenty-five squares (representing 25 different quantum-particle detectors) that are possible is the astronomically large figure of *factorial 25* (the answer to the sum $25 \times 24 \times 23 \times 22 \times 21 \times 20 \times 19 \times 18 \times 17 \times 16 \times 15 \times 14 \times 13 \times 12 \times 11 \times 10 \times 9 \times 8 \times 7 \times 6 \times 5 \times 4 \times 3 \times 2$), which amounts to just over 15.5 trillion trillion!!!!! There seemed to me to be a very real possibility that even if the model was working relatively well I'd be waiting all day (and maybe even all year or more!) for the evolution of the model to converge on a pattern representing an image-forming arrangement (**Figure 2**) – where neighbouring particle detectors (neighbouring squares) always direct attention to neighbouring points in space (represented by the coordinates that each square contains).

Since the automatic iteration facility would not work with the sort of calculation my model was doing, I had to manually iterate it, which meant only about 30 iterations per second (even with the F9 key held down constantly). That makes it only possible for the model to try out around a billion different arrangements *in a year!* If the model was a trillion times better than chance, it could still take over a thousand years to converge on an image-forming arrangement! It was therefore with tremendous satisfaction, and considerable relief, that I watched as my first trial of the fully working model threw the pixels into order in a matter of *minutes*. With just the simplest type of random mutation programmed in (swapping the positions of two randomly-chosen 'quantum-particle detectors'– squares), and with a very appropriate selection criterion (no increase in the average distance between the coordinates in adjacent squares), it achieved a fixed image-forming arrangement (see **Figure 2**, overleaf) within only a few thousand iterations.

Figure 1 shows the maximally jumbled array before the iterating program was run. The shaded squares are for illustration only. They represent regions where the amplitude of the wave function has been raised due to increased light intensity caused by a nearby object. In our early conscious ancestors, such bright regions would not have formed a subjective image of the object they were looking at. Such images (see **Figure 2**) only came into being after many generations as the benefits of a preference for short shifts in attention favoured arrangements of the system in which nearby detectors shifted attention to nearby points in space.

2 1	3 5	5 3	1 4	3 3
4 3	5 1	1 2	5 5	2 5
2 2	1 1	3 2	4 5	4 2
3 1	2 4	2 3	4 1	3 4
5 4	1 3	4 4	1 5	5 2

Figure 1. Maximally Jumbled Array at Start of Iterating Program:
Each square was made of two spreadsheet cells. The top cell contained the x-coordinate and the bottom cell the y-coordinate of a point on a Cartesian coordinate grid representing a location on the retina. The grid represents the positions of 25 detectors which, on detecting the quantum particle, shift attention to the spatial location indicated by their retinal coordinates. The shaded squares are for illustration only. They represent an increase in the particle's wave function (i.e. the colour it experiences) caused by higher light intensity on the retina, and geared to favour attention focusing on its source (see ch.7). At the start of the iterating process, all the squares were randomly jumbled up in no particular order as above. After a few thousand random swaps, one of the eight possible image-forming arrangements (see **Figure 2**) was usually obtained. This illustrates the evolutionary process by which retina-dependent variations of brightness (the grey squares) in the experience of our distant ancestors would gradually evolve to have the same basic form as the retinal image. So what was this ancestor looking at? See **Figure 2** for the answer.

1 1	2 1	3 1	4 1	5 1
1 2	2 2	3 2	4 2	5 2
1 3	2 3	3 3	4 3	5 3
1 4	2 4	3 4	4 4	5 4
1 5	2 5	3 5	4 5	5 5

Figure 2. One of the Eight Image-Forming Arrangements:
At the start of the iterating process all the squares were randomly jumbled up in no particular order (see **Figure 1**). After a few thousand random swaps, which were put back if the average distance between the coordinates in neighbouring squares was greater than before, one of the eight possible image-forming arrangements was usually obtained. The above diagram (the order of the squares, not the cross it reveals) shows one of these arrangements. The other seven can easily be deduced as the three obtained from rotating this arrangement successively by 90 degrees clockwise (while maintaining the x-coordinate above the y-coordinate in each square), and the four more obtained by reversing the order of the columns in each of the first four arrangements. The orientation of those image-forming arrangements is irrelevant due to the fact that the orientation of the wave function that forms our experience relative to other brain structures would not affect what we actually experience. Hence, in the 25-detector system thus modelled, it should only take a few thousand mutations to evolve a retinal-image-forming arrangement.

For obvious reasons, I have christened this computational model *The Blind Mindmaker Game.* It consists of a formula that randomly swaps the squares of a jumbled 5-by-5 square array representing the array of detectors that measures the position of the proposed quantum particle. Each square contains a pair of coordinates representing the position (on the retinal image, say) of the point to which the detector it stands for directs our ancestors' attention. And each swap represents a random change in the positions of two of these detectors caused by a random genetic mutation.

If, after each swap, the new arrangement meets a condition that makes it represent a *less-efficient* attention-focussing system, the swapped squares are put back again. This represents the effect of natural selection. The criterion that decides whether a mutation is kept or not is based upon the assumption of an attention-spotlight mechanism consisting of a uniform increase in the wave function that favours the particle turning up in the space represented by a particular square, but which also accidentally favours it turning up in the eight adjoining squares by the same amount. The Pythagorean distance formula (which you may remember from High School maths lessons!) is adapted to define the average shift in attention that this mechanism produces. In other words, the model just averages the distance between the coordinates contained in each of the nine central squares and the coordinates in the eight squares that surround it (dividing the total by 9 instead of 8 to include the equal chance of attention not shifting away from its initial focus). It then finds the average of the resultant values over the whole array (dividing the total by 9 again, but this time because it is averaging over the nine distinct attention-spotlight positions).

The only rules of the game are that if after a swap this average shift in attention is anything more than a fixed tolerance value of 0.6 percent above what it was before, the swapped squares must get put back. This symbolises the detrimental effect of an attention spotlight that generates larger-than-usual shifts in attention, and the 'genetic drift' resulting from the lack of any detrimental effect that would occur if the average shift in attention between members of an interbreeding population was roughly the same size.

The very small tolerance level is essential to stop the system getting stuck in a non-image-forming arrangement, but one can understand it as representing a real tolerance that would be present in the proposed system. Since the role of the attention spotlight is to keep a creature's attention focussed on or near the same *object* (rather than the same point in space) for long enough to make a useful assessment of the significance of that object, creatures whose attention spotlight caused them to shift their attention slightly further on average than their fellows would not initially be at a disadvantage provided they were just as likely to shift it to a location *in the vicinity* of the attended object. It would only be when their average shift in attention approached the average radius of that beneficial region (which would depend upon the typical image-size at which objects were most commonly assessed) that their greater average shift length would become a liability.

It is also worth noting that the maximum tolerance level in this model is fixed by the requirement that no successful swaps be possible when the squares are arranged so that the coordinates are in an image-forming order (the orientation of which is irrelevant). This is just above 0.6 percent. Of course, the tolerance could have been set *lower* than this, but that would make it hard to successfully swap the squares when most of the array was correctly ordered. The choice of 0.6 percent was a compromise between stopping the model getting stuck before an image-forming arrangement was reached, and ensuring that once reached that image-forming arrangement could not be successfully mutated.

Starting with the coordinates all jumbled up, the first trial took only around 6800 iterations to rearrange the squares into an image-forming order via purely random swaps (each square being as likely to swap with any of the twenty-four others in the array). In view of the fact that the vast majority of those random swaps were 'put back' (which required an iteration to accomplish), this amounted to only 3800 or so random mutations (including all the detrimental ones). On a second trial from a different starting point, it took just over 13000 iterations (around 7000 random mutations). Although occasionally the process did appear to get stuck in an ongoing oscillation, this occurred when the random mutations attempted to orient the array so that the diagonal of the image-forming arrangement was vertical or horizontal. As this would not happen in the malleable system the array represents where the orientation of the image is irrelevant, this can be ignored (or fixed by a pre-programmed rotation of the contents of the array).

Over all successfully converging trials so far carried out – more than three quarters of the total number – the number of random mutations needed to rearrange the array into a fixed image-forming arrangement has ranged from just under 700 to around 40000, with most trials accomplishing the task in less than 5000. And this was the case even for a maximally jumbled array – see **Figure 1** (which I jumbled manually using a well-shuffled pack of twenty-five cards to decide which squares the coordinates started in).

It is worth bearing in mind that the probability of hitting one of the eight image-forming arrangements of this array by purely random shuffling is 1 in just under 2 trillion trillion (15.5 trillion trillion divided by the 8 different image-forming arrangements that the model could converge to). In other words, the proposed evolutionary process has reduced the number of mutations that chance would require by *20-21 orders of magnitude!* – it does it a *billion trillion* times quicker than chance – which is why I think an explanation of this sort is perfectly plausible even for the kind of resolution typical of our sensory images.

I have included a relatively detailed description of that little experiment here partly to inspire more computer-literate readers who may wish to extend this model. I'd next like to see it adapted to order an array of polar coordinates on the surface of a sphere (or icosahedron), for example, or even a three-dimensional array. However, I also wanted to demonstrate the genuine potential for positive natural selection to fully account for our subjective images, which in my view are by far the most fascinating (and unappreciated) aspect of our consciousness. In view of the incredible improbability of such images coming into existence by chance, natural selection offers the only currently justifiable possibility for a scientific explanation. Philosophers who posit that our experiences are epiphenomena (and thus have no effect upon the brain) appear to me to be relying on the practically non-existent chance that they will just happen to be consistently arranged in such an image-forming way. The theory we have so far developed genuinely explains the existence of these images – and more interestingly, it does so in a manner that is far from arbitrary and *ad hoc*.

The fact that the only explanation this theory offers for one aspect of our experience (our attention spotlight) provides just the right piece of the jigsaw needed to complete the explanation of another aspect (our visual and other sensory images) is a remarkable feature of this theory. It is to my mind another indication that the theory is essentially correct. As we shall see shortly, though, an even stronger indication of this is provided by the fact that the evolutionary process we have discovered in this chapter also offers a very straightforward solution to the infamous 'binding problem' – a mystery that regularly troubles scientists and philosophers who are trying to account for the contents of our experiences.

The binding problem in philosophy is how to explain the fact that although we experience so many separate sources of data, processed separately in the brain, our experience of them seems to be woven into a single entity. We sense how one thing relates to another. The most obvious example of this is that when you look at someone speaking to you, you sense that the sounds you're hearing are coming from the moving lips that you see (or at least you will claim to *know* that they are). In chapter 10, we shall investigate how and why this situation has evolved. First, though, we need to be able to answer a much more basic question: Why is the experience containing our visual images so very different from that in which we sense our auditory data? Why shouldn't the shape and movement of those lips be encoded in *sounds* and the *voice that we hear* in colour experience? Why, for that matter, haven't both come to be encoded in a sort of mixed colour-sound sensation, or indeed a whole mishmash of other types of experience? In actual fact, for some people (known as synesthetes) such mixing does occur. Auditory data sometimes *does* get partly represented in colours! So the question really is, why is it so rare?

As we shall see in the next chapter, the answer requires us to postulate another effect of experiences upon the location of our quantum particle; and that effect is quite distinct from that of their intensity (their brightness, loudness, acuteness or salience) that we have so far been considering. Before we introduce this new effect, though, there is one final aspect of our experiences that the effect of intensity allows us to explain, and that is the vividness of our sensory experiences compared to the experiences in which the things we remember or imagine are encoded. It is the fact that imagining a favourite activity is *nowhere near* as good as doing it.

Why Sensory Images are Vivid and Memories Faint

Our memories and imaginings are obviously extremely faint and fleeting in comparison to the things we are seeing and hearing all around us. This is generally assumed to be because we don't remember things in great detail. Our brain only stores a few important features of an object or event we happen to perceive. Our memories are faint and fleeting, it is thought, because only these details can then be brought to mind later on. Don't be deceived by the apparent plausibility of this story! It is another instance of functionalism – a theory that receives no support from established science. Nothing gives us any reason to believe that nature can detect the amount of relevant memory information in some piece of your brain activity and determine the strength of your experience on that basis. We should expect such a view to be false. One can quite easily imagine having very *vivid* experiences that contain as little information as a memory contains. So we need to identify a reason why nature *favoured* consciousnesses in which memory data is instead encoded in relatively faint and fleeting experiences. We need to find an *advantage* that the organisms utilising these consciousnesses gained from this arrangement.

First let's remind ourselves of what the intensity – vividness – of an experience *does* in this theory. In chapter 7, we identified a scientific explanation for why the intensity of the light hitting our retina gets so closely represented by the intensity of an aspect of our experience – in this case, the brightness of a colour. After first assuming that our experience constitutes the wave function of a single quantum particle adapted by the brain to introduce randomness into its attention-focussing process, we realised that this match between light intensity and brightness can be explained as a product of natural selection if **the intensity of an experience makes a consciousness *more likely to select the location of that experience***. By selecting that location, it causes the particle it constitutes to be found at the corresponding location in space. And in the case of the quantum particle behind human consciousness, that location is a position in the brain that has been rigged up so that an appearance of the particle there triggers a shift in attention to a particular source of data. **Increasing the intensity of experience at a particular subjective location thus increases the chance of our particle showing up at the associated location in brain-space, and thereby triggering the shift in attention that this location has been wired up to trigger.**

We next noted that the *most urgent* sources of data that we could focus attention upon tend to be those that give off *the strongest sensory stimuli* (the strongest light or sound waves, or steepest temperature or pressure gradients). As a result, when the intensity of our ancestors' experience at each subjective location happened to vary *in the same way as the intensity of the sensory stimuli* coming from the source of data selected by that location, they were able to shift their attention more appropriately. And such creatures would thereby outbreed their competitors. It is this that explains why the intensity of our experience has come to vary, in many circumstances, in a way that closely matches the intensity variations of the stimuli being detected by our senses.

In this chapter, we further noted that the increased intensity of experience that is evident in *the salience of the object we are attending to* can be explained by a similar argument. That **increased intensity makes our consciousness more likely to**

select the locations where it occurs, and our brain's subsequent measurement of the position of our quantum particle thus becomes more likely to keep our attention focussed on the currently attended object. The evolution of this system can be explained by the fact that maintaining attention on that currently-attended object until a certain amount of data has been gleaned from it **constitutes a better information-gathering strategy than immediately shifting attention elsewhere.** Hence the same effect of subjective intensity explains the evolution of our 'attention spotlight'.

So what does all this tell us about the faintness of our memory images? Well, you may have noticed that in both these cases the *less urgent* information (or rather, the information that is *less likely to be most* urgent) has come to be represented in *weaker* (*less salient*) types of experience. If so, you may already have realised how a similar story could account for the faintness of the experiences that are often called 'impressions' or 'mental images', in which the things we remember or imagine are represented. Recalled or imagined things have come to be so much *fainter* in our experience than our sensory data about what is happening right now simply because for creatures trying to survive in the relatively hostile environments that our ancestors faced on a daily basis, **data about the here-and-now is *far more important* than any relevant memories or hypotheses their brains happen to come up with.** The association of memories and hypotheses with an object that our ancestors had detected was thus not a particularly strong criterion for deciding whether that object was the best one to attend to at that time. The real-time sensory data about that object, and other objects in its vicinity, was *a far better* indicator of its potential to bring immediate harm or benefit to those ancestors. As such, it had to have *a far greater effect* upon the amplitude of the wave function for the particle choosing their focus of attention.

It's worth noting that this doesn't mean memories were not an important factor in controlling their behaviour. After all, the brain uses *subconscious* memories and thought processes all the time to construct our experiences and control our actions. The extent to which a memory is presented in consciousness (via its perceived vividness, detail or emotional content) is not, according to this theory, a reflection of how much the brain is using that memory. It is merely an indication of how urgent the brain ranks the subject of that memory, or the memory itself (if no subject is present at the time), as an appropriate focus of attention for the current moment.

Now, you might think that the faintness of memory images should therefore mean we'd never choose to attend to them (which, as every daydreamer knows, isn't true). However, that objection fails to take into account the fact that, in this theory, our consciousness doesn't choose *experiences* to attend to but *locations in its experienced space*; and these are positions within the brain where our quantum particle will subsequently appear if our brain happens to measure its position at that moment. Although these tend to be rigged up to trigger a shift in attention to a particular point in space on or outside our body, the actual experiences in which our consciousness perceives them need not be merely those representing the sensory stimuli coming from those points in space. They could also include the fainter contribution of an associated memory-type or emotion-type experience (you will see how in chapter 10). When nothing much is changing in our environment, the occurrence of a faint memory image *in association with a particular sensory-type experience* can indeed increase the salience of a part of our experience above that of other regions. This *would* make our consciousness more likely to select that location, and thereby bring about a corresponding shift in the orientation of our sense organs. Moreover, the selected location could easily be 'inside our head' or 'beyond the horizon'. In other words, it could be a potential position of our quantum particle that *does not get used to direct attention to a location in our body or its environment.* Since evolution will almost certainly have adapted that redundant position to *some* attention-shifting role, it could easily have been adapted to switch our brain's attention to a train of thoughts – thus accounting for our ability to daydream and meditate. However, the contribution to the intensity of our experience that the strongest memory image adds cannot be anything like that typical of a moderately urgent sensory stimulus.

Just think, if our memory images were as intense as our images of the things we are currently seeing in our environment (as happens in a hallucination) we would become quite likely to focus upon a location within one of those memory images. In the theory we have been developing, this would shift our attention to the corresponding location in space – a location where nothing of any importance might be found. Doing that would reduce a creature's ability to gather relevant data quickly, making it impossible for such a creature to compete with those in whom memories had only a very *small* effect upon their experiences. Obviously, amongst our ancestors the latter must have had a slight edge over competitors whose memories and hypotheses had absolutely *no* effect. But that can be accounted for by realising that in situations where several sources of data were *equally favoured by their sensory inform-ation,* the possession of relevant memories about one of them may well make it slightly more beneficial to attend to that one first.

That the advantage of experiencing memories and thoughts is only a slight one is well supported by the fact that some people do not experience *any* mental images at all,[26] and yet have no problem thinking and remembering things. If you are not one of these

---

[26] See e.g. Sacks (2010), pp.222-6

people, that may seem like a contradiction in terms. But that is only because you are assuming your experienced thoughts are somehow playing a vital role in your brain's thought processes. According to this theory they have merely evolved to contribute a very small, and often insignificant, adjustment to our likelihood of attending to different sources of data – an adjustment that some brains have either managed to do without, or else accomplished via some alternative type of experience (using faint *feelings*, for example, where most of us would experience faint images).

The effect of the *intensity* aspect of our experience that this theory demands has thus allowed us to explain *several* notable features of the way our experiences encode information: The *faintness* of our memory images; the *salience* of the object or stimulus that we are attending to; the origin of our *sensory images*; and the very presence of *sensory information* in our consciousness. However, as I mentioned earlier, it doesn't allow us to explain why particular *ranges* of experience (such as colours and sounds) have become exclusively adapted to encode the information from particular senses. That is because each type of experience within those ranges can take on *any value of intensity,* from the most extreme to the faintest impression. Colour experience, for example, can vary in intensity from the very intense experience we get when looking at a bright light, right down to the faint impressions in which the images we imagine appear to us. And sound experience likewise from the din of the noisiest amplifier to a memory of the faintest tinkle of a dropped pin. Since each range of experience supports a full range of differing intensities, intensity *cannot* be the aspect of our experiences that is responsible for that subjective separation of our senses. Something else must be at work. In the next chapter, we shall find out what that other effect is most likely to be.

CHAPTER NINE

Why we See in Colour and Hear in Sound

It could have been Different!

To you it might seem natural that our visual information is encoded in colours whilst our auditory data is encoded in sound experience. It couldn't be any other way, could it? But if you think about it, the properties of the acoustic waves that our ears detect – their frequency, intensity and the direction from which they arrive at our ears – could quite conceivably be encoded in the variable hue and brightness of the colours within an appropriate region of our subjective *visual* field (the colour part of our experience). Similarly, the intensity, wavelength profile, and retinal location of the light our eyes detect could be fully encoded in the loudness, pitch and directionality aspects of our *sound* sensations. And why does the information from different senses even have to be represented by *different* types of experience? After all, as far as we know it isn't carried through the brain by different types of signal. The same sort of electrochemical signalling carries both the visual and the auditory data before we experience it. Although each is processed by a different part of the brain, the structures responsible are very similar. So why couldn't both our auditory *and* our visual information be encoded in the colour aspect of our experience?

Perhaps you're thinking that superposing one set of colour variations on top of another would result in the loss of some of that data (as we wouldn't be able to distinguish the auditory patterns from the visual ones). However, that would not be the case if we had half the colour spectrum representing the full range of light frequencies, and the other half the full range of acoustic frequencies. The result might actually be silently beautiful! Alternatively, one could have half the visual *field* encoding the light data and the other half the auditory data. Or one could do something similar with the pitches and perceived directions of our sound experiences. One could even encode both types of data in a psychedelic mixture of colours *and* sounds.

Now you might think all this is just silly speculation. It obviously couldn't be any different because the resultant experience simply wouldn't make any sense. However, if you do, you're not taking into account the fact that the organisation of our conscious experience (according to current scientific knowledge) has to be a product of natural selection. The process of natural selection is *completely blind* to how a creature's experience feels. It cares only for what that experience *does*. Once the effect of its experiences upon the brain proves to be most beneficial to the creature, its consciousness will stop evolving into a state of greater organisation *no matter how confusing or psychedelic those experiences happen to be*. And this is definitely going to apply to the quantum particle consciousness that we've been discussing.

Current science thus gives us no *a priori* reason why our experiences *should* make any sense.

What this means is that to account for the subjective separation of our sensory information in this theory (colours for vision, sounds for hearing, and so on) we need to identify an advantage that a creature would have gained from having more of its visual information encoded in colours and more of its auditory data in sounds. And to do that, we need to ask ourselves the question: What exactly *are* distinct types of experience? What aspect of a brain-based physical system are the distinct *ranges* of experience that we call colours, sounds, feelings, etcetera? And what are the *pure* types of experience within each such range, the ones out of which all the other experiences in that range seem to be composed – the *primary colours*, for example, or the *pure tones* of sound?

What Different Types of Experience Are

Given that our consciousness is a single quantum particle confined somewhere in our brain, there does not appear to me to be a whole lot of options. Our experience is the wave function of that particle, so our different types of experience must be aspects of that wave function. Now, that wave function gains its distinct form through the effect of something called a 'potential' (usually symbolised by the letter V in the equations of quantum mechanics). But a potential is just the cumulative influence of all the particles in the environment, and particles can affect each other *in several different ways* (through gravity, electromagnetic fields, collisions, the exclusion principle, etc.). Hence it seems obvious to me that **the qualitatively different *ranges* or *spaces* of our experience (colours, sounds, feelings, etc.) must represent different *types of*** *interaction* between our particle and others in its environment. More specifically, they must each represent **the effect upon the wave function of our particle that is caused by the *potential* for our particle to undergo the associated type of interaction**. The variations in brightness throughout our visual field, for example, must represent **the extent to which whatever interaction is responsible for our colour experience favours our quantum particle being found in each of its possible positions**. And the same is true of the variation in loudness across our *auditory field* (the directionality aspect of our sound experiences), and the variation in the strength of feeling across the *felt-space* we think of as our body.

Now, if each of these distinct ranges of experience thus represents the effect of a distinct type of interaction, **the different *pure* types of experience that occur within them (usually in complex mixtures) can only constitute the effect of distinct *ways in which that interaction can take place***. There might, for example, be a slightly different quality of experience representing each distinct possibility for the exchange of energy between the interacting particles, or each possible way in which they could be oriented relative to one another. Thus the continuum of our sound pitches ought to represent a continuum of different ways in which the interaction responsible for our sound experience can take place. And the primary colours and black of our colour experience ought each to represent the effect, upon the wave function of our particle, of one of the four (or five [27]) distinct ways in which the interaction represented by our colour experience must be able to take place.

---

[27] The exact structure of our subjective colour space is disputed. Whilst everyone agrees that one's bluest blue and reddest red are primary colours, there is some disagreement over whether to include green or yellow or both. Although in physics it is the wavelengths of light we perceive as green, red and blue that combine to make white light, the idea that green combines with red to make

When it can occur in several of these ways *at the same position in space*, a *mixture* of these colours (or pitches) arises at the associated subjective location. This postulate is essential in order to account for the huge range of distinct types of colour and sound that we experience in a reasonably economic manner, and we do clearly *feel* that rich tones and most hues are mixtures of simpler sounds or colours. To be consistent with our earlier observations about the effect of brightness and salience, the strength of each component in such a mixture must represent *the extent to which the associated way of interacting favours our quantum particle being found at the position that the subjective location of the mixture represents*.

Don't worry if all this sounds rather too technical. I have tried to be as precise as possible at this point for any physicist readers, who may well be trying to see if they can infer further details of the sort of particle we must constitute. It will be helpful to remember that colours probably arise from one type of effect upon the wave function of our particle, and sounds from a completely different type of effect. But because we do not at this stage know precisely which effects these are, this inference will not be used in the explanation for the separation of our sensory images that we shall now turn to. Instead, we will ask ourselves what effect particular types of experience might have upon the choices *our consciousness* makes that might make it advantageous for a particular range of experience to exclusively encode the information gathered by a particular sense. We will leave it up to quantum physicists to identify the *physical* effect that the subjective effect we require must be giving rise to.

---

yellow never feels right to me, whereas blue combining with yellow to make green does seem reasonable (though that is perhaps nothing to go by). Anyway, assuming all colours (including white) are the result of combining three primary colour experiences, you still need a blackest black to darken all those mixtures.

What Different Types of Experience Do

Remember, the role of a consciousness in this theory is to determine the position of the effect of the quantum particle it constitutes. In actual fact it is choosing where that effect appears *in the consciousnesses of other particles* (just as we experience other particles' effects). It does this by freely selecting a new location in its experience, which it does repeatedly. In our case, we experience this as *voluntary shifts in attention*, though only a small number of these are the result of any thought or desire. Most are purely random choices that we are totally free to make, but in which we often end up selecting relatively *salient* parts of our experience.

To understand what is being proposed in this chapter, it is essential to note that these 'voluntary selections' do not always determine the position of the *physical* effect of our quantum particle. That only happens when a *measurement* of our quantum particle's position takes place (the conditions for which are beyond the scope of this discussion). And only when that happens can our selections have any effect upon our brain or behaviour. They do, however, always have a certain effect upon *the experience of other quantum particles* centred at a location in their experience that corresponds to the point-like location we happen to be selecting in ours. Each particle's experience is really *made up* of such effects.

Another thing that's worth noting is that there is no requirement in this theory for us to *feel* as though we are selecting point-like locations. Most of the time we probably feel as though we are examining whole regions of experience, such as the shape of an object we see, or the feeling across a particular part of our body. If that is indeed the case it matters very little. The position of the effect of our quantum particle could simply be the *centre* of the space represented by that subjectively-chosen region. We are never aware of the effect we're having on the experience of other particles, which is what the position of our particle essentially constitutes in this theory. **What we *are* aware of is the effect of other particles upon our *own* experience: its varying intensity**. From the way the intensity of our experience has come to reflect the relative urgency of the information it encodes, we know that an increase in that intensity at a particular location must constitute an increase in the *probability* of our particle turning up in the associated region of space. And the only way that can happen in this theory is if it is making us *more likely to select that region*.

As we noted in chapter 7, more-urgent sorts of information are generally encoded in more-intense sorts of experience. In order to account for this by natural selection in our theory, greater intensity of experience must correspond to a larger wave function – a location where the wave function has *a higher amplitude*, and where the quantum particle is therefore more likely to be found. It doesn't take much to see that this is very probably because **we (the consciousness) are more likely to select locations in our experience that have *more intense* colour, sound, pain, etcetera, over those where the sensation is less intense**.

But intensity (salience) need not be the *only* aspect of our experience favouring us selecting particular locations. Indeed the very fact that particular types of experience have come to always represent particular types of information guarantees that the *type* of an experience must have an effect that is *distinct* from the effect of its intensity. So how could a *type* of experience affect which locations we select? What **new postulate** does this demand?

Well, the simplest possibility to my mind is the proposal that **we tend to shift our voluntary attention more often between locations in our consciousness where we find experience that is mainly of a *similar type*.** I don't just mean 'from one coloured region to another', or 'from one sound to another'. I mean from one coloured region to a region of *similar* colour, or from one sound to a *similarly pitched* sound.[28]

How the Subjective Separation of our Senses Came About

With this one elementary postulate it becomes surprisingly easy to account for the separation of our senses. The key thing to remember is the effect of our *attention spotlight* that we inferred in chapter 8: **The salience of the region of our experience encoding our current focus of attention makes us very likely to place our voluntary attention *within that particular region*.** Although we are next very likely to shift it to another location within that same region, **our new postulate makes us also likely to shift it to a location of *similar colour* (or sound or texture, etc.), either within that region, or elsewhere in our experience.** And of course, this favours attention being shifted to the associated source of data (the one selected by the resultant position of our particle).

The reason particular colours came to represent particular wavelengths of light is because whenever such an arrangement was caused by a random genetic mutation it made *similar objects* (which tend to reflect similar types of light) represented in our ancestors' experiences by *similar colours*.[29] Due to our new

---

[28] Since it has an effect upon the output of the system, this tendency must be contributing to the quantum particle's wave function. Since the same type of experience in this theory represents the same type of interaction (and in fact the very same *way* of interacting), it is currently envisaged that this tendency is what gives each interaction its fixed 'coupling strength'.

[29] Of course, our colours do not *always* represent the same wavelengths of light as the phenomenon of colour constancy (see chapter 5) clearly shows. However, in view of the fact that colour constancy is another instance of our visual experience being organised so that similar objects appear similarly coloured (even in poor illumination), its existence only supports the current hypothesis.

postulate (p.155), this would have made those ancestors **more likely to shift their attention from one object** *to another of a similar type* either nearby or elsewhere in their environment. Since this allowed their brains to immediately obtain useful information about the abundance or proximity of that type of object, it greatly improved the efficiency of the data-gathering process, allowing those ancestors to outbreed their competitors, and the new mutation to quickly spread throughout the population.

It's worth noting here that this proposed effect of similar colours could not have been adapted to this role before the attention spotlight evolved. That is because the salience of the currently attended object is what attracts our subjective attention to the colour in that part of our experience, which is essential before that tendency to select a similar colour elsewhere can favour shifts in attention to a different object with similar subjective properties.

Of course, a similar explanation will account for the association of *other* particular types of experience with *other* particular types of sensory stimuli. However, this observation does not yet rule out particular auditory frequencies becoming represented by particular *colours*, and particular wavelengths of light by particular pitches of *sound*. Nor does it preclude the possibility of both auditory and visual information being represented by distinct *sets* of colours (or separate *ranges* of pitch). With a little bit of thought, though, we soon discover a very good reason for why we should expect natural selection to gradually eliminate such alternative arrangements.

The problem with having both light and acoustic stimuli represented by particular instances of the same range of experience (e.g. particular colours) could simply be the fact that when those representations occur *at the same subjective location* – as they would if the stimuli were coming from the same object (see chapter 7 for why) – **they would *mix together***. As explained earlier (p.153), such mixing is essential to account for how all the many possible colours arise from the small set of primary colours and black that appears to constitute the basic elements of our colour experience. Hence the colours encoding the visual information about a particular object would *blend* with the colours representing its acoustic vibrations (noise). That would not be a disaster as long as the same objects always made the same noises. They'd then still be represented by the same colour. But since the noise an object makes (as in the acoustic pressure waves that it produces) is linked with its movement, it tends to vary a lot more than the light it reflects, and it varies in different circumstances. As a result, if both the noise and the light were represented by colours, the colour of the object would change significantly whenever it was making a different noise. Since our new postulate (p.155) will only impart an advantage if similar objects tend to be represented by *similar* colours, creatures in which auditory and visual data were both encoded in colours would be at a disadvantage compared to competitors whose consciousnesses were more like our own. As a result, the latter would outbreed the former, and the encoding of auditory information in a *completely distinct range* of experience from visual information would become the norm.

I think it is wonderful that such a simple postulate can provide such a satisfactory explanation for the subjective separation of our senses! Although the story doesn't yet tell us why colours rather than sounds were used for vision, it does account for why *one* – and *only* one – complete range of experience was used, which is the main problem. The exact range that came to be used could be just an accident – a random bias in favour of the interaction responsible for colour in the structures that entered the visual data into the wave function.

Separation and Binding

The subjective separation of our senses is a fascinating example of apparent design in the structure of our conscious experiences. And as we have seen, our theory accounts for it as a product of the gradual process of natural selection, just as its perfect nature (in most people most of the time) suggests we should expect.

But that association of distinct ranges of experience with distinct senses is not generally regarded as the most puzzling feature of our experiences. Most neuroscientists and philosophers appear to think it is somehow simply a consequence of the fact that the information from distinct senses tends to be processed in distinct regions of the brain. It perhaps seems logical to them that separate neural structures might result in distinct types of experience. For them, the most baffling aspect of the sensory information in our consciousness is not the fact that it is separated according to its sensory origin into distinct ranges of experience. It is the fact that those distinct ranges of experience appear to be appropriately *connected together* to form a unified whole – an amazingly holistic representation of the human organism interacting with its environment. How can this *be* if all that information is processed in separate parts of the brain?

As I mentioned in chapter 8, this is commonly referred to as 'the binding problem'; and as we shall discover in the next chapter, a very straightforward solution to it simply falls out of the theory we have been considering. Part of the problem is of course solved by the fact that in this theory our consciousness is indeed a part of the brain where all this information comes together. But that, by itself, does not account for the appropriate way in which it is all connected up in our experience. It does not explain why, for example, when we look at a person talking to us the sound of the person's voice doesn't seem to be coming from everywhere around us, or from the person's stomach, or from the ceiling, or from behind us. Something more is needed to explain the fact that we accurately feel (or *know*) it to be coming from the person's lips. As we shall now see, the inferences we have made in this chapter concerning the physical nature of colour and sound experience, allow a perfect evolutionary explanation for this further instance of design-like structure in our experience. It is worth remembering that this aspect of our experience is largely the one responsible for the amazing fact that we (a quantum particle according to this scientifically-defensible theory) actually feel like the human organism in whose brain we reside!

CHAPTER TEN

A Simple Solution to the Binding Problem

The Questions we still need to Answer

Why do our experiences make sense? Why do we feel that the sound experiences in which a person's voice is represented are coming from the part of our colour experience (our subjective visual field) in which the image of the person's lips is located? As we saw in the previous chapter, the distinct *ranges of experience* that we call colour and sound are most likely to constitute the effects of distinct *types of interaction* by which other quantum particles affect the form of the wave function that our experience constitutes. So the question can be broken down into the following two parts:

(1) How can experiences in one *subjective domain* (e.g. our visual field) feel as though they are connected to certain

experiences in another *completely distinct* one (e.g. the sound aspect of our consciousness)?

and

(2) Why do those connected experiences encode the images or patterns of things that happen to be similarly connected in our environment (such as the light and acoustic stimuli coming from the same object)?

Taking into account the conclusions we reached in the previous chapter concerning the physical nature of colour and sound experience, and the sort of explanation (natural selection) that applies to other instances of apparent design in nature, we can rephrase these questions as follows:

(1) What aspect of an interaction links instances of one *type of interaction* to instances of a *completely distinct* type of interaction?

and

(2) What advantage did our ancestors gain from having data from different senses that happens to be about the same object encoded into the wave function of their quantum particle via such linked aspects of the distinct interactions responsible for inputting that sensory data?

The Subjective Glue

A fascinating thing about this theory of consciousness is that it offers only one really obvious answer to question (1). The only thing that could connect two completely distinct types of interaction is the potential for them to occur *at the same place* (and time). In other words, **our sense that an image we see is connected to a sound we are hearing can only be due to the fulfilment of one condition: The interaction responsible for the colour experience must be favouring the quantum particle being found *at the same position in space* that is simultaneously favoured by the interaction responsible for the sound experience.**

The seemingly more difficult question is (2): How could it have benefited our ancestors to have auditory and visual data about *the same object* (or *the same external location*) encoded via interactions that favoured the quantum particle turning up in *the same region* of the space over which its wave function extends?

As you have probably already realised, this is *not* a more difficult question at all! The answer is blatantly obvious! If you have understood the theory so far, you will remember that our ancestors' attention-focussing system has evolved until each potential position of the quantum particle directs attention to a *distinct* point in space (see chapter 7). In other words, **each point in space gets attention directed to it by *a single* position of that particle.**[30] And crucially, **all the sensory information coming from that point in space has been adapted to appropriately adjust the amplitude of the wave function for the appearance of the particle *at that single associated position*.** In view of this it is no surprise that the sound coming from an object feels connected to our visual image of that object. This is simply a straightforward consequence of the fact that the proposed system will evolve until the auditory and visual information coming from the same point in space always affects the amplitude of the wave function for *the*

---

[30] In actual fact, it is a region of potential positions so tiny that we can easily speak of it as a single position.

same potential position of the quantum particle that we constitute. Eureka!

Not only does this explain the perceived *spatial* connections between our subjective representations of auditory and visual stimuli, it explains their *synchronisation* as well. In chapter 5, we observed that the different lengths of the nerve fibres coming from sensors in different parts of our body results in some sensory signals taking much longer to get to our brain than others do. Consequently, the only way our brain can represent the arrival times of our sensory stimuli accurately is by delaying the construction of our experience until enough time has elapsed for signals from peripheral parts of our body to arrive. But why does it *need* to do this? Why doesn't it just let the signals that get there first alter the wave function as soon as they arrive, and allow other signals to alter it later on?

Since you now know the purpose of that representation, you can probably see why it doesn't do that. It evolved to maximise the efficiency of a randomly shifting focus of attention by keeping its probability of selecting each potential source of data as close as possible to its optimum value. **An accurate representation of the relative timing of our sensory stimuli was favoured by evolution because it allowed the resultant probabilities to *better reflect the relative urgency of the associated sources of data*.** For example, when the arrival of intense auditory and intense visual stimuli from the same point in space was accurately represented by a simultaneous increase in the wave function's amplitude for positions that direct attention to that point, our ancestors tended to shift their attention more efficiently. They were more likely to examine that point in space next, and thereby better placed to acquire the wealth of possibly urgent data that the simultaneous visual and auditory signals coming from it were providing.

They would not have been so likely to attend to that location next if the associated visual and auditory stimuli had been represented at different times because the intensity of the colour experience would not then have been supplemented by the intensity of the sound, and its location may not therefore have stood out against other bright regions of their visual field. And the absence of a simultaneous burst of colour a moment later when the sound occurs would similarly make that location less likely to be selected than that of other sounds. It's important to remember that the common origin of those two signals makes them increase the wave function's amplitude *for the same positions* of the quantum particle. When this happens *simultaneously*, those two separate increases in the wave function's amplitude combine to make the quantum particle highly likely to turn up at that position. As a result, creatures in whom that simultaneous representation occurs would become highly likely to attend to the source of those signals – which would often have proven beneficial (after all, a source of intense light that also crackles loudly is usually going to be a more urgent source of data than a brighter source that makes very little noise). And, as I have already mentioned, they would experience those signals to be both simultaneous *and connected*.

Why Our Experiences Make Sense

The importance of this observation is that it doesn't just apply to visual and auditory data. The same simple story can account for the accurate connections we perceive between our visual data and the data from our senses of touch and proprioception (our sense of the position and orientation of our limbs and other body parts). It can explain the connection we experience between the images of words and our memories of what they sound like, and perhaps even our memories of what they mean. It could also account for the link between memories of taste (or smell) and visual images – or memories – of the food with which the taste (or smell) is associated. That's because the faintness of the sensations in which memories are represented could allow the taste memory to be combined with the visual image without causing us to think we are actually consuming that food – a sensation that would require the touch and proprioceptive experiences that we call 'our mouth and tongue' to be combined in a similar way with appropriate textures and a *strong* version of the taste experience.

As you can see, *all* the different sensory and memory data a brain can access about each object it calculates to be relevant will almost inevitably be adapted to influence the amplitude of the wave function *for the same potential positions* of our quantum particle. It will thus come to be experienced as connected. This observation has the potential to account for our complete sense of what we are and what other things are. It explains how we accurately experience one thing as being related to another, and thereby intuitively understand the world around us. And it accounts for how memories can be linked together in our experience to form the thoughts we think. Hence, to my mind at least, it does indeed solve the binding problem that has baffled philosophers and neuroscientists for decades!

There is, however, one aspect of what things mean to us that this explanation does *not* account for – or at least, not by itself. It is our sense of the *value* that things have (technically known as 'valence'). It is our sense that some things are nice (the taste of chocolate) and other things nasty (an intense pain). And it is the observation that the nasty experiences seem confined to circumstances that are *bad* for us – particularly those that would have reduced our foraging ancestors' chances of raising healthy offspring. To account for this, a further ingredient is needed that is not found among the postulates we have so far considered.

In the next chapter, I shall make a suggestion as to what that ingredient is, and I will show how that suggestion allows our fairly accurate sense of the value of things – our feeling that tissue damage, bereavement, loneliness and so on are bad, whilst warmth, comfort, friendliness and such like are good – to be fully accounted for in the current theory. As with the postulate introduced in chapter 9, I will not be speculating as to what aspect of the quantum-mechanical description of the proposed system this postulate could account for. Although that would be a fascinating topic for discussion, it is one that would be too technical to explore in this book. And besides, as far as justifying this explanation of consciousness is concerned, it is at present unnecessary. No other theory of consciousness comes close to the completeness and scientific nature of the explanation for our experiences that this theory provides. The ease with which it explains the observed phenomena, and the extent to which that explanation is similar to the scientific explanation for the most-similar successfully-explained phenomenon, give me sufficient grounds for confidence that it is at least on the right lines. It is therefore up to physicists to interpret quantum mechanics in a way that is *consistent* with this theory.

With that in mind, let us now identify what pains and other unpleasant sensations *do*, so that quantum physicists can start to work out what they are. We shall also consider what's special about *pleasant* sensations, and why they tend to be associated with *good* things. And surprisingly, in the process of doing all this, we will even discover a very plausible reason for the commonly reported sense that time slows down during traumatic situations.

So many assume the problem solved:
"To *protect* the organism, pain evolved".
But unless a feeling can affect a choice,
one might as well feel a desire to rejoice!

Because if your consciousness hasn't an effect
upon your brain's response to damage that your pains could correct,
then even if your body suffered terrible abuse,
there would be no *need* for pain, as pain would have no *use*.

And if a fundamental law connects my feeling of pain
to a certain physical event that happens in my brain,
if the feeling has no effect, then what cruel chance or charm
made *that* event a part of my detector of harm?

C. S. Morrison (The Problem of Pain, v.9-11)

CHAPTER ELEVEN

The Purpose of Pain

Nature is neither Cruel nor Kind

When you stub your toe, why does your toe feel sore? That may seem like a silly question. You might think it's just because you've damaged it (or at least come close to damaging it). Damage is bad for you, so you might think it logical that the signals informing your brain about the damage get represented in nasty sensations. Nature seems to demand it. Without this, our experience wouldn't make much sense, would it?

But that hypothesis is a *functionalistic* one, and as we saw in chapter 5, current science gives us no reason to believe in a functionalistic theory of consciousness, pain, or anything else, and many reasons to *dis*believe such a theory. Why *should* signals carrying information about damage get represented in nasty experiences? And why are those experiences so unbelievably horrible. More to the point, how does nature *recognise* events that constitute damage, or distinguish signals carrying damage information from similar signals recording temperature changes or the texture of a sock? After all, the neural signals carrying information from damage sensors work in exactly the same way as those carrying other types of information. The only real difference is in the stimulus that first triggers them, which in the case of damage signals is the detection of certain chemicals released by tissue in circumstances that are likely to prematurely end its beneficial contribution to an organism's physiology.

As a consciousness whose quality of experience is highly dependent upon keeping that organism up and running, we call that damage. However, it is important to remember that this thing that we call 'damage' is nothing but a slightly different arrangement of the particles that a biological (or artificial) structure consists of. The new arrangement does make the structure somewhat less useful to an organism who relies upon it, but that reduction in usefulness would not normally manifest itself until the organism has tried to use the damaged part (which will usually be sometime after its 'damage sensors' have registered the occurrence of whatever physical or chemical stimuli they have evolved to detect). So how does nature know to make the activity of these sensors give rise to pain, as functionalism demands? It seems to me that nature would have to remember that the activation of these sensors *in the past* was followed by defective function!

Pain doesn't therefore appear to be arising from damage itself, but from the operation of sensors for certain chemicals that abnormally-deformed human tissue tends to release. Since these chemicals *needn't* have evolved to indicate damage, for this to be an example of functionalism nature would have to have *learned*, perhaps over the course of human evolution, that these chemicals signify damage, which seems to me to be an extremely unscientific hypothesis.

From a scientific perspective, the connection of pain with damage ought instead to be regarded as an example of apparent design in a biological structure, and every example of this sort of thing that science has explained has been accounted for as a product of positive natural selection. In other words, it is a situation that has arisen gradually due to the fact that small steps toward it had a positive influence upon the reproductive capabilities or prospects of the creatures carrying the genes that code for these small changes. Hence we ought to assume that this is how the pain-damage connection came about. We ought to assume that pain sensations have some effect upon the brain that proved advantageous when our ancestors were damaged, and not advantageous – or even downright detrimental – in other circumstances.

Okay, so perhaps pain causes us to stop doing the action that's resulting in the damage, or to avoid repeating that action. After all, once you've stubbed your toe into an object, you're certainly a lot more careful the next time you approach that object.

I find this hypothesis doubtful for the following reasons: Firstly, as we discussed in chapter 5, our conscious experience lags about half a second behind the events that are represented within it. It takes that long for the damage signals from the stubbed toe to reach the brain and be connected up with the appropriate visual and auditory signals to form our experience of that event. By that time, due to reflexes triggered by our spinal cord and signals from parts of the brain responding quickly and unconsciously to the visual and auditory data, our body has already successfully retracted the foot from whatever obstacle was damaging it and stopped us in our tracks. Hence, the pain can't be there to make us choose to stop. If it can, our body will stop us doing the damaging thing automatically before our consciousness even learns about it. So could the pain be there to stop us choosing to do it again?

I think that too is unlikely. The reason is that in order for us to choose to do something, the thought of doing it must be represented in our consciousness. Our theory so far suggests that we make this choice through focussing attention upon that thought. But it is obviously our brain that constructs this thought. In order to encode memories of pain within it, or to link it to pain sensations that were currently being experienced, our brain would have to know that the proposed action was going to result in damage. And if it knows that, why would it give us the option of choosing to perform it in the first place? Why offer us the option of doing it, and at the same time try to put us off with pain sensations and memories, when it could simply *not* offer us the option of doing it by not supplying the necessary thought (or by making that thought so faint and fleeting it would be very rarely attended to)?

Now, I'm not saying that pain isn't there to stop us doing something that could be damaging to us. Indeed, its association with instances of damage indicates that it *must* play such a role. All I'm saying is that it isn't there to make us *choose* not to do the damaging things. The brain is perfectly capable of doing that on its own. The role of pain has to be something much-more-subtle than this. And as we shall now see, the theory of consciousness we have so far constructed offers major clues as to what that role might be.

For a start, pain sensations are intense – they are perhaps the most intense sensations we have – and in our theory of consciousness, locations where intense sensations occur constitute regions of space where our quantum particle's wave function has a *high amplitude*. In other words, they are positions where our quantum particle is very likely to be found. And crucially, when it appears there, it triggers a shift in our attention to the source of the damage signals.

So have pain sensations become associated with damage simply so as to draw our attention immediately to the location of the damage? That would certainly have benefited our ancestors because their brains would then have been able to make an immediate assessment of the cause of the damage, which would help them calculate how to avoid it in future. Nevertheless, I don't think this is the full story. My reason is that there are other extremely-intense sensations that would serve this purpose just as effectively. If diverting our attention to the location of the damage were all that was required, wouldn't an *ear-splitting sound* or an *extremely bright colour* be sufficient? Remember, we are not talking about a noise or burst of light being detected by our ears or eyes here. We are talking about the damage signals being represented in our consciousness by these alternative types of experience. Hence the fact that we might not be looking at our toe when the damage was incurred would not stop these sensations occurring in an associated part of our consciousness.

Another reason to think there's more to it than this is the fact that pain is an example of an *unpleasant* experience, and there are quite a few different examples of such experiences (fear, frustration, despair, hunger, sickness, to name but a few). Very frequently we find that these experiences are connected with circumstances that are likely to be *detrimental* to us – reducing our health or prosperity, or the health or prosperity of our close relatives. Moreover, where that doesn't appear to be the case, it is usually possible to identify sources of the unpleasant experience that would have proven detrimental to our distant human ancestors. As is to be expected with products of evolution, whilst they are perfectly suited to the circumstances in which they evolved, it takes a long time for them to disappear after circumstances change in a way that makes them no longer required. The presence of this close association between unpleasantness and detrimental nature strongly suggests that unpleasant sensations have some other effect, over and above that of their intensity, which proved to be advantageous in detrimental circumstances (and of no benefit in circumstances that were not detrimental).

In the light of these considerations, pain must have some other effect that caused it to be adapted to represent damage data in preference to other intense experiences: An effect brought about by its *unpleasantness*, and which ought therefore to be exerted (perhaps to a lesser extent) by those other types of unpleasant experience too.

What Unpleasantness Does and Why it was Useful

The proposal that I think works is that **whenever a consciousness shifts its voluntary attention to an unpleasant part of its experience, the unpleasantness makes it tend to shift that voluntary attention away to another location sooner than would otherwise be the case (the effect increasing with greater intensity).** It doesn't *like* being there.[31] That sounds logical, doesn't it? And it is also fairly consistent with introspection. When you stub your toe, you don't enjoy attending to the stubbed toe. You can't help it because it's so intense. But you don't enjoy it and are always looking around you for other things to focus upon. The question is: How could this have been consistently beneficial in

---

[31] This contribution to the wave function still needs a physical interpretation. I currently suspect that it lies behind the tendency of quantum particles to prefer lower energy states.

detrimental circumstances, and not beneficial in circumstances that were benign?

To answer that question, we need to consider what effect this change in the shifting pattern of our voluntary attention would have on our behaviour. Remember, in shifting that voluntary attention we are effectively choosing the position where our quantum particle will be found when our brain measures it. Although we quickly shift our voluntary attention away from the painful part of our experience, we are nevertheless drawn back there frequently due to its intensity, and quickly shift away again. Consequently, the brain's measurements of the position of that quantum particle are still quite likely to direct its attention to the location of the damage. However, due to the fact that we spend less time in the painful region, they are also likely to direct it to the sources of other stimuli as well. Moreover, since the intensity of pain will override the effect of the attention spotlight discussed in chapter 8, frequent measurements of the quantum particle's position are not likely to find it at a location that will direct the brain's attention back to where it is currently focussed (unless it happens to be already aimed at the location of the damage). As a result, our attention will shift more frequently and more randomly. It is this greater randomness in a creature's focus of attention that I suspect to be the real reason unpleasant experiences proved to be advantageous in detrimental circumstances.

Why this would be beneficial is easy to understand when you consider that those circumstances are obviously ones the brain hasn't anticipated in advance, and therefore doesn't immediately know how to deal with. If it had anticipated them, you wouldn't be in them. Since its current focus of attention has got it into the damaging circumstances, and since it doesn't immediately know how to escape from them, the best thing it can do is to shift its attention a bit more randomly and hope that it hits upon a solution. Consequently, when a genetic mutation caused our ancestors to shift their attention more randomly in unanticipated circumstances that were detrimental to them, their brains were more likely to stumble upon a way out of those circumstances, and they consequently survived more often to pass on that mutation to future generations.

Now, you might be thinking that simply reducing the salience of the attended object (see chapter 8) would have the same effect. And to some extent you would be right. Doing that would certainly increase the randomness in the creature's focus of attention. A drop in the intensity of the region of our experience that directs our attention to the vicinity of the currently-attended object or stimulus would clearly increase the chance that we will direct our attention elsewhere. There is, however, a crucial difference in the way pain does this that confers an important additional advantage.

To see what that is, you need to recall the postulate introduced in chapter 9, that **a consciousness is more likely to shift its voluntary attention** *between locations of similar experience*. When a consciousness shifts away from a location of pain, it is more likely to select locations of similar experience elsewhere. These might be pain-type feelings, too, but they could also be locations where the consciousness experiences the *same colour* (or from which it hears the *same sound*) as it was experiencing at the location of the pain. In the highly evolved attention-focussing system we are now considering, these are obviously more likely than other locations to direct the creature's attention to other sources of potential harm, thereby allowing its brain to make an accurate assessment of the danger it needs to escape from more quickly than would otherwise be possible. It is this that ultimately explains why we evolved to feel pain when damaged.

How Time Slows Down

Interestingly, the benefit of having a more-rapidly-shifting focus of attention in dangerous or detrimental circumstances may also enable this theory to explain the intriguing fact that many people who have endured extremely painful or traumatic situations report that time appeared to *slow down* during their ordeal. Although they are just reliving a memory when they report this, the fact that this memory appears to take longer to play back than memories of equally long periods of pleasant experience is something that needs to be accounted for. Assuming (as our theory obviously suggests) that experienced time is in fact physical time (just as our experienced spaces – the potential positions of our quantum particle – are physical spaces within the brain), it does suggest that the experience itself took longer to happen. And in the current theory, that is perfectly possible.

The key thing to remember is that just as relatively large spaces on our body are represented by extremely tiny spaces in the brain, longish time intervals could easily be getting represented in the attention-focussing system by extremely *short* time intervals. We don't actually know how much real physical time *the experienced duration* that we think of as 'a second', for instance, takes up. It only represents one second because that is how long the events represented within it take to happen when they occur in the outside world. Our subjective representation of these events (the changes in the wave function that forms our experience of them) might be proceeding much faster than the events themselves did. Provided our subjective representation of every other second always happens just as quickly, we would not notice anything unusual.

Now, you might think there'd be a problem because our experience would soon catch up with real time. When that happened, the brain would run out of sensory data to represent, and would have to wait for more. But that would only be a problem if our experience were continuous. In the current theory, our brain is frequently measuring the position of our quantum particle; and when it does so, our experience must temporarily cease. For all we know, it might be absent for the best part of every second, and only brought into existence momentarily whenever the brain decides that a random shift in attention is called for. That very brief moment would be what we experience as that second in time (though in actual fact it would be the one that finished half a second before). And since we don't experience anything (not even nothing) in the intervening period, that experienced second would flow naturally into the next one.

We would only notice something strange if the brain began representing periods of time that were *shorter than usual* using the same length of experienced time. And crucially, that is exactly what the brain would need to do in this theory if it wanted to make our random shifts in attention occur *more frequently* (as it would in dangerous situations that it didn't know how to escape from). The shorter intervals between measurements would mean it had shorter intervals of sensory data to encode within the wave function of the quantum particle. Since the brief moment of indeterminate duration between the isolation of the quantum particle (when a moment of experience begins) and the ensuing measurement (when it stops) would not be easy to adjust, the brain would instead have to *slow down the representation* to ensure that when each measurement took place the probability of its outcome was still dependent upon the full set of sensory data. As a result, when memories of these experiences were played back against the backdrop of normal sensory experience, the remembered events would appear to have taken longer than usual to happen.

Hence, as well as accounting for the association of unpleasant experience with potentially detrimental circumstances, the fairly obvious benefits of having a more rapidly and randomly shifting focus of attention in those circumstances also allows this theory to explain why we seem to have evolved to endure those experiences *for longer than expected.*

The Pleasantness-Benefit Correlation

Of course, genetic mutations could equally well have caused our ancestors to shift their attention more randomly in *benign* circumstances too (by, for example, causing *tactile* stimuli or *visual* stimuli to be represented in unpleasant sensations). However, the very definition of benign circumstances means those in which what creatures are currently doing is of some benefit to them. Random shifts in their attention are likely to interrupt that current action, and they would thereby prevent those creatures benefiting any further from it. Since this would put those creatures at a disadvantage compared to their competitors, the mutations that caused it are likely to be removed from the gene pool. The creatures who have these mutations will tend to raise fewer healthy offspring than their competitors who don't, eventually resulting in a population that no longer have these mutations.

But what would happen if a creature sustained a mutation that actually *reduced* the shifting of its attention in benign circumstances? Clearly that creature would tend to stay focussed upon a task that it was benefiting from *for longer than its competitors would.* Such a mutation would therefore *improve* its chances of passing on its genes to future generations (provided of course that the same mutation didn't also reduce that shifting of attention when its circumstances were detrimental, or have any other undesirable side-effects). In view of this, any mutation that reduced the shifting of a creature's attention purely in benign circumstances via a non-detrimental change in structure is likely to be retained. As we shall now see, this is exactly how we should expect to explain the association of *pleasant* experience with beneficial circumstances in our consciousness. It is why we tend to like stimuli similar to ones that frequently benefitted our ancestors.

Pleasantness obviously seems to be the opposite of unpleasantness. But why? The most probable reason is that it is having the opposite *effect* upon our consciousness. As we have just seen, the simplest explanation for why unpleasant experiences have come to indicate the occurrence of detrimental circumstances is that unpleasantness makes our consciousness shift its voluntary attention more randomly, resulting in greater randomness in our focus of attention. When that effect was confined to detrimental circumstances via a mutation an ancestor of ours received, it proved to be beneficial, causing that ancestor to stumble upon a way out of such circumstances sooner than its competitors. Since pleasantness ought to have the *opposite effect* to unpleasantness, we can postulate that the occurrence of pleasant sensations *reduces our tendency to shift our attention away from its current focus.* In other words, when we focus upon a pleasant part of our experience we tend to stay there for longer. We *like* it there. As a result, when a mutation caused a pleasant experience to arise from a stimulus that always indicated the occurrence of a beneficial circumstance (for our ancestors, that is), those ancestors were less likely to be distracted from the activity that was benefiting them. Since this would have improved their chances of raising healthy offspring, genes causing pleasant experience to arise from the detection of intrinsically beneficial circumstances became commonplace.

Summing Up

I think it is truly remarkable that the current theory allows so simple a postulate as greater or less randomness in the shifting of attention to fully explain the obvious correlations between pleasant experience and beneficial circumstances, and between unpleasant experience and detrimental circumstances, that are such an important feature of human consciousness. As with the perfectly scientific explanation for our visual images described in chapter 7, the simple reason for the existence of our attention spotlight detailed in chapter 8, the satisfying account of the subjective separation of our senses that chapter 9 related, and the straightforward solution to the binding problem identified in chapter 10, this final demonstration of this theory's power convinces me that it is correct. No other theory of consciousness comes close to accounting for these facts. Functionalists, for example, might claim to have explained the images in our visual experience by saying something like 'our colour experience *arises from* the visual information it encodes'. But such dubious pronouncements neglect to mention that the information they are referring to isn't the image on one's retina. It is information obtained from that retinal image by some other part of the brain. And from what we know about the brain so far, we would not expect that information to be stored in perfect retinal-image-like patterns.

To explain the visual images we experience, the functionalists who believe that visual processing gives rise to colours must therefore account for why these colours are not arranged in the form of the neurons and neural structures that are known to process visual information in the brain. They must explain why they appear instead to be organised in patterns very similar to the patterns formed by light interacting with photoreceptor cells on our retina. No functionalistic theory I am aware of provides a convincing reason for this. And by a similar argument, one can also see that no functionalistic theory accounts for the human-body-like form that the tactile and proprioceptive information in our experience takes. Functionalism simply cannot explain why we feel like a human being rather than a set of brain cells. Yet most theories of consciousness invoke some form of functionalism in an effort to do precisely that.

In contrast, the theory we have constructed over the previous six chapters offers a perfectly scientific reason for why the experiences of a brain-based consciousness should be expected to evolve a humanlike form. Beginning with the defensible assumption that our subjective spaces represent the potential positions of a single quantum particle, it tells us how this aspect of reality could come to represent spaces within a human body and its surroundings, how it could come to be so full of sensory and memory information, and why the experiences encoding that information would come to highlight the object or stimulus that the human brain was attending to. It then reveals that these experiences would almost inevitably come to be arranged into a form that very closely resembles the spatial patterns of the sensory stimuli they represent. And it entails that sensory stimuli coming from the same object, together with memories and ideas about that object, would evolve to feel connected. Moreover, with just two more basic postulates, it explains why distinct ranges of experience would become exclusively associated with particular senses, and why unpleasantness would become a warning of detrimental situations, and pleasant experience a reward for good things.

It is important to note that it is at present the only theory of consciousness that does this. There are other theories that attribute consciousness to supposed quantum processes taking place in the brain. But these offer no scientific mechanism that would account for why the consciousness thus generated feels like a whole human being. Their justification tends to be that they explain the *existence* of our consciousness, and the fact that it feels as though it affects our brain's activity. Its image-forming nature – the most surprising feature of our experiences – is left completely unaccounted for. It is as though the proponents of these theories presuppose that any sensory information contained in a conscious part of the brain will automatically be encoded in sensory-image-like forms. More likely, it is because the presuppositions implicit in these theories (such as the hubristic assumption that we constitute something big like a vast network of coherent quantum particles stretching right across the brain) make that amazing image-forming nature impossible to account for in any consistent scientific way.

As we have just seen, the view that our experience is actually the wave function of a single quantum particle being used by our brain to introduce randomness into our focus of attention – a view that I call *PSI-psychism* (or *Position Selecting Interactionism*) after the Greek letter "psi" conventionally used to denote the wave function – allows this and all its other features to be accounted for as straightforward products of natural selection. Positive natural selection, and the fortunate occurrence of the circumstances that allowed the adaptation of the proposed quantum particle, are the Blind Mindmaker. They account for all the features of the human mind without requiring the universe, nature or pre-existent conscious souls to be able to see and know what brains and senses are, and understand how the information they gather is organised, and without requiring brains and senses to know what *experiences* are. Since that is exactly how current science *says* we should expect these features to be explained, we have every reason to believe that this theory is accurate. It is, in any case, the only means of explaining those features that current science offers us.

In view of this, I think we have good reason to take this theory of consciousness seriously and explore its implications. We have absolutely *no* rational reason to regard it as just a crazy idea. It may *sound* crazy, but that is only the verdict of intuitions that have evolved to make us think that we, as consciousnesses (streams of experience), are something more than just a tiny particle getting used by the human brain to impart a non-detrimental level of randomness into human behaviour. Those intuitions are a product of the neural structures that keep that randomness in check. To fully appreciate what science says we are most likely to be, we need to overcome such intuitions and trust what successful scientific theories themselves are telling us when we consider how they explain structures with similar sets of properties. And that is precisely what we have been doing throughout this book.

PART THREE

THEOLOGICAL IMPLICATIONS

The God who made the world and all things in it,
he, being Lord of heaven and earth,
doesn't dwell in temples made with hands.
He isn't served by men's hands, as though he needed anything,
seeing as he himself gives to all life and breath, and all things.
He made from one blood every nation of men
to dwell on all the surface of the earth,
having determined appointed seasons,
and the boundaries of their dwellings,
that they should seek the Lord,
so that perhaps they might reach out for him and find him,
though he is not far from each one of us.
For in him we live, and move, and have our being.

Acts 17:24-28

CHAPTER TWELVE

The GOD Prediction

Why the Universe is Likely to be Conscious

From a theological perspective, it is really interesting that identifying consciousness with the wave function of a quantum system appears to be the only *scientific* means of explaining it. That is because the main criterion for a system to enter into an indeterminate 'quantum' state is for it to become *completely isolated from its environment*. When nearby particles interact with a quantum particle in a way that affects further particles with implications for what a human experimenter observes, the wave function of the quantum particle 'collapses' – which simply means the particle instantly comes to have a fixed position or energy (or one that is not nearly as uncertain as it was). Hence to have properties that are completely indeterminate, quantum systems must not undergo such interactions. They must not constantly affect their environment in ways that have potentially measurable consequences. And one system that doesn't appear to be constantly interacting with an external environment is the universe itself.

Since the universe we inhabit seems to be governed everywhere by the same set of fundamental laws – and since we have no evidence of frequent events that break these laws – it is fairly reasonable to suppose that it either doesn't have an external environment (by far the simplest position) or isn't regularly interacting with one. As a result, we can be fairly confident that the universe too will have a wave function and therefore a consequent experience. Indeed, modern cosmological theories often attribute the Big Bang – the explosion believed to have begun the universe – to a spontaneous quantum event, an event caused in this theory by *the free choice of a consciousness*. And since we have no undisputed evidence of anything outside of the universe, it is reasonable to suppose that the form of its wave function – and therefore the form of its experience – is the form of the universe itself (including the distribution of all the matter contained therein). As we shall see shortly, there is also reason to believe it will include the universe's past. Hence we are already beginning to see how this scientifically-consistent theory of consciousness entails the possibility of a universe-wide consciousness – a being who experiences everything that happens, and has happened, within the universe, and who even started it all off.

The really big question is: Could such a being do anything significant *after* the Big Bang? Would it be able to intervene in the course of evolution in a measurable way? Remember, we're talking about a consequence of a scientific theory here, not a supernatural being. Any capability we attribute to it must be allowed by the established laws of physics, and must be entirely consistent with what our theory of consciousness predicts.

Why a Cosmic Consciousness needn't break the Laws of Physics

To understand what a universe-wide consciousness ought to be capable of, we must consider what other non-human consciousnesses in our theory do. Recall from chapter 7 that these make free choices that determine the position of a quantum particle. Their experiences (as the wave function of that particle) ensure that some positions are more likely to be chosen than others. Given that the universe has a consciousness, the following question then arises: What *free choice* is the experience *of the universe* influencing? If the universe has no external environment, or is constantly isolated from such an environment, its wave function never collapses. Consequently, its predicted free choice cannot be fixing the position of the universe itself (whatever that might mean). Nor can it be physically altering the paths of any particle, since that would break the hallowed 'conservation of energy' law of physics. The only possibility, as far as I can see, is that its free choices are *collapsing the wave functions of other quantum systems.*

Now if you are familiar with the various interpretations of quantum mechanics that scientists have put forward over the last century, you will know that in some of these the collapse of the wave function is not a real process. According to the aptly termed 'many worlds' interpretation, for example, when the position of a quantum particle is measured it doesn't actually lose any of its other potential positions as it appears to. Instead, an infinite number of new parallel universes supposedly spring into being, in each of which that one quantum particle is found to occupy a different position! In fact, every single measurement of a quantum particle's position is reputed to cause such an infinite proliferation of universes branching out from our own in which identical copies of your consciousness and my consciousness exist.

Whatever you think of such rather uneconomical hypotheses is not important for this discussion because the fact that we don't experience our consciousness existing in an infinite number of universes means that from our perspective the wave function constituting our experience *must* collapse when a measurement of the position of our particle is made. Something must therefore determine the moment when that happens. And since we don't experience the measurements that our brain must be performing on our particle, it must take place at the very instant these occur.

Due to the fact that all other processes we know of appear to be formed out of the effects of *fundamental* particles – particles like electrons, quarks and photons that are currently thought not to be composed of anything smaller – I have speculated that this process is also caused by fundamental particles. I have tentatively proposed that it is caused by a free choice made by one of the truly fundamental constituents of a quantum particle or system. If so, it would be very reasonable to attribute this wave-function collapsing ability to the universe itself – the very first 'particle' to ever exist, and thus a genuinely fundamental one.

What is interesting about this final conclusion is that by causing the collapse of other wave functions, this universe-wide consciousness could intervene in the universe's evolution *without breaking the laws of physics*. That is because due to an experimentally verified effect known as the 'quantum Zeno effect' it could fix the trajectory of a particle anywhere in space simply by repeatedly collapsing the wave function of that particle. Such particles could then be used to bring about chosen changes in an organism's genome; or even alterations in a human being's thoughts at a crucial moment in world history. Remember, due to the completeness of the information content of its experiences, this universe-wide consciousness would not need a brain to plan such actions. It could simply choose the goals of its actions from events that it observes elsewhere in the universe that (due to its complete knowledge of their history) it would automatically know how to bring about in other places.

This is why I am so confident that a genuinely scientific explanation for human consciousness entails the existence of a GOD (a Goal-determining Omniscient – or Omni-*sentient* – Decision-maker, if you like acronyms). That GOD is not needed to account for the existence and organisation of human experience, which is best explained as a product of the fundamental laws of physics (suitably reinterpreted), chance, and natural selection. But the only scientifically-consistent hypothesis that allows human consciousness to be explained by these processes turns out to *predict* the existence of that universe-wide consciousness. Thus, just as modern quantum theory predicted the Higgs boson (the so-called 'god particle' that gives other particles mass), or Einstein's theory of gravity predicted the existence of black holes (objects so heavy and dense that even light cannot escape from their surfaces), this scientific theory of consciousness is likely to predict a GOD.

Invoking a GOD in Science

The significance of this is that this GOD ought therefore to be considered a rational possibility. Scientists should take the possible existence of this being as seriously as they take the possible existence of the particles and processes entailed by their most reasonable explanations of other phenomena. Hence, just as it is reasonable to invoke the action of a black hole to account for some otherwise inexplicable astronomical observations, it ought to be considered perfectly reasonable to propose the action of that GOD to account for similarly inexplicable phenomena that have all the hallmarks of the activity of an intelligent being.

Whilst many scientists would still be loath to invoke a God as an explanation for such things, that is just because those scientists don't believe there *is* a God. As we have seen in this chapter, though, that atheistic presupposition is a prejudice arising from their failure to treat the facts about human experience in the same way they treat the facts about every other complex aspect of a biological organism that appears to be perfectly designed to encode biologically-gathered information. By treating consciousness (and colour and sound and warmth and coldness and hardness and softness and sweetness and bitterness and happiness and sadness and pain and pleasure, etc., etc.) as something that emerges in a magical way from the complexity of a brain, and nowhere else in the universe, they illegitimately prevent scientific theories, and the models that support them, from predicting the existence of God or any other consciousnesses that might possibly exist in nature. As we have seen in this chapter, when that illegitimate assumption is removed, and human consciousness treated like every other complex design-like aspect of a human being, the theory that emerges turns out to predict the existence of a consciousness in whose experience *everything* is represented.

This is not an irrational conclusion, but a logical consequence of attempting to explain the design-like structure of human consciousness in the same way science explains the structure of every other information-carrying part of our brain activity. Other scientifically-trained philosophers have arrived at very similar views. Chief among them is the British astrophysicist Sir Arthur Eddington, whom we met in chapter 4. In the tenth chapter of *The Nature of the Physical World*, he also argued that 'the universe is of the nature of a thought or a sensation in a universal mind'.

Hence, our best scientific theories strongly favour the view that there is a consciousness experiencing all things that probably exerts a consciously-controlled influence in a freely chosen manner. Remember, such a consciousness wouldn't need eyes or ears or hands to experience things because everything is *already represented* in its experiences, including the light each thing reflects and the sounds that it makes. Nothing needs to be detected. It experiences all things in the same way you experience the part of your brain activity that your experiences constitute (though unlike yours, its experiences wouldn't be moulded into the shapes and forms of sensory stimuli, and would not therefore feel like a human body and what it detects – they would instead feel just like the universe that they constitute, and the material structures within it).

Of course, such a consciousness would need to be continually supplied with *memories* before it could act in a creative way. However, it is possible that it may not need any machinery – biological or otherwise – to provide that capability. That's because there is reason to believe that such a being would simply *continue to experience the past of the universe* as well as its present. The reasoning behind this claim is complex, but you might be able to appreciate where it comes from by realising that you also continue to experience a bit of the past. How else could you possibly experience something moving, such as when you turn a page of this book. You couldn't possibly have any impression of the movement of the page if you were not somehow aware of where it was a moment before now. And your impression of its movement is not like a blurred photograph, as it would be if your experience of the previous moment were simply superimposed onto your experience of the present moment. Hence you must at all times be clearly conscious of the form of your experience a moment before the present (though how this can be is not easily comprehended).

In the theory we have developed, this is best interpreted as the period during which the wave function of our particle evolves in between the brain's measurements of that particle's position.

Since the consciousness of the universe extends over vastly more space than the tiny region of the brain where yours is confined, and since it doesn't get collapsed by regular measurements, it seems reasonable to expect that its intrinsic sense of the past extends much further back in time than yours does – perhaps even as far back as the Big Bang itself. If so, it wouldn't need any means of retrieving memories of what its past actions had done. It just wouldn't ever forget them. And it could thereby choose to act in ways that in the past had constructive consequences. That would make it pretty much an *omniscient, creative being* – a being who knows everything that can be known at each moment in time and can act according to that knowledge.[32] It is for this reason that I can confidently conclude that a Goal-determining Omniscient Decision-maker (GOD) is predicted by our best scientific theories.

Since 'being predicted by our best scientific theories' is considered reasonable grounds for believing in many things (black holes, Higgs bosons, the Big Bang, etc.), it ought to be considered reasonable grounds for believing in a GOD too. As a result, I am entirely confident that there are independent, scientific reasons for believing that a GOD exists, making it perfectly justifiable for me

---

[32] Although some might claim that this is not a *Christian* conception of God, I disagree. According to *Acts 17:28*, the foremost Christian evangelist – St Paul – claimed that in God 'we live and move and have our being'. In Collossians 1:16-17, Paul also claimed that 'in him all things were created: things in heaven and on earth, visible and invisible, whether thrones or powers or rulers or authorities; all things have been created through him and for him. He is before all things, and in him all things hold together'. The universe-wide consciousness predicted by a scientific explanation for consciousness is entirely consistent with these early Christian beliefs. Interestingly, the way in which that GOD remembers things by continually experiencing the past is recalled by Jesus' answer to the Pharisees in John 8:58: 'Before Abraham came into existence, I am!'

to posit the influence of that intelligent being when no more-reasonable explanation for a phenomenon is forthcoming.

Possible Evidence of a GOD

There are, of course, very few phenomena for which this is the case. However, I am convinced that the number of such phenomena isn't zero. In particular, I think that the action of a GOD is the only reasonable explanation for the historical fulfilment of three prophecies that are found in the Old Testament book of Daniel (a pseudonymous work that was very obviously forged in the second century BC, but which contains three prophecies that were clearly intended to predict events far beyond that time as a means of countering scepticism about the book's authenticity). Wherever these prophecies came from, they happen to make specific and time-limited predictions that appear to me to have come true to a rather astonishing extent. Moreover, the nature of the predicted events are such that they could not have been deliberately brought about by humans, and their occurrence is far too much of a coincidence to be reasonably dismissed as chance.

My reasons for this conclusion are covered in my book *Unexpectedly Foretold Occurrences*, so I shall not go into any further detail here. However, it is relevant to note that the one thing common to all three of these prophecies is that they predicted events pertaining to the emergence of a new world religion that were definitely fulfilled by the rise of Christianity. Moreover, they clearly portray this new religion as originating *from God himself*.

In the light of this, it may be no coincidence that Christian theology is so easy to reconcile with this scientific explanation of consciousness, as you will see in the next two chapters.

Ah soul, so airy, dear and dainty,
My body's guest and choicest friend,
To what strange places will you wander,
All pallid, stiff, and bare out yonder,
Where all your wonted jests must end.

Emperor Hadrian (138 AD)

Historia Augusta: Life of Hadrian 25,9
Translation by Fred. A. Dixon

CHAPTER THIRTEEN

Till Death do us part...and beyond

Your Place in Nature

Although it is very difficult not to think of yourself as a human being, we discovered in chapter 5 that what you experience as your human body and limbs are not your *real* body and limbs at all. They are patterns of some mysterious type of brain activity triggered by nerve impulses coming from those parts of your body. If your body and limbs were completely removed and a machine inserted into your brain to maintain exactly the same patterns of brain activity – *not* something you should ever try by the way! – then (provided your eyes were closed) you'd still feel just the same. You'd experience what neurologists would in those circumstances call a *'phantom'* body and limbs, but which is really just the same set of feelings you had before you were decapitated. How do I know? Because there are numerous reports of amputees continuing to feel their missing limbs after surgery – sometimes *long* after surgery. The feeling of those limbs must arise from their brains, and the same no doubt applies to all body parts. Hence, you are not actually a whole human being, or even very much of one. You are really just some part of a human being's brain activity.

Although modern science doesn't appear to tell us much more than this about what we are, we know what the activity of relatively large chunks of a brain looks like from brain scans, and it certainly doesn't resemble the images that a person in a scanner might be made to see. Nor does it look remotely like the shapes of the body and limbs that such a person feels, the surfaces he or she is touching, or the things that person may say they are imagining. Moreover, the information present in our experience at any moment in time has been calculated to be vastly less – *millions of times* less – than the information the brain must be processing in order to generate it. Hence, we are in fact very likely to be an *extremely small* part of our brain's activity as the theory developed in chapters 6-11 predicts.

It is true that vast regions of the brain are getting used in the calculations that *generate* the patterns (visual images, sounds, feelings, etc.) that we experience. However, we do not experience those calculations. We only experience their *end-product* – the *output* of the calculations – and the part (or parts) of the brain where that output emerges may well be extremely small. Yet it is in that part of the brain that we each reside.

But what do I mean by this 'we'? I mean the set of *experiences* in which those output patterns are encoded: The set of colour experiences that our visual images are made of, together with the set of sound experiences that encode what we hear, the tastes and smells that encode chemical data, and the set of feelings that form the perceived shape, orientation and state of our body. These are the things that we actually consist of (together with the fainter impressions of our thoughts and memories and the meanings that link it all together). Throughout this book, we have called that set of experiences our *consciousness*,[33] but it is essentially everything that we are.

Current theories of how our brains work tell us nothing about what that consciousness is. Nor do they tell us what an experience is, or how the many different types of experience that our consciousness consists of come about. On the other hand, in view of the fact that each of those things appears to be organised to encode particular types of brain-based information in an extremely appropriate way, scientists ought to be pretty sure about something (though few will publicly admit it): They ought to be pretty confident that, whatever these things are, they have a *very real effect* upon our brain activity – an effect that was strong enough to have an impact on the behaviour of our ancestors.

As I explained in chapter 6, what the organisation of our experiences ought to imply for a scientist familiar with current theories of how our brains developed is that consciousnesses (whatever they are) must *do something* that depends upon what they are experiencing, and which is able to affect the brain in a beneficial way. If they did not do anything, they could not have become adapted to a biological role through natural selection (which is currently the only known process that can account for high levels of design-like organisation in biological structures).

---

[33] The word 'consciousness', as defined here, is in my view synonymous with the words 'soul' and 'mind'. It should not be confused with the word 'spirit' (as used in the Bible, for example) which one can roughly define as 'a state of mind (consciousness/soul) – or a manner of conscious thought – that tends to bring about some type of behaviour or action'. Thus an 'evil spirit' is a state of mind – or way of thinking – that brings about actions or behaviour that are evil (whether or not it is implanted through 'possession' by a mischievous supernatural mind that is continually in such a state as was commonly thought in ancient times).

And if different *parts* of a consciousness – different *experiences* – did not do *different* things, even if they were adapted to a biological role, their adaptation by natural selection would not be able to account for the amazingly appropriate and meaningful way our experiences encode information. Yet that is the only way to explain this example of complex design-like organisation *in a manner that is similar to how science says all other brain-based structures that encode sensory information came to be organised.* This is why, in chapter 6, I was able to conclude that, whatever consciousnesses are, they must definitely do something to our brain activity that depends upon what they experience.

We do of course *feel* as though we do something that's influenced by our experiences. However, as I explained in chapter 6, feelings can be deceptive. It is the fact that the only remotely scientific way of explaining consciousness *requires* it to do something to the brain that gives us a genuine reason to believe we do indeed do something. And we should also note that what we *actually* do (direct our brain's attention according to chapter 8) may well not be what we *think* we do. Just like our feelings, our thoughts too are often mistaken.

Now, most scientists will accept that we should expect our experiences to be made out of ordinary matter. That at least does not appear to be an overly contentious claim. To give rise to experiences in an intelligible scientific way, though (the same way ordinary matter gives rise to *other* sorts of phenomena according to established theories), ordinary matter must have properties that can combine to *form* experiences. That is because different distributions of basic properties like charge and mass is what gives rise to *all the other* properties of matter that scientists measure and document. However, no distribution of charge or mass or any other physical property (as it is currently defined by scientists) has the potential to form an experience of the colour red, or of a sound or a pain. In fact, one cannot conceive of properties that could combine to form an experience that are *not themselves experiences* (little specks of red, quavers of sound or pinpricks of pain, for example).

What this means is that experiences themselves, and therefore the consciousnesses that experience them, should be expected to exist *at the bottom level of reality*, just as our theory requires. The existence of basic instances of such phenomena – devoid of biological information – cannot therefore require a brain. And as we saw in chapter 3, there really isn't any good reason to think it *should* require a brain. It is the biologically acquired *information* present in our experiences that results from the complex organisation of the brain – not the experiences themselves. In other words, we need a brain to ensure that our colour experiences form images that match those formed by light hitting our retina; and we need a brain to ensure that different types of stimuli are always represented by different types of experience, and the same type of stimuli by the same type of experience. But nothing we currently know suggests a brain is needed to bring those basic types of experience *into existence*.

This is why it is perfectly reasonable to suppose that a genuinely scientific explanation for human consciousness could predict the existence of a GOD (a consciousness that arises from the universe as a whole, rather than from a part of a brain, and which therefore experiences everything the universe contains and applies its effect anywhere it chooses). As we discovered in chapter 12, the only scientifically-justifiable explanation for our consciousness *does indeed entail the existence of such a being.* Interestingly, as we shall now see, it also entails that it may be possible for our consciousness to live on after our brain dies.

Of course, the *information* (the set of images and patterns) in our experiences obviously does require a living brain to ensure that it represents our body's sensory information about the real world outside it. However, as we noted in chapter 3, we have no reason to think that experiences that *don't* contain such images and patterns can't exist without a brain's input. If my consciousness (the quantum particle that I ultimately constitute according to chapter 7) were not connected up correctly to the brain in which it is doubtlessly located, its experiences would not be organised to represent the shapes, sounds and feelings of familiar objects and people. However, that does not mean that it – *I* – wouldn't have *some* kind of experience.

In fact, before consciousnesses became adapted to the attention-directing role that our consciousness plays, according to chapter 8, we should expect that they had experiences that *did not contain any sensory information at all*. Or at least, we should expect that whatever sensory information happened by chance to be encoded in their experiences would not have been encoded in a way that made the consciousness feel like it was the organism whose senses were gathering that information. As we saw in chapter 6, that highly organised and meaningful experience – which we now possess – ought to be regarded by scientists as a product of millennia of evolution. In its place, the experience of those un-adapted consciousnesses (the countless trillions of quantum particles that make up the universe we inhabit) would be merely a meaningless barrage of different types of sensation. They would not know anything at all about the things producing those sensations, apart from the fact that they produce those sensations.

Whilst that might be all there is to know about the *intrinsic nature* of these things, it does not provide any information about the sorts of structures these things are parts of, or what they are doing to each other. That's because information that is not available in the direct experience of a consciousness needs to be made available and encoded in the right mixture of experiences for it to make any sense (which is one of the jobs our brain has evolved do). Even the brain-based quantum particles that formed the primitive consciousnesses of our first conscious ancestors would have had that simple and meaningless sort of experience. Since their experiences were not organised to form patterns resembling those ancestors' sensory stimuli, they would not even have known they were a part of a living organism. And they would have been restricted to doing whatever it is that consciousnesses do to their surrounding matter in response to the meaningless mixtures of sensations they were continually bombarded with. They would have continued to choose the position of the particle they constitute (see chapter 7) in a way that was statistically dependent upon their experience (the form of which would simply have reflected the form of that particle's wave function).

Why there almost certainly is Life after Death

By this point, a rather worrying thought has probably occurred to you. If you are something as small as a quantum particle, it is possible that your brain's death will not mean the end of your existence. Although that particle might for a time cease to be suspended in the isolated superposition of states that forms your experiences, it could easily come into such isolation at some future time causing your experience to re-emerge. And it's worth noting that even if that were millions of years in the future, you wouldn't notice any of that time passing. On death, your experience will instantly change from its current rich and meaningful representation of a human being to its next form. And unless you are incredibly, incredibly lucky, that is very unlikely to be the form of another quantum particle directing the attention of an intelligent organism. If pure chance determines where your experience next emerges, you are far, far more likely to become one of those un-adapted quantum particles experiencing the meaningless barrage of sensations that un-adapted consciousnesses must naturally experience according to evolutionary theory.

Of course, if consciousnesses are quantum particles as we concluded in chapter 7, we have every reason to expect there to be trillions of trillions of other consciousnesses that exist in this pitiful state even today. These are the ones that were not adapted by human or animal brains to perform the sort of task we happen to perform (random shifts in attention according to chapter 8). It is perhaps somewhat comforting to note that these consciousnesses will not be mourning their predicament. They won't even know that their experience could be any different. Since a brain is almost certainly needed to mould the experiential qualities of such consciousnesses into coherent thoughts and memories, these consciousnesses will just get on and do whatever it is they do without even thinking about it. And of course, so will you if you become one of these consciousnesses after your brain's death.

You might at first think that such an existence would either be extremely tedious or frighteningly unpredictable. After all, one wouldn't be able to predict whether the next experience that comes along is going to be a nice one (a new colour say) or a really nasty one (a terrible pain). However, these consciousnesses wouldn't have any means of evaluating their experiences or anticipating what was to come. We only have that ability because we are appropriately connected up to the human brain, an incredibly powerful supercomputer, which carries out those functions for us and shows us the results. Each of these is suitably encoded in the set of experiences that we call emotions such that those which aren't in our favour get represented in unpleasant experiences like frustration or worry.[34] Hence, within these un-adapted consciousnesses the feelings that we call frustration and worry *wouldn't ever arise in response to their hopeless predicament.*

In fact, their experience, from their point of view, may not be all that unpleasant. You see, it is likely that the intensity of unpleasant experience that we get in detrimental situations (those that are very likely to be reducing our body's chances of survival or our genes' chances of being passed on to future generations) is a product of evolution designed to make us act in a way that helps our body escape the damaging circumstances. Hence, although our feelings of acute pain and terror are no doubt related to something un-adapted consciousnesses naturally experience, they are probably a significantly *amplified* version of that natural quality. Without the amplification provided by the ordered structure of the brain, such extremes of one type of experience would probably be exceedingly rare.

Of course, at present there is no scientific consensus on what our consciousness actually is. However, we do have a relatively

---

[34] Technically our brain doesn't evaluate the actual *experience*. After all, science tells us it evolved by natural selection, and natural selection would only make a brain care about an experience if that experience made our ancestors less able than their competitors to pass on the genes for their brain to future generations. It evaluates the circumstances giving rise to the experience. But each of these evaluations tends to reach a similar conclusion to one of the evaluations – like the unpleasantness of pain or the sweetness of sugar – that have been hardwired (by natural selection) into the system that generates the quality of our perceptions. As a result, they demand a similar sort of response from that system, and they therefore give it an experience that has a similar – though far from identical – quality (because that's what provokes the appropriate response). Hence if a perception feels unpleasant it tends to be accompanied by an evaluation (worry, say) that also feels unpleasant. And if a perception feels nice it is often accompanied by an evaluation (say, happiness) that also feels nice.

good idea of what other parts of a human brain are made of and how they came to have their organised structure, and we have no reason not to expect that a similar story applies in the case of our consciousness. The interesting thing is that, as we have seen, the required story does suggest that our consciousness could be something so small and requiring so little organisation that it is capable of 'living on' after our body's death, or else re-emerging by chance at a future time when the matter and energy that forms it comes together in other circumstances. But it also warns us that the experience we can expect to have in those circumstances will be *nothing like* the meaningful human perspective on reality that we currently enjoy.

For every consciousness that was adapted to the particular role in the human brain that we each currently serve, there must be countless trillions that were not so adapted. The experiences of these consciousnesses will not be supplied with biologically gathered information conveniently encoded in appropriate sensations and impressions, and they will not therefore form any meaningful sense of the world around them, or any consistent thoughts or memories. Compared to our current rich experience of human life, the experience of these consciousnesses will be frighteningly impoverished. Although it will probably not be terribly painful (perhaps far less painful than our own can often be), their existence is nevertheless an extremely dull and meaningless one compared to what ours is. Yet, as we have seen, it is exactly the sort of existence that science says each one of us can expect to end up experiencing after our body dies. To escape it we would have to become incorporated into precisely the same region of the brain in another organism – perhaps even another human being – and there doesn't appear to be much chance of that happening.

The Good News

Is there no hope then? Well, from what we discovered in chapter 12 of this book, there might be. But it requires action. If, as I argued in chapter 12, the GOD predicted by this theory of consciousness was behind the rise of Christianity, it could be the case that the only thing in the whole universe that has the power to save us from that fate really is offering us that opportunity. According to the New Testament, the message of Christ is that we are indeed all destined to end up condemned to such a meaningless eternal existence, but God is offering us a way to escape that fate. God is offering us eternal *life* – of the fun and meaningful sort that most of us currently enjoy most of the time – which he intends to provide for us by putting us in charge of a brand new and imperishable body at some future date. All we need to do, according to the New Testament writers, is to believe that Christ was who he said he was and obey his commands. If we do that, according to the apostle Paul, our current stream of experience will be instantly transformed on death into an even richer and vastly more meaningful and joyful one – an experience often referred to as 'heaven'. Since Christ's commands are things like 'love one another', 'love your neighbour as yourself', 'do unto others as you would have them do unto you', 'love your enemies', 'pay your taxes', 'repent for all the bad things you've done', they are generally seen as ethically sound (even if difficult to put into practice). It is *believing in Jesus* that many people nowadays find problematic.

However, the New Testament makes it clear that God is not asking us to take a *blind* leap of faith, or accept a historical claim as fact in a disinterested way. For those who really desire to believe in Christ and take a genuine interest in what is written about him, and who try to obey his teaching, God promises to reveal his reality *directly into their experience*, just as he appears to have done to the writer of those prophecies that I mentioned in chapter 12. That is what will allow them to believe in Christ fully, regardless of their sceptical nature. Hence, what we must do to gain that promised salvation, according to the New Testament, is develop a passionate *interest* in Christ, and a willingness to give his claims the benefit of the doubt, on the understanding that one of these claims is that such doubts will eventually be removed.

Is God Cruel or Unfair?

One might, of course, think it rather unfair of God to grant that promised salvation only to people who fulfil those criteria. However, God must draw the line somewhere. That is because for every consciousness who has enjoyed life as a human being (or some other consciousness-using creature) we should expect there to be countless trillions who have not. In fact, at the smallest level, matter may well be *made* of such consciousnesses, as the British astrophysicist Sir Arthur Eddington rightly concluded (see chapter 4). Indeed, that is precisely what the scientific theory of consciousness that we developed in chapter 7 entails. If that is the case, then any material body we may be put in charge of at some future time will have to be made of such consciousnesses too. Hence, it would be far fairer of God to give some of those *other* consciousnesses a chance to have the rich humanlike experience that we currently enjoy. We have no right to have a second go.

If the Christian gospel is correct on this issue, God is therefore making an exception in our case *purely out of his love for us*, and his compassion for those who recognise the likely continuation of their consciousness after death, and the extremely impoverished nature of the subsequent experiences that chance is likely to give them. But he does not force us to choose the life he offers.

This is not immoral of God because in granting any one of us a second chance to experience a rich intelligent life, he is denying that opportunity to some other consciousness who has not yet had that privilege. Although that in itself may seem immoral, in my opinion God gets away with it without becoming unrighteous because of one important consideration: By promising this opportunity of eternal life to those of us who realise the poverty of their future existence, he is alleviating the despair that this realisation inevitably causes in minds controlled by brains that have evolved to represent detrimental situations in unhappy feelings. And a God who wants to be considered righteous is committed to alleviating suffering *wherever possible*.

Of course, this argument is vulnerable to the famous objection that if God is so committed to alleviating suffering, then why is there so much of it in the world? Surely such a powerful being could instantly intervene to prevent each and every instance of suffering. And come to think of it, could he not have prevented the evolution of whatever dastardly biological structures cause us the negative experiences that suffering ultimately consists of? I don't mean the nerves that carry damage signals to the brain, or the neural systems that register unfavourable circumstances. I mean the unknown structures that encode the resultant information in unpleasant experience. Wouldn't the morally perfect God of Jesus Christ have intervened to ensure that this information was encoded in experiences that, if not exactly pleasant, were at least somewhat less intense?

In the light of these considerations, many philosophers have concluded that if there is a God, of the all-knowing and all-powerful sort that my theory of consciousness predicts, then that God can't possibly be *morally perfect* (i.e. righteous) as the God of Jesus Christ is supposed to be. However, the scientific interpretation of the gospel message that we have identified in this chapter seems to demand that God is indeed morally perfect. Only a morally perfect God would be committed to relieving suffering whenever it was in the best interests of the suffering mind. And only a morally perfect God would be committed to being fair to all consciousnesses despite his (or her) love for those that had already participated in an intelligent human life. Hence, in the final chapter of this book, I shall indicate why the suffering that there is in the world is not irreconcilable with the view that there is an all-knowing and all-powerful being who is also morally perfect. The key observation that has been missed by the philosophers who deny this claim is the fact that suffering is not physical damage or extreme reactions. It is merely *a state of consciousness that the consciousness hates being in.*

CHAPTER FOURTEEN

Overcoming Evil

Why God allows Suffering

The world is indeed full of pain and anguish. Millions of innocent people suffer all the time from disease, disability, loss, fear and hardship. Many philosophers nowadays think that a God who has the power to detect and prevent that suffering, either doesn't exist, or can't be morally perfect. However, I am not so sure this follows. My reason is that if God exists (and I have shown why I think he does in chapter 12) then he has clearly used the process of *natural selection* to develop humans and other creatures. Whilst we can totally expect such a being to have guided and perhaps even started that process on earth, it is important to remember that natural selection adapts whatever works best of the structures that mutations (random or otherwise) present to it. Since I think natural selection shaped our consciousness as much as it shaped the rest of our brain, the intensity of pain for damage, and the heaviness of unpleasant emotion in unfavourable circumstances, is simply what most helped our ancestors survive and raise healthy offspring.

I think we should be grateful that those negative experiences worked best in circumstances that were *un*favourable, rather than in those that increased our ancestors' chances of survival. Otherwise suffering would not be limited to those comparatively rare occasions where our body is enduring serious deprivation or hardship from which no escape seems imminent. Nevertheless, one might think a God who allows suffering *even in these circumstances* cannot be morally perfect because he surely has the power to limit that suffering, either by some kind of brain surgery, or by making the world so perfect that such situations never arise.

To my mind, if we are to hold onto the belief in a morally perfect God, there must be some potential benefit to the sufferer from their suffering that would be removed were God to bring it to an end. And the idea that such situations make us cry out to a possible God for help seems to me to be the answer. If we did not see or know suffering, then we are unlikely to fear any future existence, and therefore unlikely to qualify for the alleviation of that fear that the Christian God's promise of resurrection is intended to accomplish. Remember, a morally perfect God wants to eliminate suffering, but only if that is in the best interests of the sufferer. Due to the existence of countless consciousnesses who have never experienced the life of an intelligent organism, he can only justify the promise of resurrection (which is clearly in the interests of every human being in view of the impoverished experience we are likely to go back to after death) as a means of alleviating suffering. And the only sort of suffering that would be alleviated by such a promise is the fear of what one might experience after one's body's death. Hence, by preventing suffering, God would eliminate *that* fear, which would not be in the best interests of the consciousnesses of human beings.

What About Animals?

Of course, one might protest that animals suffer constantly at the claws – or guns – of predators, or from hunger, cold, forest fires, etcetera; and yet, lacking the type of thinking that language makes possible, they presumably can never dread what happens to them after their body's death.

However, my answer to that one is the question: Do we really know that animals suffer? Do we even know that they are conscious beings? They may writhe around like we do when damaged, but how do we know that this writhing behaviour is accompanied by an experience of agony or despair. It may simply be a reflex favoured by natural selection because, out of all the types of behaviour that random mutations allowed in those circumstances, this one turned out to be the one that most increased their ancestors' survival chances (or those of their offspring). It is important to remember that this is a *scientific* question looking for a *scientifically justifiable* answer. It is clear to me that from a moral perspective we must always assume that all animals do suffer, and treat them in a way that minimises any potential suffering they may happen to endure. But that does not mean the answer to the scientific question is yes. Even if it turns out that we have reason to doubt the existence of suffering in animals, the fact that we can never know anything with absolute certainty means that my moral answer will still be the same. So the question is, from what science has shown us, do we really know that animals suffer?

When pressed, most philosophers will probably admit that we do not. Unless they are functionalists, they would observe that animals' brains are structured differently from ours, and we therefore have no reason to assume that they give them the same set of experiences. Although animals obviously do react to tissue damage in ways that resemble the reactions of humans in pain, we have no reason to think that these reactions are actually caused by the *experience* of pain (other than our obvious moral obligation to ensure that we treat them with the respect that the mere possibility of this demands). These reactions could simply be nature's way of getting them out of the damaging situation as quickly as possible.

Indeed, that is what our scientific theory of consciousness says they are (see chapter 11). This does not mean they don't experience pain in those situations. But in order for them to do so, our theory says they would at least have to have an attention-focussing system controlled by a quantum particle. How abundant that development is within life on earth is an open question. It may eventually be answered via observation and experiment.

But even if it does turn out that some animals are conscious, there is no guarantee that pain experiences will have been adapted to represent any of their sensory information. That happened in our ancestors, according to chapter 11, because it made their attention shift more randomly in detrimental circumstances, increasing their chances of spotting a way out. However, there are other ways of increasing that randomness that would not involve the effect of pain. If there are consciousnesses controlling some non-human animals in the form of the quantum randomness-generator proposed in chapter 7, it is quite possible that natural selection would have favoured one of those other methods of handling detrimental circumstances. With much smaller brains, and a less variable environment, it is even possible that relying upon a *deterministic* calculation was a more economical survival strategy. The consciousnesses of those animals would then only operate when their circumstances were favourable. If that were the case, there'd be no selection pressure favouring the adaptation of the effect of unpleasantness that we inferred in chapter 11, and therefore no reason to expect those animals to evolve to feel pain.

Whilst I personally am reluctant to believe that animals are completely without consciousness, I have no problem with the possibility that they do not experience extremes of suffering in circumstances where a human being would. Indeed, I rather hope that that is the case. If it is, it renders the fact that animals cannot fear an afterlife irrelevant as an objection to the solution to the problem of suffering proposed in this chapter.

It is thus conceivable that suffering has a morally justifiable purpose: It makes one fear the possibility of an impoverished afterlife, allowing God the chance to offer the promise of eternal life as a means of alleviating that fear.[35] And it goes without saying that a morally perfect God should be expected to keep his promises.

However, a morally perfect God should also be expected to honour the free choices that people make. Consequently, we should not expect such a being to grant eternal life to anyone who doesn't take up that offer. He will rightly conclude that such a person doesn't really fear (or recognise) the impoverished state of his life after death, and isn't suffering as a result. And since there was no acceptance of that promise of eternal life, God has no obligation to keep it. Indeed, he is obliged by fairness to allow

---

[35] This would be a very reasonable interpretation of Romans 8:20-22, which says, 'The creation was subjected to vanity, not of its own will, but because of him who subjected it, in hope that the creation itself also will be delivered from the bondage of decay into the liberty of the glory of the children of God. For we know that the whole creation groans and travails in pain together until now.'

some other consciousness its first chance to experience the life of a human being, and must therefore deny that chance to the person who did not choose to take up his offer. On the other hand, according to the gospel message, he willingly grants it to *anyone* who does so choose (see John 8:51, for example).

By insisting that we first choose to obey Christ's teaching, he shows us that he only wants to save those who are willing to live with each other from now on in peace and harmony – thus again alleviating human suffering. However, from the moment we make that decision, and turn away from attitudes and actions that cause disharmony (i.e. suffering), he does not hold any of our past deeds and attitudes against us, and we immediately qualify for the salvation he is offering.

A Scientific Theology

Although inferred from scientifically justifiable ideas about the nature of consciousness, everything I have proposed so far in this chapter is perfectly consistent with the picture painted by the New Testament writers. And, as far as I can see, it is also consistent with the claims that these writers make about God. God is a loving and compassionate being. Even though he is both omniscient (or at least omni-sentient) and omnipresent – experiencing and able to act upon everything in the universe – he cares about other consciousnesses, and wants to alleviate, in the kindest possible way, the despair that those used by brains that are aware of their consciousness's eternal predicament are likely to undergo. Something we would describe as 'hell' does exist (though souls who inhabit that impoverished state of existence are not in constant agony). It is what matter naturally experiences when not raised to the unique position within the human brain that we currently occupy. Although we are each likely to return to that state after our body's death, God is offering us a way to avoid that otherwise inevitable fate if we want to. That salvation involves God putting us in charge of a body again, and the brain of that body will presumably be made to supply us with memories of our past existence (so that we will know who we were). Hence it constitutes a *resurrection,* rather than just a reincarnation, which is presumably why God needed to demonstrate that this was possible through the death and resurrection of Christ and Lazarus.

Of course, some portrayals of hell in the New Testament suggest it is a fiery place (or a very *dark* place) where people get thrown to suffer in agony for all eternity, all the while remaining aware of their predicament and the joy they could have had if they'd been a better person. I personally find these portrayals impossible to reconcile with my unshakable conviction that the God of Jesus Christ is a God of love and compassion. As such, he cannot be a sadistic person. A sadistic or vengeful nature is a rather undesirable by-product of the evolutionary process – it is presumably a genetically-programmed strategy for eliminating competition, or threats to one's survival. As a result, it is not going to be an attribute of the universe-wide consciousness predicted by the scientific theory of consciousness that we've identified. Nor is it likely to be an attribute of the morally perfect God that Christ describes. No matter how much that God abhors sin (i.e. moral imperfections – such as allowing a sadistic nature to control one's actions), he is not going to single out individual human consciousnesses for eternal punishment like a great big bully. If he did that, his moral perfection would be compromised. However, his moral perfection would be equally compromised if he were to resurrect such consciousnesses at the cost of others who have not yet had the chance to try living the sin-free human life that the God of Jesus Christ wants us to live. And what non-resurrection means for us, according to our scientific theory of consciousness, is that we go back to the impoverished and meaningless sort of experience that almost all quantum particles constantly undergo.

But if that is true, why do the portrayals of hell in the New Testament suggest an angry, punishing, sadistic sort of God? My current view on these portrayals is that they are there precisely *because* God loves us. They are there to frighten us into making the right decision. They also portray what that natural state of matter would be like if we could experience it with our brain intact, and compare it with memories of the rich experience we currently enjoy, knowing that we will never be able to have such a beautiful quality of experience ever again. If that were the case, we really would suffer for all eternity. That is because the production of negative feelings in our consciousness is our brain's natural reaction to such hopeless circumstances (see chapter 11). It improved our ancestors' chances of escaping them. However, I definitely do not think God is going to supply the unredeemed on judgement day with an imperishable body tailor made to survive for eternity in a blazing fire, and with a brain intricately designed to generate feelings of intense pain and suffering all that time, even though the body attached to it is indestructible. The God portrayed by the stories of Jesus is simply not like that.

That is not to say that God won't judge us. A judgement where all human beings are resurrected would clearly fulfil certain prophecies about Jesus that the Bible contains. And for reasons given in my book *Unexpectedly Foretold Occurrences* (see chapter 12), I do not think God is averse to fulfilling such prophecies. Hence a 'Last Judgement' is something we might reasonably expect this God to bring about – though right now I can't think of what *good* it would serve (and am perfectly open to the possibility that these prophecies are wrong).

If it does happen, though, I don't think it will be about punishment. Instead, it could be God's way of introducing those who have accepted his offer to the new life he is granting them, and *for their edification* showing their reward to those who sneered at their commitment, or treated them badly in life. The newly resurrected bodies of those people may even be humanely destroyed by a sudden blast of intense heat, as one of the pictures of that Last Judgement suggests. However, if this unlikely-sounding situation happens, I suspect God will have made the brains of the people to whom this fate applies unable to generate pain and fear at that moment – since he is, after all, a God of love and compassion. Any such spectacle will be for the edification of those who were being saved (to give them closure, as the modern expression goes) rather than for God. A morally perfect God would not gain the slightest pleasure from such an act, and would be adamantly opposed to causing suffering to any consciousnesses it involves. It would be merely what he must do in order to be fair to the many consciousnesses who have not yet had their first chance to experience the rich and meaningful life of an intelligent organism, and to remove any source of future pain from the saved without removing their memories of their first life and the experiences that gave it meaning.

Whilst I am sceptical about the authenticity of the biblical passages upon which this doctrine is based, I am not in the least bit sceptical about the restricted promise of salvation found everywhere in the New Testament. To be fair to other consciousnesses, a righteous GOD is obliged *not* to resurrect consciousnesses that have already experienced intelligent life. He can only justify such a course of action as the fulfilment of a promise made to alleviate the suffering of those who fear what is to happen to them after death. And he must allow us the freedom to choose whether or not to take up that promise – a commitment to Christ being the sign of our assent. That said, I am also open to the view that God will grant eternal life to the loved ones of those of us who do choose to believe in Christ and are thus saved (especially if we ask him to). It seems to me that Christ appears to be promising this in Matthew 25:40 and 10:42, and John 16:23 and 15:7. Moreover, I find it hard to see how the redeemed could ever be genuinely happy knowing that their loved ones weren't among them. Consequently, God can justify raising those others (and remain morally perfect) on the grounds that it removes this potential source of further suffering for those who have qualified for his salvation, without requiring him to delete their memories of those loved ones.

Remember, according to this theology he was only able to grant that second chance of a rich intelligent life to the latter as a means of alleviating the suffering that was caused by their fear of death and hell. As a result, God is under no moral obligation to similarly raise the consciousnesses of any other human beings. Although the consciousnesses of these unfortunate individuals will therefore be reduced to an eternal barrage of meaningless mixtures of sensations, the fact that they will not be trapped within a brain any more means that nasty feelings will no longer be amplified in response to their predicament, and they will no longer recall anything they experienced before. So the saved will have no need to worry that other people were in any kind of ongoing agony (a worry that might otherwise have necessitated further resurrections). As it says in the book of Revelation, 'He will wipe every tear from their eyes'. God couldn't genuinely comfort his people if they knew other people were in constant torment. Hence, the experiences of those people, though formless and meaningless, won't constitute suffering. They will in fact probably be far *less* painful than many of the experiences that they endured when they were part of a human brain.

Nevertheless, according the New Testament writers, the experience of those who, during their human lifetimes, choose to accept the salvation that Christ has on offer is going to be *billions of times better.*

The Potential Profitability of Prayer

If you have properly understood the argument of this book, you will already be interested in that gospel message. That is because the scientific nature of my theory of consciousness, and the lack of any scientific alternative explanation, makes that theory *very likely to be true*; and if it is, something of the nature of the Christian gospel is our only hope of avoiding a meaningless eternal existence. Nevertheless, many readers will no doubt feel that they don't know enough to decide whether the claims made in this book are sufficiently plausible. I have tried to put forward the evidence that I believe justifies them in as clear a manner as possible. But I recognise that academic opinion, may seem quite opposed to the conclusions I have drawn. Due to the unscientific functionalism that infects discussions of consciousness, I expect that many academics will reject this theory as too counterintuitive, or too incomplete, or too radical to warrant serious consideration. I therefore suspect that some readers will be reluctant to go against what they see as the weight of academic opinion on those matters.

If that is you, you will be pleased to know that there is another way to come to a knowledge of this GOD (if 'He' really exists as the evidence in this book appears to be suggesting). It is a very *practical* way because it involves performing a little experiment and patiently awaiting the results. Moreover, that experiment won't take too much time to do, and does not require any expensive equipment. In view of the fact that this predicted universe-wide consciousness experiences everything, including the thoughts in your mind, it is perfectly justifiable for us all to ask that GOD for the knowledge we require by *saying a prayer*.

With any other concept of God, one might rightly wonder how such a being could possibly 'hear' a prayer. But with this being, if he exists, we can be fairly sure he can. That's because he experiences literally everything. Although you might think this means the tiny part of that experience that constitutes the thoughts in your mind will be completely swamped by the rest of it, that need not be the case. Complex consciousnesses like ours may well constitute highly distinct forms of experience in its mind. And such a being could easily have an ability to zoom in. The evidence I hinted at in chapter 12 strongly supports this possibility. To that being, your mind (along with the minds of the six billion or so other intelligent occupants of planet earth) is a far more interesting place than much of the rest of its experience. Hence, provided we fill our mind with that prayer and seriously will that being to hear us over and above the cacophony of the other such voices he must be simultaneously aware of, there is a good chance that he will. According to the gospels, God is looking out for exactly this sort of signal, and promises to respond with the information we need to help us make the important destiny-determining decision that's ours to make. In John 14:13-17, Christ tells his followers:

Whatever you ask in my name, I will do it, that the Father may be glorified in the Son. If you ask anything in my name, I will do it. If you love me, keep my commandments. I will pray to the Father, and he will give you another Counselor, that he may be with you forever: the Spirit of truth, whom the world can't receive; for it doesn't see him and doesn't know him. You know him, for he lives with you, and will be in you.

And in Luke 11:9-10, he emphasises the importance of persistence:

Keep asking, and it will be given you. Keep seeking, and you shall find. Keep knocking, and it will be opened to you. For everyone who asks, receives. He who seeks finds. To him who knocks it will be opened.

Hopefully, what I have shown you in this book will encourage you to do just that. If I'm right, you will thereby obtain your free ticket to a second rich and interesting intelligent life – one that promises to be far more permanent and joyful than the one you are currently experiencing. As the Old Testament prophet Isaiah apparently said:

Hey! Come, everyone who thirsts, to the waters!
Come, you who have no money, buy, and eat!
Yes, come, buy wine and milk without money and without cost.
Why do you spend money for that which is not bread,
and your labour for that which doesn't satisfy?
Listen diligently to me, and eat that which is good,
and **let your soul delight itself in richness**.
Turn your ear, and come to me.
Hear, **and your soul will live**.

(Isaiah 55:1-3)

On my itchy nose, a scratch occurred.
As my hand approached, a scrape was heard…
And seen… And then my fingernail
Brushed a dense invisible veil.

Yet fear was not allowed to rise,
Nor curiosity guide mine eyes.
My hand was not released to flail,
Nor grasp at any ghostly shawl.

Instead, each feeling and sight and sound
Reverberated round and round,
For a time well learned when the brain was young,
Adjusted often as my limbs grew long.

The nasal touch delayed the most,
For half a second, it would coast;
The sight and sound for not much less,
The veil a quarter of that at best.

Then signals from my feet were met,
And all combined in a neural net,
As though they'd only just been caught,
Their pattern read, and memories sought.

Then instantly, within my mind,
I scratch my nose, an itch to end,
Unaware that I had settled that score
Half a second or so *before*.

C. S. Morrison (Delayed Gratification)

CONCLUSION

The main purpose of this book was to show you that the mysterious but design-like representation of information by experience that we call our 'consciousness' can be fully accounted for in a manner perfectly consistent with how science currently explains complex aspects of living organisms that appear designed for some function. Explaining it does not require one to invoke bizarre functionalistic laws, or postulate the existence of illusions that appear out of nowhere and aren't made of ordinary matter.

The existence and use of appropriate types of experience (what philosophers call *qualia*) to exclusively represent our body's sensory stimuli, accessed memories, action priorities, and assessments of its circumstances, in an internally felt space and time, can be fully accounted for *without invoking any laws or substances that aren't motivated by current physical theories*. It can be explained as a consequence of selection pressures resulting from the adaption of a single quantum particle to a certain decision-making role in the brain of our distant ancestors. The only proviso is that we must assume that the wave function of that particle actually describes *the effect of a pattern of experience* upon a free conscious choice – a choice that determines the position of that particle within the region of space over which its wave function extends (which in this case will obviously lie somewhere within the brain[36]).

Since nobody knows what the wave function actually describes, the view that it is a pattern of experience is a good one. As far as I am aware, it is the only view that attributes the wave function to *any* known part of nature. But as we have seen, it more-or-less entails that our experience will continue in some form for a very long time after our body's death. And since quantum particles that aren't connected to brains can't have experiences that carry suitably organised sensory data, we have no scientific reason to expect our experience in those circumstances to be particularly interesting and enjoyable.

Not wanting to leave you dolefully contemplating this rather bleak prospect, I have taken the liberty of showing you the one implication of this theory that offers us a ray of hope for a better afterlife: The GOD prediction. And I have tried to show why I think this predicted GOD will take the trouble to save you (and possibly your loved ones) from this rather gloomy fate if you want that. Remember, it is only gloomy from our perspective. Quantum particles are too busy navigating their way around the effects of other quantum particles to care whether or not their variety of experience could have been any different, and they have no

---

[36] The fact that according to current quantum theory there is the tiniest of probabilities that a confined quantum particle could appear somewhere other than its region of confinement does not contradict this view. Although it does suggest that a part of our experience will represent space beyond that part of the brain, the minuscule nature of the probability of the particle turning up in that space demands that this part of our experience be so weak as to be pretty much unnoticeable. I suspect that its existence probably contributes to our natural sense that the space of our experience is unbounded.

memory of any prior intelligent, humanlike existence they might have had.

Nevertheless, it may still be something you'd like the opportunity to avoid if such an opportunity does exist. I for one would far prefer to have another experience of being the consciousness of an intelligent organism rather than an eternity of trouble-free, but meaningless, memory-less, and thoughtless wanderings through an ocean of formless and shapeless patterns of sensation.

Remember, if we are the essence of a single tiny particle as my scientific explanation of our experience demands, then there is probably not another choice. That particle is going to exist on for a very long time regardless of what happens to our bodies after death; and unless a very real God who constantly knows its whereabouts positions it at the required location in the brain of an intelligent organism at some future time, it is extremely unlikely to end up in such highly privileged circumstances ever again.

We are extremely lucky to have had even one opportunity to experience this pinnacle of knowledge, and exceptional richness of subjective life, that our current role in the highly-evolved brain of a language-using species allows us to have. And it is for this reason that we cannot expect a righteous God to automatically grant us that opportunity a second time. There are uncountable numbers of other consciousnesses that have not yet had even one taste of that richness of intelligent life; so even though God loves the individual intelligent consciousnesses he has created here on earth, he cannot justify resurrecting them at the expense of some of those others.

One of the fascinating things about Christian theology is that it recognises the one loophole that allows God to do this. That loophole is our fear of the impoverished afterlife that awaits us, and the need for a righteous God to alleviate suffering wherever he can do so without compromising the most important of ethical principles: *Do unto other consciousnesses only what you would have them do unto you if you were in their shoes.* God could remove that fear of what awaits us in many ways: He could make us believe that there's no such bleak prospect ahead. He could make us stop thinking about it, or cause us to think that our experiences cease at death, or that a rich paradise inevitably awaits us all. But these courses of action are not what he would have us do to him if he were in our shoes. Consequently, he removes this form of suffering in the only way that satisfies that overarching ethical principle. He offers us the opportunity to be resurrected if we so choose.

There are, of course, strings attached. We have to be committed to following Christ's teaching ("Do unto others as you would have them do unto you!", for example). Although that may at times seem difficult, the emphasis on repentance in the New Testament suggests to me that God is more interested in our *willingness* to do this than the extent to which we succeed. Those strings are in fact only to be expected. God would not be reducing suffering if he were committing himself to resurrect people who were unwilling to abide by rules designed specifically to prevent suffering. And if we did not have to make a choice to accept this offer of resurrection, God would not be offering it purely to those who are suffering from this fear (as his righteousness requires).

Our willingness to make that choice is the evidence that we are enduring this form of suffering in the first place, and therefore the criteria that God chooses to abide by when selecting those he will resurrect. Some scriptures do, of course, suggest that the resurrection of loved ones is also promised to those who follow Christ. If so, this is easily understood as God's means of alleviating another very obvious form of suffering in those for whom this form of relief can be justified – the people who currently fear what will happen to them after death, and who are not likely to be responsible for further suffering after their resurrection. Such people may clearly be suffering from the thought of not seeing their loved ones again – a form of suffering that, as far as I can see, allows God to promise the resurrection of those loved ones too (even if they are already deceased).

As I explained in chapter 13, the extent to which the Christian gospel makes sense when viewed in the light of what science tells us about our consciousness is extremely encouraging. It is encouraging because it could indicate that the God predicted by my scientific theory of consciousness was responsible for that gospel message (for further evidence of this, see my book *Unexpectedly Foretold Occurrences*). And one of the key features of that gospel message is its promise of *resurrection* – being put back in charge of an intelligent organism (possibly equipped with our favourite memories) – which is our only hope of escaping the meaningless and mostly formless 'eternal' experience that the vast majority of quantum particles almost certainly undergo.

Let's remember, though; what you think of these theological implications is completely irrelevant to the task of assessing the merits of the theory of consciousness that this book proposes. That theory – *Position Selecting Interactionism* – explains all the main facts about the way our experiences are organised to encode information. It explains their existence, their information-content, the salience of the attended object, the faintness of memories, why experiences form sensory-image-like patterns, why distinct ranges are associated with distinct senses, and why we sense what they all mean. Moreover, it achieves all this in exactly the way science suggests we should expect. For this reason, I think we have very strong grounds to conclude that it is probably the correct position.

Looking down through patchy clouds,
I glimpse some tents and sprawling crowds,
A city of canvas covers the land,
Its populace scattered through streets unplanned.

Imperceptibly, they begin to gather –
A trickle at first, and then another;
Like floodwater pooling in empty fields,
Dammed by vast canvas shields.

They mill around and turn each way,
Seeming almost still from far away.
Then suddenly, each pool starts to sway,
A ripple runs through it like wind on hay.

They turn to face the nearest shield.
Then, all as one, a cheer they yield.
Separate oscillating patterns appear
In synchrony before each weir.

Then Wow! by processes I can't see,
From synchronicity comes a song.
A single voice, both clear and free,
Rises from each gathered throng.

Does synchronicity free that song,
In the same way neurons yield our minds,
Their in-step firing real thought finds
If neuroscientists be not wrong?

Of course not! Those folk crowd and cheer
Because the song is coming and the time is near.
It's the song that makes them one to wave.
And neurons, likewise, *for minds* behave.

C. S. Morrison (The View from Above)

POSTSCRIPT

Consciousness Explained

Although we have reached our conclusion, I can't resist returning one last time to the theory of consciousness that this book has put forward to head off certain potential objections that may not have been sufficiently covered in the main text or footnotes. I shall begin with those I expect to hear from the many philosophers who believe that consciousness arises from – and only from – a complex working brain due to something a part of that brain is doing. Remember, these philosophers never tell you how that happens. They never tell you where this emergent entity comes from, or what it is made of. And they never explain how it miraculously emerges with just the right information and organisation to make it feel like the whole human organism. They may say it's an 'illusion' – but what they really mean by this is that its real *magic*. Illusions that aren't real magic don't come from nowhere but must get constructed by a part of the brain (or a stage magician). And even illusions must be made of something, otherwise the brain would not be able to construct them. One of

231

these philosophers is Daniel Dennett, who claims that a theory (like my one) which assumes the existence of consciousnesses outwith a brain cannot be considered to *explain* consciousness (see e.g. Dennett 1993 p.454). It can't be considered to explain consciousness, according to Dennett, because it assumes the existence of consciousness to begin with.

I think you'll agree that we are talking about two different consciousnesses here. The consciousness being explained is *human* consciousness – the complex, information-carrying, image-forming entity that we each ultimately constitute. The consciousnesses we are assuming to exist are the extremely 'simple' (as in 'unorganised') ones whose experience has a form identical to the forms imposed upon the wave functions of quantum particles by all the various potentials they encounter. To claim that a theory showing how human consciousness evolved out of those simple consciousnesses *isn't an explanation of consciousness* is like claiming that explaining the magnetism of a bar magnet out of the magnetism of its atoms isn't an explanation of that observed magnetism. Of course it is! It would be far less of an explanation to assume that the magnetism of the bar magnet just emerges from nothing whenever someone tries to pick up metal objects with it.

Just as the same kind of force evident in the behaviour of that bar magnet is inferred to be present in its atoms, modalities of experience similar to ours (colours, sounds, feelings, etc.) are inferred to be present in the simple consciousnesses postulated in chapter 7. However, in these consciousnesses such things do not represent the detection of light, acoustic pressure waves, or contact with external surfaces, and they don't form images of the world outside the region of space in which the quantum particle that experiences them is mainly confined. Nor are they organised to recur at appropriate future times as memories of what was experienced before, or thoughts of what might lie ahead. And their pleasantness or unpleasantness contains no information about how good or bad the current situation is. To start by assuming the existence of only these very simple instances of consciousness, and show exactly how and why one of them would develop into a consciousness that feels very like a human organism, is, I think, an admirable example of plausible and defensible explanation. It *does* fully explain consciousness, as we know it to be.

One might still quibble that the existence of the simple consciousnesses of quantum particles has not been explained – so consciousness is still a mystery. However, if you do, you would be neglecting the fact that explaining something in science does not always mean identifying its origin. When James Clerk Maxwell explained light as *electromagnetic waves*, he wasn't making a claim about the origin of light. He was simply *identifying* this observed phenomenon (light) with that predicted consequence of a scientific theory (electromagnetic waves). He based this identification upon the fact that the measured speed of light was the same as the speed of the waves predicted by his theory of electromagnetism. This is exactly what our theory does with the phenomena of consciousness and qualia. It identifies these observed phenomena as aspects of the wave function of a single quantum particle (an entity predicted by quantum theory); and it does this on the basis of the similarity between the random yet pattern-dependent effect of a consciousness (required by evolutionary theory) and the random wave-function-dependent effect of an individual quantum particle upon its environment. This is just like the way Maxwell identified light with electromagnetic waves on the grounds that the speeds were the same. And we should also note that just as the wavelike properties of light (diffraction and interference) further supported this identification, the three-dimensional subjective space of our experiences supports the identification of our consciousness as the wave function of a *single* quantum particle (the only system for which the wave function is defined in a *three-dimensional* 'configuration space').

Indeed, Daniel Dennett is applying this same method of inference to human consciousness when he identifies it as the workings of his "von Neumannesque" 'Joycean machine' (Dennett 1993 p.210). He bases this conclusion mainly on the grounds that the sequential one-thing-at-a-time nature of conscious experience reminds him of the "von Neumann bottleneck" – Dennett 1993 p.214 – a place at the heart of every digital computer where bits of information must be processed sequentially rather than in parallel. However, as far as I can see, Dennett's chosen analogy here is not the explained phenomenon that has *most* features in common with human consciousness – which is one of the reasons I have little confidence in his conclusions.

Although a temporal ordering of data and a single shifting focus of attention are indeed features of our conscious experience, the one feature of consciousness that strikes me more powerfully than any other is the sheer quantity of information that appears to be present in our experience at each moment in time. Whilst some have suggested that much of that information isn't *actually* present – it just appears as though it is because attention shifts so rapidly – the fact that it appears to be there suggests to me that in some sense it really is there. Whatever information is necessary to generate that appearance must actually be simultaneously present in our experience. If one assumes that it isn't, the appearance simply cannot be explained. The fact that all this information seems to be there, all combined within the same entity and obviously contributing to its output (because otherwise it couldn't have been put there in such an organised way by natural selection), is reminiscent of what in quantum mechanics is known as a *superposition.*

Quantum versus Classical Computation

'Superposition' is a term used by quantum physicists to talk about the unseeable physical system that a wave function describes. It expresses the view that one gets from both the maths and the results of recent experiments that such a system isn't actually in any single state (as one would intuitively expect it to be), but somehow exists in multiple states at the same time. It exists in what those physicists call a *superposition* of states (which can include seemingly impossible combinations like rotating clockwise and counter-clockwise at the same time). No-one can ever *see* it existing in this way, because as soon as you look at it with a suitable measuring device, it is always found to occupy only one of those potential states.

The many different potential states (or configurations) of such a system each constitute a possible measurement outcome with a certain probability value that can be obtained from a knowledge of the system's wave function. But you don't actually *need* to know that wave function to work out what that probability value is. All you really need to do is carry out the same measurement on a large number of identically prepared versions of the system, and count how often the state you're interested in comes up as a fraction of the total number of identical measurements you've carried out.

This is how an output is obtained from a superposition by an innovative new device known as *quantum computer*, which uses the fact that a quantum particle can be in many states at the same time to make it carry out a whole lot of simultaneous calculations.

Quantum computers (a technology currently in its infancy) make use of superpositions in an attempt to speed up problem-solving tasks – and they do this precisely because a superposition can be made to carry out many calculations *in parallel* rather than sequentially. A quantum computer is thus quite different from the sort of machine Dennett imagines consciousness to be. Yet the quantity of information we feel to be present in our experience at each moment in time is, in my view, much more reminiscent of the superposition used by a quantum computer than the bit-by-bit nature of the digital computers Dennett has in mind. The only resemblance between a quantum computer and Dennett's 'Joycean machine' is that a quantum computer must measure many identically-prepared versions of the same quantum system in order to 'read off' the statistical distribution that encodes the result of its calculations (just as Dennett's Joycean machine must probe the multiple drafts generated by the parallel architecture of the brain). However, if our experience *is* the wave function of such a system, we would experience *first-hand knowledge* of that distribution. We would know that distribution *before* our brain carries out any measurement upon a large number of identically-prepared particles in order to read it off (which is just as well since according to this theory the brain does nothing of the sort). The superposition-like nature of our experience is thus strong evidence that its origin lies in quantum mechanics, as I propose, rather than in the pattern-dependent switches of a classical computational device.

Of course, if you understood the theory developed in chapter 7, you will have noted that our consciousness isn't part of a *true* quantum computer in that theory. At no time does the brain measure the position of hundreds of identically-prepared versions of the quantum particle we constitute, and it therefore never 'sees' the statistical distribution that has the form of our experiences (and which would constitute the output of our consciousness if it were a true quantum computer).

Now you might be worrying that if our brain doesn't 'see' that distribution, we shouldn't be able to *talk* about our experiences. But if so, you can immediately lay that concern to rest. Our brain doesn't *need* to 'see' that distribution in order to form an accurate description of it, because it *already knows* what that distribution is. After all, it *created* it out of the sensory and memory information it had already gathered and processed. It is not using that distribution to calculate anything, but to prevent a random influence upon our behaviour becoming detrimental. We are thus a type of quantum computer, but one that *doesn't have* a deterministic output. The brain doesn't need to 'see' the full statistical pattern that would arise from measurements of many identically-prepared versions of the quantum system that we constitute because it is not using the output of our system to calculate anything. It is using our quantum particle to impart a non-detrimental level of randomness into its attention-focusing process. The calculations that aim to ensure that the level of randomness remains non-detrimental are performed elsewhere, and their output is what *determines* our experiences (and no doubt also the content of what we say when we talk about them).

Experimental Evidence for PSI

As well as the superposition-like nature of our experiences, there are in fact other observations that suggest our brain is using a quantum superposition in its decision-making. For example, Belgian theoretical physicist Diederik Aerts recently observed that the logic of human decision-making has a form more typical of 'quantum logic' than 'classical logic'.[37] Although this does not entail that those decisions were definitely made by a quantum device, it does mean that the sort of outcomes a quantum device would generate *did prove beneficial to our ancestors*. Which means that if it were possible for the brain to adapt such a device, one would expect it to have done so.

Pointing out these similarities between quantum processes and consciousness is all very well, but they don't constitute *scientific* evidence for or against the theory I have proposed. Hence, another potential objection to this theory is the fact that I have not stated specific ways in which it could be tested. Remember, in order to be really confident of the accuracy of a scientific theory, one ought to look for unexpected things that it predicts (such as measurements for which it predicts practically un-guessable values). One could then perform experiments to test those predictions. A positive result would rightly give one great confidence in the theory's accuracy, and a negative result would show that it needs modification or abandonment.

Although I suspect that the theory I have put forward in this book will eventually yield predictions of this nature, further development is needed. Its current predictions are fairly obvious and therefore probably something of which I could have had foreknowledge (either from my own subjective experience or from suitable journals). For example, it predicts that one's attention should shift in a more rapid and more random way when we are in pain than when we are not in pain. Hardly something you weren't expecting, is it? It also predicts that we are more likely to attend to the objects that are more salient in our experience than to other objects. Again, not particularly un-guessable.

---

[37] Aerts (2009)

Something that might be worth looking for is the effect of *experience type* proposed in chapter 9. There I argued that the separation of our senses can be explained if we tend to shift our voluntary attention between subjective locations where the same type of experience is occurring more often than between locations of different types of experience. An experiment ought to show this if it is carefully designed to eliminate the effect of salience as much as possible. One could, for example, station a subject in a quiet room and ensure that his (or her) visual field is composed purely of a stationary patchwork of equally small primary-coloured squares (perhaps on a large or very close computer monitor). These would have to be adjusted in intensity until the subject reports that they are equally bright, and each primary colour would have to be equally abundant and evenly distributed over his or her visual field. Although it is difficult to eliminate the proposed effects of memories and emotions (particularly the latter, as memories are faint), one could ask the subject to look for a black dot that will appear in one of the squares. Eye trackers could then record what he or she is attending to. Since many of the eye's rapid movements (saccades) are subconsciously generated, one can't simply count saccades that go from one colour to a similarly-coloured location, and those that go from a similar colour to a different colour. Remember the delay of around half-a-second mentioned in chapter 5 between the eye's reception of visual data and the representation of that data in consciousness (which must precede any shift in attention influenced by that visual data). Due to that delay, the eye may well move off the colour that is being presented to consciousness as the focus of attention *before* the quantum particle has a chance to 'keep' attention focused upon that colour. Consequently, the effect of the quantum particle in those circumstances will usually be to cause a saccade *back* to a location of that colour. If the postulate in chapter 9 is correct, this ought to cause a peak in the number of times attention is focused on the same colour as it was around half-a-second or more before. Unfortunately, it is hard to be more precise than this due to our lack of knowledge of the exact time between the reception of visual data and the consciously-caused saccade. But that peak does seem like something fairly unexpected that could be looked for.

Due to the effect of the attention spotlight proposed in chapter 8, one would need to discount all shifts that went back to (or stayed fixed on) the same square as half a second or so before (though these ought to similarly form a peak in the data that could be sought in a separate experiment). One could also use just two distinct colours of square in each trial, as the same effect ought still to be discernible. The experiment would then need to be repeated with different pairs of colours to prove that any effect was not just a peculiarity of one combination of qualia.

I am not aware of such an experiment having yet been performed. But it doesn't seem all that difficult to do. When some researcher does carry it out, I will be eagerly awaiting the results. A null observation would entail a rethink of chapter 9, and probably some of chapter 11 too. On the other hand, it probably wouldn't cause me to abandon the entire theory. The other postulates it involves are easily seen to be consistent with experience – and, as I have emphasised throughout this book, there is at present *no reasonable scientific alternative*.

Of course, even the existence of that proposed effect could have been guessed, so a positive result can hardly be regarded as confirmation of the whole theory. For that, it will require scientists to attempt to identify the quantum particle involved, work out where it is located in the brain, and try to gently manipulate its wave function artificially (though I will not be putting myself forward as a subject when that time comes!). But this will require physicists and neuroscientists to be persuaded that our experience really is likely to be the wave function of such a particle.

Interpreting the Wave function according to PSI

An objection I expect to hear from physicists is the claim that we do not need to identify the wave function of a quantum system as anything at all – far less something as familiar to us as experience. They will point out that the mathematics of quantum theory will work just as well without the attribution of any such physical meaning. And they will argue that this point was made a long time ago by the founders of modern quantum theory. It is, after all, an inherent aspect of the so-called 'Copenhagen Interpretation' championed by Nobel prize-winning Danish physicist Niels Bohr.

However, such an objection completely misses the point. The identification of the wave function as experience, in my theory, is not being made to improve our understanding of quantum physics, but to allow a scientific explanation for human consciousness. Whether or not it is helpful to quantum physicists is *completely irrelevant*. It has been forced upon us because if we didn't make that identification we could not possibly explain the information-content and organisation of our experiences as a product of positive natural selection without invoking brand new substances and influences that are not motivated by any scientific theory (and which are practically ruled out by current observations). On the other hand, the fact that making that identification allows us to do this *so easily*, and the fact that there appears to be no other means available, is a strong indication that it is the correct view – an observation that physicists would do well to take notice of.

I think most physicists would agree that what we are calling our consciousness must be some piece (or spread) of matter somewhere in our brain. If so, our experiences are what that matter *really consists of.* Some part of the matter in our brain thus really consists of experiences. And as Eddington pointed out in 1928 (see chapter 4) we have no scientific knowledge of what the rest of it really consists of (science only tells us what it does to our measuring devices; and our experiences only tell us what it does to our sense organs). It is therefore only reasonable to assume that it consists of experiences too. And as we have seen, the only way to divide those experiences up into separate consciousnesses in a manner that will allow a scientific explanation for human consciousness, is the proposal that a single consciousness is the wave function of a single particle.

If that is true, we would be in the intriguing position of being the only instrument available that can see a superposition evolve in real time without needing to perform a series of identical measurements upon a very large number of identically-prepared quantum systems. Admittedly we are limited to the one example of a superposition that the quantum particle behind our experiences represents. Moreover, its Schrödinger evolution in between our brain's measurements of its state most probably constitutes only a very *brief* time interval – the 'now' moment in which we actually experience changes taking place (as opposed to memories of changes that *have* taken place). As soon as our attention spotlight shifts to something we chose to attend to, we can be sure our brain has already measured the position of our quantum particle and shifted our focus of attention accordingly. Nevertheless, the fact that we know what this very brief period of Schrödinger evolution feels like, allows us to infer what longer periods of such evolution *ought* to feel like. Moreover, from the identification of experience-type with interaction-type made in chapter 9, the relatively diverse nature of our experiences suggests that the particle we constitute can interact with surrounding matter in a considerable variety of ways. We should therefore expect it to be a fairly *complex* particle (a *composite* particle or 'bound state') – and because of this, we might reasonably expect to be able to infer the experience of simpler particles in terms of subsets of what we experience.

Whilst that might not contribute anything to the mathematical procedures by which quantum physicists predict experimental results, it may suggest future directions of research and reveal directions that are likely to be unproductive. If, for example, a fundamental constant of nature were shown to depend upon how likeable a particular type of qualia is compared to other types, it would mean that seeking an overarching theory that accounted for that constant may be a waste of time. There may be *no* deeper reason for how nice a particular type of qualia feels. Similarly, it might be found that the laws of physics reduce to some particular ordering of simple and satisfying subjective principles like 'minimising unpleasantness', 'maximising pleasantness', and 'balancing stability and variety of experience'. If the arguments we considered in Part 3 are correct, that is probably what we should expect. Something along these lines would certainly be consistent with the attributes of the universe-wide consciousness that Christ claimed to represent.

The N-particle Wave function

Since I have so far only been talking about the wave functions of *single* particles, it is possible that a reader familiar with quantum physics could be thinking that I've misunderstood the nature of the wave function. Hence, I'd like now to address the main area from which misunderstandings may arise about what my theory of consciousness says about quantum reality.

Although it does predict that the experience of a consciousness is the wave function of a *single* particle, it doesn't have nothing to say about the multi-particle wave functions of quantum field theory. The three-dimensional space that we experience is essentially a very small region of physical space somewhere within our brain. But that is only because the quantum particle we constitute is confined there by the effects of the particles forming the surrounding neural structures – effects that manifest themselves in all the qualia we experience (and I suspect particularly the qualia we call 'feelings'). For free quantum particles, the three-dimensional space they experience is the *whole universe* (though where they are more likely to be found is represented by more-salient qualia, and any regions from which they are excluded, by no qualia at all). The 3N-dimensional nature of the configuration space of the N-particle wave function (where N stands for a very large number such as the number of particles in the universe) is caused by the fact that each and every particle chooses its location from an experience in which the whole of 3-dimensional space is represented (though newly created or recently observed particles will experience a local region of that space in much-more-salient qualia than the rest of it, making them more likely to be found there). And as we shall see shortly, they each affect the experience of all the others in a way that is statistically governed by the spread of qualia that they themselves are experiencing (a spread of qualia that we have identified as the single particle wave function).

This of course begs the question: Where does all that qualia come from? And to that question there can be only one answer: From the effects of other consciousnesses. When the consciousness of a quantum particle chooses a position in space by selecting a location in its experience, what it is really doing is positioning an effect in the experience of other consciousnesses – *all* other consciousnesses in which that region of space is represented, and which belong to particles capable of interacting with that quantum particle. The effect in question must obviously be a change in the experience of those other consciousnesses centred on the location representing the chosen position in space. And a corresponding change should occur in all the modalities of experience that represent interactions that both particles 'feel'. Not all these particles will experience exactly the same change of qualia. If the choosing particle is an electrically charged one, for example, the consciousness of a particle with opposite electric charge will presumably experience an increase in the salience of the qualia representing the electric interaction in regions close to the chosen location, whereas one with like charge will experience a corresponding *decrease* in the salience of that qualia (This is what makes it less likely to be observed in that region of space, yielding the conclusion 'like charges repel').

The relative magnitude of those changes will depend upon how likely the two particles are to be near each other – which will in turn depend upon where they were last observed to be, and how long it had been since that last observation took place. An observation will be experienced as a moment when the effects of certain particles suddenly become very salient (their salience tending to reduce afterwards, in the case of free particles, until another observation takes place). The salience of the effects of other particles is what proximity in space *means* in this theory.

Since the locations of these effects are shifted randomly and frequently by the consciousnesses of the particles that produce them, one might think they ought to yield a rather chaotic experience. However, we must remember that the effects of individual particles are usually only very slight changes in experience, and these are mainly confined to the locations that are salient in those particles' experiences. Due to the fact that our consciousness experiences the effects of millions of particles, the ability of the neural structures that confine it to hold those particles in a more-or-less fixed position allows these tiny shifting effects to accumulate to form the stable patterns that encode our sensory information so wonderfully well. It is the fact that each quantum particle experiences its distribution of probability across space, and affects the experiences of 'all' other quantum particles in a way that is statistically dependent upon that distribution, which allows a single wave function to describe the N-particle system.

One criticism that has been levelled at this theory is that it claims the effects of individual particles will be slight but doesn't specify a spatial scale by which that claim can be justified. Given that the wave function in principle extends throughout all space, why does so much of our experience come from the tiny bit of brain space where our quantum particle is confined? Shouldn't that be dwarfed into insignificance by experiences from the rest of the universe? My answer to these criticisms is that a particle senses the universe in much the same way we sense depth in our visual experience, or extent in the felt-space we call the body. It 'looks out' from the location it was previously measured to be at, and its fields of experience are taken up with the effects of the particles that have most influence upon where it is next likely to be found. If it was confined in an exceedingly tiny space by only a few nearby particles, then the effects of these particles will dominate its experience. In our case, judging from the resolution of our visual images, the cavity in which our particle roams free is relatively large. Millions of particles in the cavity walls have a fairly equal influence on where it is next likely to be observed. Their effects encode our visual experience and our sense of our body's surface. The effects of particles further out are so slight we are only vaguely aware of them as our constant sense that there is an infinite universe beyond that subjective body and environment. Since the resolution of our visual and tactile experience is something that could be estimated via experiment and verbal report, it should be possible to estimate the number of particles responsible. Only by doing that can we gauge the size of the space over which our wave function mainly extends, and thereby establish a true spatial scale for our experience.

What constitutes an observation in this theory hasn't yet become clear (as is also the case in quantum physics). But since there is obviously no special place in this theory for human consciousness, it is presumed to be a choice made by the consciousness of one of the elementary constituents of the observed or observing particle. Such a real 'wave function collapse' does appear to be implied by the theory because something must account for the fact that we don't experience the brain's measurements of the position of the quantum particle we constitute. It is thus presumed that during the moment when the elementary constituents of our particle are interacting with those of another, our experience temporarily ceases to exist – being restored only when our particle is released (by which time the brain has adjusted our experience to favour its new focus of attention). The purpose of the experience of a composite particle or 'bound state' appears to be that of choosing which external elementary particles appear salient to the consciousnesses of its elementary constituents. Without it those elementary constituents would only experience- and affect the experience of- each other. It is presumably a continuation of their experience of- and affects upon-each other, even after a composite particle has split in two, that constitutes quantum entanglement (the 'spooky action at a distance' – or 'EPR paradox' – that Einstein, Podolsky and Rosen first drew attention to).

Admittedly this suggestion, and the others I have made in the same paragraph, are sketchy and preliminary. They are not intended to be permanent conclusions or essential assumptions, but ideas that I am putting on the table in an effort to inspire experts in quantum physics with the confidence that a consistent interpretation of quantum theory can be constructed that permits the explanation for human consciousness that I have put forward in chapters 6-11 of this book. Much more work still needs to be done to complete that interpretation. However, I hope I have demonstrated that it is at least possible to interpret quantum mechanics in this PSI-psychistic way.

Inference from the Best Methodology

Some philosophers will no doubt still complain that their functionalistic theories are more intuitive than PSI-psychism. They will perhaps argue that, in the case of consciousness, intuition is as valid as any other means of assessing the likelihood of a given theory, and dismiss my arguments to the contrary as merely my own intuitions. It is therefore important to finish this postscript by pointing out that the justification for my theory comes from *science*; and if it is valid, it is therefore far more trustworthy than any that comes from human intuitions. We know this, not only because of the successful nature of modern scientific theories, but because of the huge number of different explanations that human intuitions have generated for consciousness. Since many of these are mutually incompatible, they cannot all be right, and so we are forced to conclude that human intuitions are definitely leading intelligent and well-informed people to *false* explanations of consciousness. We therefore have no reason to think that our intuitions will lead us to an accurate view. Hence, if a more justifiable method of deciding between theories of consciousness can be found, we ought to allow it to dictate our views.

Although one could argue that in basing my explanation for human consciousness upon the scientific explanation for the most similar explained phenomena I have simply used my own intuitions as to which approach to follow, there is a way of defending this approach that is entirely independent of intuitions. That is because when it is not possible to experimentally test a set of possible explanations for a given phenomenon, one can still objectively define the *most likely* explanation for that phenomenon. One can define it as 'the explanation that follows from the *most successful method of generating explanations*[38] *for phenomena we already know how to explain that have much in common with the phenomenon in question*'. The success of that explanation-generating procedure at generating explanations for those most similar explained phenomena will give us good reason to believe that when applied to human consciousness the explanation it yields will be accurate (to the level of accuracy typical of the explanations it yields for those physical phenomena).

---

[38] The method in question must also be *objective* (intuition-free), and must lead to only a single *possible* explanation for each phenomenon to which it is applied, and it must also be *topic-independent*. It must apply the same rules to explain consciousness as it applies to construct explanations for physical phenomena because otherwise its success at explaining physical phenomena would be no grounds for confidence in the explanation it yields for consciousness ('Explain physical phenomena in the way stipulated by the latest textbooks' is an example of a method that is *not* topic-independent). I therefore like to refer to this procedure as the Top-performing Objective Possibility-yielding Topic-Independent Procedure (the *TOP TIP* for explaining consciousness!)

Since the method of analogy that I have used to obtain my theory of consciousness ('Explain it in the way that is most like how the most similar explained phenomenon is accounted for but which doesn't make false predictions'[39]) also yields scientifically acceptable explanations for countless phenomena that have many features in common with human consciousness, I can confidently conclude that my theory of consciousness has a high likelihood of being accurate (to the level of accuracy that applies to those other explanations). And since any objective method of generating explanations that happens to yield a *functionalistic* explanation of consciousness *isn't* going to be very successful when applied to physical phenomena, I can justifiably conclude that functionalistic explanations are not nearly as likely to be accurate.

I call this argument *Inference from the Best Methodology*. As far as I can see, the only way round it for the functionalist is to insist that the really successful method of generating explanations that yields functionalism simply hasn't been found yet. Until it is, I think I am justified in concluding that PSI-psychism is by far the most likely explanation for consciousness that our current state of knowledge gives us. And I therefore have every reason to take its implications extremely seriously.

---

[39] In fact, to ensure that it is the most successful method, I need to define it somewhat more specifically than this. The most precise definition I have so far come up with is the rather less eloquent sequence of four constraints that follows: *(1) Consistency* - Explain it in the same way science accounts for the explained phenomenon that has, firstly, the most features in common with it, and secondly, the least number of different features, replacing each mechanism or formula that yields a false prediction with the most likely alternative mechanism or formula that does not. *(2) Adequacy* – If there remain features that aren't yet accounted for, reapply (1) to the full set of those remaining features and then apply (2) again. *(3) Likelihood* – Remove or replace any mechanisms or formulae selected by (1) for which a more likely alternative is suggested by (2). And *(4) Parsimony* – Remove any unnecessary assumptions. I have dubbed this method the *Sequence of Consistency-, Adequacy-, Likelihood- and Parsimony- Ensuring Laws (The SCALPEL)*.

SELECTIVE BIBLIOGRAPHY

Aerts, D. (2009). 'Quantum structure in cognition', *Journal of Mathematical Psychology*, 53, 314-348.

Aerts, D., Aerts, S. and Gabora, L. (2009). 'Experimental evidence for quantum structure in cognition' in P. D. Bruza, D. Sofge, W. Lawless, C. J. van Rijsbergen and M. Klusch (Eds.), *Proceedings of QI 2009-Third International Symposium on Quantum Interaction, Book series: Lecture Notes in Computer Science*, 5494, pp. 59-70.

Aerts, D., Broekaert, J. and Gabora, L. (2011). 'A case for applying an abstracted quantum formalism to cognition', *New Ideas in Psychology*, 29, pp. 136-146.

Albertazzi, L. (2007), 'At the Roots of Consciousness: Intentional Presentations', *Journal of Consciousness Studies*, 14, No. 1-2, 2007, pp. 94-114.

Al-Khalili, J. (2008), *Quantum: A Guide for the Perplexed* (London: Phoenix Illustrated).

Al-Khalili, J. & McFadden, J. (2014), *Life on the Edge: The Coming of Age of Quantum Biology* (Great Britain: Bantam Press).

Armstrong, D. M. (1981), 'The Causal Theory of the Mind', in Chalmers, D. (2002), *Philosophy of Mind: Classical and Contemporary Readings* (Oxford University Press), pp. 80-87.

Arndt, M. & Zeilinger, A. (2008), 'Buckyballs and the Dual-Slit Experiment', in Al-Khalili, J (2008), *Quantum: A Guide for the Perplexed* (London: Phoenix Illustrated).

Ashcroft, A. (2013), *The Spark of Life: Electricity in the Human Body* (UK: Penguin books).

Aydon, C. (2003), *Charles Darwin* (London: Robinson, Constable & Robinson).

Ayer, A. J. (1980), *Language, Truth and Logic* (Great Britain: Pelican Books).

Beeckmans, J. (2007), 'Can Higher Order Representation Theories Pass Scientific Muster?', *Journal of Consciousness Studies*, 14, No. 9-10, 2007, pp. 90-111.

Berkeley, G. (1710), *The Principles of Human Knowledge*, in Warnock, G. J. ed.(1962), *The Principles of Human Knowledge With Other Writings* (UK: Fontana).

Blackmore, S. (2002), 'There is no stream of consciousness', Journal of Consciousness Studies, 9, No. 5-6, pp.17-28.

Blackmore, S. (2003), *Consciousness: An Introduction* (Great Britain: Hodder & Stoughton).

Block, N., Flanagan, O. & Guzeldere, G. eds. (1997), *The Nature of Consciousness: Philosophical Debates* (United States: MIT Press).

Bohm, D. (2005), *Wholeness and Implicate Order* (Great Britain: Routledge).

Braddon-Mitchell, D. & Jackson, F. (1996), *Philosophy of Mind and Cognition* (Blackwell).

Bramsden, B. H. & Joachain, C. J. (1992), *Introduction to Quantum Mechanics* (Great Britain: Longman UK Ltd).

Brooks, M. (2009), *13 Things that Don't Make Sense* (Great Britain: Profile Books Ltd).

Brooks, M (2012), *The Secret Anarchy of Science* (Great Britain: Profile Books Ltd).

Bruce, V. (1998), *Unsolved Mysteries of the Mind* (Great Britain: Psychology Press).

Carlson, N. R. (2004), *Physiology of Behaviour, 8th Edition* (United States: Pearson/Allyn & Bacon).

Carter, R. (1998), *Mapping the Mind* (Great Britain: Weidenfeld & Nicholson).

Chalmers, D. (1997), *The Conscious Mind: In Search of a Fundamental Theory* (New York: Oxford University Press).

Chalmers, D. (2002), 'Consciousness and Its Place in Nature', *Blackwell Guide to the Philosophy of Mind*, Stich & Warfield, eds (Blackwell), reprinted in Chalmers, D (2002), *Philosophy of Mind: Classical and Contemporary Readings* (Oxford University Press).

Chalmers, D. (2002), *Philosophy of Mind: Classical and Contemporary Readings* (Oxford University Press).

Churchland, P. M. (1999), *Matter and Consciousness* (United States: The MIT Press).

Collins, F. S. (2006), *The Language of God* (New York: FREE PRESS, Simon & Schuster).

Corabi, J. (2008), 'Pleasure's Role in Evolution: A Response to Robinson', *Journal of Consciousness Studies*, 15, No. 7, 2008, pp. 78-86.

Crick, F. (1994), *The Astonishing Hypothesis* (London: Simon & Schuster).

Cytowic, R. E. (2003), *The Man Who Tasted Shapes* (Great Britain: Imprint Academic).

Damasio, A. (2000), *The Feeling of What Happens* (London: Vintage).

Darwin, C. (1859), *On the Origin of Species* (London: John Murray).

Davies, P. (1993), *The Mind of God: Science and the Search for Ultimate Meaning* (London: Penguin Books).

Davies, P. (2003), *The Origin of Life* (London: Penguin Books).

Dawkins, R. (1996), *River out of Eden* (London: Phoenix).

Dawkins, R. (2005), *The Ancestors' Tale* (London: Phoenix).

Dawkins, R. (2006), *The God Delusion* (London: Bantam Press).

Dawkins, R. (2012), *The Magic of Reality* (Great Britain: Black Swan).

Dennett, D. C. (1988), 'Quining Qualia', in Marcel, A & Bisiach, E (1988), *Consciousness in Contemporary Science* (Oxford University Press), repr in Chalmers, D. (2002), *Philosophy of Mind: Classical and Contemporary Readings* (Oxford University Press) pp.226-46.

Dennett, D. C. (1993), *Consciousness Explained* (London: Penguin Books).

Dennett, D. C. (1996), *Kinds of Minds: Towards an understanding of Consciousness* (London: Weidenfeld & Nicolson)).

Dennett, D. C. (2001), 'Surprise, surprise', *Behavioural and Brain Sciences*, 24, No. 5, p.982.

Earl, B. (2008), 'What Does the Evidence Tell Us about the Biological Value of Consciousness? Comment on Robinson 2007', *Journal of Consciousness Studies*, 15, No. 7, 2008, pp. 87-94.

Eddington. A. S. (1928), *The Nature of the Physical World* (New York: The Macmillan Company).

Edwards, J. C. W. (2006), *How many people are there in my head? And in hers?* (Great Britain: Imprint Academic).

Farmelo, G. (2002), 'The Planck-Einstein Equation for the Energy of a Quantum' in Farmelo, G (2003), *It Must Be Beautiful: Great Equations of Modern Science*, pp. 1-27 (London: Granta Books).

Feynman, R. P. (1990), *QED: The Strange Theory of Light and Matter* (London: Penguin Books).

Feynman, R. P. (1992), *The Character of Physical Law* (London: Penguin Books).

Ford, J. (2008), 'Attention and the New Sceptics', *Journal of Consciousness Studies*, 15, No. 3, 2008, pp. 59-86.

Frische, O. R. (1972), *The Nature of Matter* (London: Thames & Hudson).

Frith, C. (2007), *Making Up the Mind: How the Brain Creates Our Mental World* (Blackwell).

Gadenne, V. (2006), 'In Defence of Qualia-epiphenomenalism', *Journal of Consciousness Studies*, 13, No. 1-2, 2006, pp. 101-14.

Gazzaniga, M. (2012) *Who's in Charge: Free Will and the Science of the Brain* (UK: Constable & Robinson).

Ghirardi, G. C., Rimini, A. & Weber, T. (1986), 'Unified Dynamics for Microscopic and Macroscopic Systems', *Phys. Rev,.* D34, 470.

Goldstein, E. B. (1996), *Sensation & Perception: 4th Edition* (United States: Brooks/Cole Publishing Company).

Goswami, A. (1995), *The Self-Aware Universe: How Consciousness Creates the Material World* (New York: Tarcher).

Greenfield, S. (1998), *The Human Brain: A Guided Tour* (London: Phoenix).

Greenfield, S. (2002), *The Private Life of the Brain* (London: Penguin Books).

Gribbin, J. (1996), *Schrodinger's Kittens and the Search for Reality* (London: Phoenix).

Gribbin, J. (2003), *Science: A History 1543-2001* (London: Penguin Books).

Griffin, G. R. (1998), *Unsnarling the World-Knot* (Los Angeles: University of California Press).

Hartelius, G. (2007), 'Quantitative Somatic Phenomenology: Toward an Epistemology of Subjective Experience', *Journal of Consciousness Studies*, 14, No. 12, 2007, pp. 24-56.

Herbert, N. (1994), *Elemental Mind* (New York: Plume/Penguin Books).

Hofstadter, D. R. & Dennett, D. C. (2000), *The Mind's I* (New York: Basic Books).

Horgan, J. (2000), *The Undiscovered Mind: How the Brain Defies Explanation* (London: Phoenix).

Hume, D. (1777 / 1902), *An Enquiry Concerning Human Understanding* (Project Gutenberg E-text).

Jackson, F. (1982), 'Epiphenomenal Qualia', *Philosophical Quarterly*, 32, pp. 127-136, in Chalmers (2002) *Philosophy of Mind: Classical and Contemporary Readings* (Oxford University Press), pp 273-280.

James, W. (1890), *The Principles of Psychology*, 2 vols (H. Holt).

Johnston, D. & Jenks, G. S. eds (1876), *Translations, literal and free, of the dying Hadrian's address to his soul* (Google books online version).

Katz, B. F. (2008), 'Fixing Functionalism', *Journal of Consciousness Studies*, 15, No 3, 2008, pp. 87-118.

Kentridge, R. W., De-Witt, L. H., & Heywood, C. A. (2008), 'What is Attended To in Spatial Attention', *Journal of Consciousness Studies*, 15, No. 4, 2008, pp. 105-11.

Krauss, L. M. (2001), *Atom: An Odyssey from the Big Bang to Life on Earth... and Beyond* (USA: Little, Brown & Co).

Kuhn, T. S. (1971), *The Structure of Scientific Revolutions*, Second Ed, Enlarged (University of Chicago Press).

Lee K. C. (2011) 'Macroscopic non-classical states and terahertz quantum processing in room-temperature diamond', *Nature Photonics* 6, 41–44 (2012), online edition.

Libet, B. (2005), *Mind Time: The Temporal Factor in Consciousness* (New York: Harvard University Press).

Linden, D. J. (2011), *Pleasure: How Our Brains Make Junk Food, Exercise, Marijuana, Generosity & Gambling Feel So Good* (Great Britain: One World Publications).

Lipton, P. (2004), *Inference to the Best Explanation, 2nd Edition* (London: Routledge).

Lloyd, S. (2007), *Programming the Universe: A Quantum Computer Scientist Takes on the Cosmos* (London: Vintage).

Mandik, P. (2009), 'Beware of the Unicorn', *Journal of Consciousness Studies,* 16, No. 1, 2009, pp. 5-36.

Manousakis, E. (2007). 'Quantum theory, consciousness and temporal perception: Binocular rivalry'. doi: 0709.4516 (http://arxiv.org/ PS_cache/ arxiv/pdf/0709/0709.4516v1.pdf).

McAlpine, K. (2010), 'Hot Green Quantum Computers Revealed', *New Scientist,* 6th February 2010, p.12.

McFadden, J. (2000), *Quantum Evolution: The New Science of Life* (Great Britain: HarperCollins).

McFadden, J. (2013), 'EM Fields and the Meaning of Meaning: Response to Jonathan C. W. Edwards', *Journal of Consciousness Studies,* 20, No. 9-10, pp. 168-176.

McGinn, C. (2006), 'Hard Questions: Comments on Galen Strawson', *Journal of Consciousness Studies,* 13, No. 10-11, 2006, pp. 3-31.

Midgley, M. (2014), *Are You an Illusion?* (Great Britain: Acumen).

Miller, A. I. (2002), 'Erotica, Aesthetics and Schrodinger's Wave Equation' in Farmelo, G (2003), *It Must Be Beautiful: Great Equations of Modern Science,* pp. 110-31 (London: Granta Books).

Miller, K. A. (2007), *Finding Darwin's God* (New York: Harper Perennial, HarperCollins).

Mole, C. (2008), 'Attention and Consciousness', *Journal of Consciousness Studies,* 15, No. 4, 2008, pp. 86-104.

Morrison, C. S. (2010), 'Identifying The Most Likely Explanation of Consciousness (Part 1): IBM and The SCALP Method', *Toward a Science of Consciousness 2010 Program book,* Abstract 46, p.62 (University of Arizona Centre for Consciousness Studies).

Morrison, C. S. (2011), 'Psi-psychism: The Most Likely Explanation of Consciousness and Quantum Phenomena', *Toward a Science of Consciousness 2011 Program book,* Abstract 198, pp.135-6 (University of Arizona Centre for Consciousness Studies).

Morrison, C. S. (2012), 'Psi-psychism: Explaining Consciousness without Magic or Misrepresentation', *Toward a Science of*

Consciousness 2012 Program book, Abstract 8, p.49 (University of Arizona Centre for Consciousness Studies).

Morrison, C. S. (2014), 'Psi-Psychism: The Most Likely Explanation of Consciousness?', *Toward a Science of Consciousness 2014 Program book*, Abstract 252, p.185-6 (University of Arizona Centre for Consciousness Studies).

Morrison, C. S. (2016), 'Psi-psychism: How a Single Particle could Evolve to Feel Like a Human Being', *The Science of Consciousness 2016 Program book*, Abstract 269, p.180 (University of Arizona Centre for Consciousness Studies).

Morrison, C. S. (2016), 'Psi-psychism: How a Single Particle could Evolve to Feel Like a Human Being', Preprint.

Morrison, C. S. (2016), *Unexpectedly Foretold Occurrences: Scientific Evidence that there is a God who Loves You (and why scholars don't discuss it)* (United States: CreateSpace Independent Publishing Platform).

Nagel, T. (1974), 'What Is It Like to Be a Bat', *Philosophical Review* 83:435-50, reprinted in Chalmers (2002) *Philosophy of Mind: Classical and Contemporary Readings* (Oxford University Press), pp. 273-280.

Papineau, D. (2001), 'The rise of Physicalism', in Gillett, C. & Loewer, B. M. eds. *Physicalism and its Discontents* (Cambridge University Press).

Papineau, D. (2006), 'Comments on Galen Strawson', *Journal of Consciousness Studies*, 13, Nos 10-11, 2006, pp.100-109.

Pearle, P. (1989), 'Combining Stochastic Dynamical State-vector Reduction with Spontaneous Localisation', *Phys. Rev.*, A39, 2277-89

Penrose, R. (1990), *The Emperor's New Mind* (London: Vintage).

Penrose, R. (2002), 'The Einstein Equation of General Relativity' in Farmelo, G. (2003), *It Must Be Beautiful: Great Equations of Modern Science*, pp. 180-212 (London: Granta Books).

Penrose, R. (2005), *Shadows of the Mind* (London: Vintage).

Pinker, S. (1995), *The Language Instinct* (London: Penguin Books).

Pinker, S. (1998), *How the Mind Works* (London: Penguin books).

Popper, K. (2002), *The Logic of Scientific Discovery*, (London, Routledge).

Putnam, H. (1973), 'The Nature of Mental States', in Chalmers, D. (2002), *Philosophy of Mind: Classical and Contemporary Readings* (Oxford University Press), pp. 73-79.

Pylkkänen, P. (1989), *The Search For Meaning* (Great Britain: Crucible).

Ramachandran, V. S. & Blakeslee, S. (1999), *Phantoms in the Brain* (London: Fourth Estate, HarperCollins).

Ramachandran, V. S. (2003), *The Emerging Mind* (London: Profile Books).

Rees, M. (2000), *Just Six Numbers* (London: Phoenix).

Roberts, A. (2014), *The Incredible Unlikeliness of Being: Evolution and the Making of Us* (London: Heron books).

Rowlands, P. (1992), *Waves Versus Corpuscles: The Revolution That Never Was* (Great Britain: PD Publications).

Rosenblum, B. & Kuttner, F. (2007), *Quantum Enigma: Physics Encounters Consciousness* (London: Gerald Duckworth & Co Ltd).

Russell, B. (1927), *The Analysis of Matter* (London: Kegan Paul).

Russell, B. (1997). *Collected Papers,* vol. 11. Edited by J. C. Slater and P. Köllner, London: Routledge.

Russell, P. (2005), *From Science To God: A Physicist's Journey into the Mystery of Consciousness* (USA: New World Library).

Sacks, O. (1970/1998), *The Man Who Mistook His Wife for a Hat and Other Clinical Tales* (New York: Touchstone, Simon & Schuster).

Sacks, O. (2010), *The Mind's Eye* (London: Picador).

Schwitzgebel, E. (2002), 'How well do we know our own conscious experience? The case of visual imagery', *Journal of Consciousness Studies,* 9, No. 5-6, pp. 35-53.

Schwitzgebel, E. (2007), 'Do You Have Constant Tactile Experience of Your Feet in Your Shoes? Or Is Experience Limited to What's in Attention', *Journal of Consciousness Studies,* 14, No. 3, 2007, pp. 5-35.

Searle, J. R. (1998), *The Mystery of Consciousness* (London: Granta Books).

Simons, P. (2006), 'The Seeds of Experience', *Journal of Consciousness Studies,* 13, No. 10-11, 2006, pp. 146-50.

Skrbina, D. (2005), *Panpsychism in the West* (Cambridge, MA: MIT Press, 2005).

Skrbina, D. (2006), 'Realistic Panpsychism', *Journal of Consciousness Studies,* 13, No. 10-11, 2006, pp. 151-7.

Smart, J. J. C. (2006), 'Ockhamist Comments on Strawson', *Journal of Consciousness Studies,* 13, Nos 10-11, 2006, pp. 158-62.

Stamenov, M. I. (2008), 'Language is in Principle Inaccessible to Consciousness. But Why?', *Journal of Consciousness Studies,* 15, No. 6, 2008, pp. 85-118.

Stannard, R. (2012), *Science & Belief: The Big Issues* (Oxford: Lion Hudson).

Stapp, H. P. (2007), *Mindful Universe: Quantum Mechanics and the Participating Observer* (New York: Springer).

Strawson, G. (1994), *Mental Reality* (USA: The MIT Press).

Strawson, G. (2006a), 'Realistic Monism: Why Physicalism Entails Panpsychism', *Journal of Consciousness Studies*, 13, No. 10-11, 2006, pp. 3-31.

Strawson, G. (2006b), 'Panpsychism? A Reply to Commentators with a Celebration of Descartes', *Journal of Consciousness Studies*, 13, No. 10-11, 2006, pp. 184-286.

Sutton, C. (2002), 'The Yang-Mills Equation' in Farmelo, G (2003), *It Must Be Beautiful: Great Equations of Modern Science* (London: Granta Books).

Swaab, D. F. (2015), *We Are Our Brains: From the Womb to Alzheimer's* (Great Britain: Penguin Books).

Trusted, J. (1979), *The Logic of Scientific Inference: An Introduction*, (London: The Macmillan Press Ltd).

Van Leeuwen C. (2007), 'What Needs to Emerge to Make You Conscious?' *Journal of Consciousness Studies*, 14, No. 1-2, 2007, pp.115-36.

Varela, F. J. (1999), 'Present-Time Consciousness', *Journal of Consciousness Studies*, 6, No.2-3, 1999, pp. 111-140, in Varela, F.J & Shear, J. (2002), *The View from Within: First-person Approaches to the Study of Consciousness* (Great Britain: Imprint Academic), pp. 111-140.

Wegner, D. M. (2002), *The Illusion of Conscious Will* (Cambridge, MA, MIT Press).

Weinberg, S. (2002), 'How Great Equations Survive' in Farmelo, G (2003), *It Must Be Beautiful: Great Equations of Modern Science*, pp. 253-7 (London: Granta Books).

Wikman, K. G. (1989), 'The Mystery of Mathematics' in Pylkkanen, P (1989), *The Search for Meaning: The New Spirit in Science and Philosophy* (Great Britain: Crucible).

Wilczek, F. (2002), 'The Dirac Equation' in Farmelo, G. (2003), *It Must Be Beautiful: Great Equations of Modern Science*, pp. 132-60 (London: Granta Books).

Wilczek, F. (2009), *The Lightness of Being: Big Questions, Real Answers* (Great Britain: Allen Lane).

INDEX

C

F

G

H

Q

R

S

ACKNOWLEDGEMENTS

The ideas presented in this book have been developed and modified over more than ten years, and I owe a huge debt of gratitude to all the many physicists, biologists, psychologists, chemistry professors, neuro-scientists, artificial intelligence researchers, theologians, LSD experimenters, transcendental meditators, poets and philosophers who have taken the time to discuss it with me at the Toward a Science of Consciousness conferences in 2010, 2011, 2012 and 2016. In particular I wish to thank Philip Goff, Sam Coleman, Jason Ford, Bruce Mangan, Brent Allsop, Jon Cape, Marcus Abundis, Dave Chalmers, Gustav Bernroider, Dean Radin, Susan Blackmore, Allyssa Ney, Keith Elkin, Andres Emilsson, Max Goff, Philip L'Hommedieu, James Tee and Arlene Lee. I would also like to thank Galen Strawson, and Jonathan Edwards, whose published work was particularly influential in the development of my theory. I am also grateful for the emails I have received from interested individuals in response to my conference abstracts, and to the anonymous person who assigned me to certain helpful email groups. Most of all I'd like to thank Ruth for the many hours she has spent proof-reading this book, and reading through all my earlier efforts, Jim for our frequent discussions, Alison for her helpful advice, Tom for the gift of several helpful books, and Fiona and Amie for helping me finally get these ideas into print.

OTHER BOOKS BY C. S. MORRISON

UNEXPECTEDLY FORETOLD OCCURRENCES
Scientific Evidence that there is a God who Loves You
(and why scholars don't discuss it)

Published in 2016 by *CreateSpace Independent Publishing Platform.*
164-page paperback available on Amazon.com.
ISBN: 978-1-5377280-4-9

A RHYME, RHYMES AND HALF A RHYME
A Collection of Poems celebrating the Book of Daniel

Published in 2017 by *CreateSpace Independent Publishing Platform.*
122-page paperback available on Amazon.com.
ISBN: 978-1-9737506-4-2

SURPRISED BY THE POWER OF DANIEL
The Miracles that brought a Skeptic to Faith

Published in 2018 by *QualiaFish* Publications.
346-page paperback available on Amazon.com.
UK Edition: ISBN: 978-1-9993393-2-6
Special Iona Edition: ISBN: 978-1-9993393-0-2

Printed in Great Britain
by Amazon